Inside
Internet
Security

**What hackers
don't want
you to know ...**

Jeff Crume

Addison-Wesley

An imprint of **Pearson Education**

Harlow, England · London · New York · Reading, Massachusetts · San Francisco
Toronto · Don Mills, Ontario · Sydney · Tokyo · Singapore · Hong Kong · Seoul
Taipei · Cape Town · Madrid · Mexico City · Amsterdam · Munich · Paris · Milan

PEARSON EDUCTION LIMITED

Head Office:
Edinburgh Gate
Harlow CM20 2JE
England
Tel: +44 (0)1279 623623
Fax: +44 (0)1279 431059

London Office:
128 Long Acre
London WC2E 9AN
Tel: +44 (0)20 7477 2000
Fax: +44 (0)20 7240 5771
Website: www.aw.com/cseng

First published in Great Britain in 2000

ISBN 0–201–67516–1

British Library Cataloguing-in-Publication Data
A CIP catalogue record for this book can be obtained from the British Library.

Library of Congress Cataloging in Publication Data
Applied for.

10 9 8 7 6 5 4 3 2 1

Designed by Claire Brodmann Book Designs, Burton-on-Trent
Typeset by Pantek Arts, Maidstone, Kent
Printed and bound in the United States of America

The Publisher's policy is to use paper manufactured from sustainable forests.

Inside

Internet
Security

To my wife and daughter
   whose love sustains me each day

   and

To my mother
   my first teacher

Permission acknowledgements

The Publisher wishes to thank the following for permission to reproduce material in this book.

Quote p.2 from F.T. Gramp and R.H. Morris (1984) 'Unix Operating System Security', AT&T Bell Labs Technical Journal, Vol 63, No 8, October, pp. 1649–1672. Copyright © 1984 AT&T. All rights reserved. Reprinted with permission.

Figure 2.3 BusinessWeek cover from 23 September 1996. Reproduced with permission from Business Week, a publication of McGraw-Hill Companies.

Quote p. 86 from Pogo reproduced with permission from Okefenokee Glee & Perloo, Inc.

Quote p. 102 reproduced with permission from Cliff Stoll.

Figure 10.2 cartoon reproduced with permission, © 1993 *The New Yorker Collection*, Peter Steiner from cartoonbank.com. All rights reserved.

Figure 10.3 cartoon by Nik Scott (http://toons.net). Reproduced with permission.

Figure 11.5 reproduced with permission from RSA Security, Inc.

Figures 12.2 AntiSniff and *16.1* L0phtCrack: copyright © 1994, 1995, 1996, 1997, 1998 LHI Technologies. Permission to use, copy and distribute documents and related graphics delivered from this World Wide Web Server is hereby granted. All other rights reserved.

Quote p. 151 reproduced with permission from Medill News Service.

Figure 17.3 reproduced with permission from International Computer Security Association, www.icsa.net.

Quote p. 227 reproduced with permission from IBM Corporation.

Quote p. 245 reproduced with permission from Counterpane Internet Security, Inc.

Figures B.5 and B.6 reproduced with permission of Network Associates. Copyright © 2000 Network Associates Technology Inc. All rights reserved.

Some of the definitions in the Glossary were adapted from Webopedia, internet.com Corp. which can be found at http://webopedia.internet.com.

Special permission to use:

    CA-98.10 Buffer Overflow in MIME-aware Mail and News Clients, © 1998

    CA-97.28 IP Denial-of-Service Attacks, © 1997

    CA-96.21 TCP SYN Flooding and IP Spoofing Attacks, © 1996

    CA-96.26 Denial-of-Service Attack via PING, © 1996

    CA-98.01 smurf IP Denial-of-Service Attacks, © 1998

    CA-99.17 Denial-of-Service Tools, © 1999

    CA-99.04 Melissa-Macro-Virus, © 1999

    CA-2000-02 Malicious HTML Tags Embedded in Client Web Requests, © 2000

    CA-2000-01 Denial-of-Service Developments, © 2000

by Carnegie Mellon University, in *Inside Internet Security: What Hackers Don't Want You To Know* is granted by the Software Engineering Institute.

CERT® Advisories are available on the Internet. Readers may learn about the latest updates at http://www.cert.org.

One evening, my eight-year-old daughter said excitedly, 'Dad, I want to tell you something.' She then announced with great pride that she had a 'secret password', which was only for her use in the school's computer lab and, since it was a secret, she was not going to tell me what it was, no matter what! She derived great satisfaction from knowing something I didn't (not the first time or the last, I'm sure!). She had been frustrated that I would not tell her the password needed to operate my laptop computer. The fact that this system contained confidential corporate information and that divulging it could cost me my job and my employer far more was lost on her. How could I keep such a secret from her? She wasn't going to tell anybody! Her indignation had now, at least to some extent, been quenched by the fact that the shoe was now on the other foot.

After letting her revel in this great personal triumph for a few moments, I mentioned that the book she had seen me working on for the past year had a whole section on secret passwords and how computer hackers can often figure them out. She was astonished. Why would I want to tell people how to steal passwords? I explained that I wanted to help people understand how to choose better passwords so that they couldn't be stolen so easily. I added that such information is something that hackers would rather not have everyone know because it could make their job a lot more difficult. 'Oh, so that's why you called the book *What hackers don't want you to know ...*, right?' she responded. 'That must mean you're an "unhacker".' I confessed that I hadn't thought of it that way, but I guessed she was right – maybe it was time to change my business cards ...

My introduction to hacking came when I was in high school in the late 1970s. It began with writing password stealers on the school's DEC PDP-11 minicomputer. Programs were written in the BASIC programming language and accessed via 300 baud acoustic coupled modems which caused garbage to be spewed across the screen if someone slammed the door to the computing lab. From that environment, which sounds unbelievably ancient and crude by today's standards, my compatriots and I streamed together almost unintelligible lines of code that could perfectly emulate the logon sequence and trick unsuspecting users into giving up their passwords. It was quite a thrill when we got them to work.

A key difference between me and the other guys that hung out in the lab after school, though, was that I never felt the need to actually steal another person's password. In other words, it was sufficiently exciting for me merely to *know* that I *could* do it so I never felt the need to break any rules. The paradoxical lesson of martial arts training is that *you learn to fight so you won't have to*. In other words, the mastery of the skills leads to confidence, which leads to self-control, which makes violence essentially unnecessary.

I first peeked inside the mind of a hacker during those pre-Internet days. I was fascinated by what some of the truly gifted hackers could do and equally taken by their reaction to it. The insatiable curiosity, astonishing ingenuity and singular focus on accomplishing a seemingly impossible task were qualities that inspired admiration. On the other hand, the delicate egos, secretive nature, antisocial behaviour and questionable ethics stripped away any remaining illusions. In any case, though, I owe a debt of gratitude to these technologically brilliant classmates who whetted my appetite for computers and the security issues that inevitably come with them, for in doing so they unknowingly provided me with a great deal of material for this book.

About the author

Jeff Crume is a Certified Information Systems Security Professional (CISSP) with 18 years' experience as a programmer, software designer and IT security specialist working for IBM and its Tivoli Systems subsidiary. During this time he has been involved in the development and technical support of systems and network management products such as NetView. His work in this area resulted in a US patent on loop detection.

In addition, he has consulted with companies around the world as they develop secure e-commerce payment systems, and designed networking infrastructures intended for e-business.

Jeff is a frequent speaker at international conferences and has published articles on cryptography and virtual private networking.

Acknowledgements

A special word of thanks to those who contributed in various ways to this project. It is only through their support and personal sacrifice that this book became a reality.

Dick Baker
Valory Batchellor
Dave Chess
David Gamey
Joe Martin
Bob Nevins
Jenni Scott
Bill Stephenson
Andrew Yeomans

Contents

18   Hackers don't want you to know that ... *active content is more active than you think*   185

19   Hackers don't want you to know that ... *yesterday's strong crypto is today's weak crypto*   191

20   Hackers don't want you to know that ... *the back door is open*   202

21   Hackers don't want you to know that ... *there's no such thing as a harmless attack*   208

Trademark notice

AtGuard™ is a trademark of WRQ, Inc.

ActiveX® and Outlook® are trademarks of Microsoft Corporation.

CERT® and CERT Coordination Center® are registered in the US Patent and Trademark Office.

Eudora and Eudora Pro are registered trademarks of Qualcomm, Inc.

Finjan SurfinGate™, SurfinShield™ are trademarks of Finjan Software Ltd.

SecureWay® and IBM are registered trademarks of IBM Corporation.

Java™ and Java 2™ are trademarks of Sun Microsystems, Inc.

Javascript™ is a trademark of Sun Microsystems, Inc., used under licence for technology invented and implemented by Netscape.

L0pht® is a registered trademark of @stake, Inc. L0phtCrack™ and Antisniff™ are trademarks of Directed Doodling, Inc.

Netscape Communicator is a trademark of Netscape Communications Corporation.

Network Associates and Dr. Solomon's are registered trademarks of Network Associates Inc and/or its affiliates in the US and/or other countries.

Tivoli® is a registered trademark of Tivoli Systems Inc.

Introduction

Magic or just a trick?

Have you ever watched a magician saw a woman in half and then put her back together unharmed? Of course, that's not what really happened. We all know that. But the appearance was convincing enough to make it seem real.

In case you hadn't figured it out, there were actually two women in the box. You saw one get in but you didn't see the other one who was already in there hiding behind an unseen barrier. What you have really just witnessed was the legs and feet of one woman dangling out of one half of the box and the head and arms of another protruding through the other half. Nobody got hurt because the magician merely sawed through a section of the box that was empty in the first place. Not so amazing after all, is it?

Your reaction to this behind-the-scenes glimpse might be, 'That's not magic, it's all a trick!' Of course it is. The magic is in the *illusion* not in what *really* goes on. Now that you know the trick, it doesn't seem like magic at all. What once looked like a miracle now is quite anticlimactic.

Hacker tricks are a lot like magic tricks in one sense. Once you know how the exploit is performed, it doesn't seem so mysterious any more. With the 'magic' revealed, the whole thing may seem rather mundane. In this book you will learn some of the tricks of the hacker trade that allow them to break into systems on a regular basis. When you know how this stuff works, you may be tempted to dismiss it, saying, 'There's no magic here – no great secret has been revealed.'

That would be a mistake. Unlike magicians, hackers really do hurt people. The fact that you know how these well-known, tried and true exploits work may take the magic out of it for you. That's not so bad, though, because it is only then that you can begin going about the task of building appropriate defences so that you don't become the next victim.

In fact, it is not the intention of this book to reveal closely guarded secrets of the hacker underworld. They change from day to day so their value has a short shelf life anyway. Of more use is the underlying *principles* that keep cropping up time and time again in various attacks. The focus, then, is on the lessons that can be learned from these recurring fundamentals – the hacker classics, if you will.

Most of the information discussed here is widely available already. The real purpose is to make sure that it gets into the right hands. For far too long it has seemed that only hackers made use of this knowledge. Now the defenders of legitimate business systems have equal access and can turn the tables on the bad guys.

Striking the right balance

There is a fine line between helping administrators protect their systems and providing a cookbook for bad guys.

Grampp and Morris (1984)

This is the conundrum facing anyone who attempts to write on the subject of **Information Technology (IT)** security. There's simply no point in talking about how something can be improved unless you first explain how it is deficient. In order to motivate people to fix things you must first convince them that those things are actually broken. In order to avoid reoccurrence, you must also explain not only *that* something is broken, but *what* causes it to break. In such discussions you run the risk of being second-guessed for providing the ammunition that hackers need to launch an assault against legitimate business systems.

The point that is often missed in such debates, however, is that *the hacking community already knows this stuff*. It's widely available on the Internet for free to anyone with enough initiative to simply go and get it.[1] The problem is that the 'good guys' are so busy attending to the day-to-day needs of the business that only the 'bad guys' have time to take advantage of this fact. The intent of this book is to help 'level the playing field' by bringing the good guys up to speed. Only when the defenders of corporate IT systems learn what hackers already know can they mount effective defences against cyber-attacks.

To this end, many references to hacker Web sites and tools have been included for your perusal. These glimpses inside the hacker's bag of tricks can lead to a better understanding of both the problem and its solution. Since this information has already been released in a public forum, the intent here is merely to point you in the right direction.

This book is *not* designed to scare, but to *inform*.

This book is *not* designed to scare, but to *inform* – although it may do a bit of both. When delving into the depths of the numerous vulnerabilities facing IT systems, it's easy to become overwhelmed. The temptation is to throw up your hands and give up because the task seems insurmountable. Resist that temptation. To give in is to play right into the hands of the hackers, who are counting on the fact that you're too busy to bother with them as they probe your systems looking for soft spots. It really is possible to conduct secure e-business without tying up all the company's resources in security countermeasures.

Like children terrorized by the fear that there are monsters under the bed, corporate IT can become paralyzed into inaction when it comes to doing business over the Internet. Unlike imaginary monsters, the monsters of IT security are real and

---

1. With the wide availability and ease of Internet access, even the effort required for the 'go' part has been almost eliminated.

they can do real damage. However, both real and imaginary threats can be dealt with when properly illuminated. Shining a flashlight under the bed proves the irrationality of a child's fear. Of course, there's nothing irrational about being concerned about IT security threats, but overwhelming fear of such things makes for an unhealthy business environment. We fear what we don't understand. Another way of looking at it is that fear is, to one degree or another, based on ignorance. I hope that this book will help shine a light on the monsters of IT security. Armed with a better understanding of the problems and their solutions, you can drive away the monsters and ultimately realize the tremendous benefits of doing business in a digital world.

'Hacker' disclaimer

Since hackers are real people, and since no two people are exactly alike, the reader should understand that broad generalizations regarding hackers (see Chapter 3 for a detailed discussion of the term 'hacker') will not necessarily apply in all cases. A case in point is the use of the masculine pronoun when speaking about a hacker. Such 'broadbrush' treatment may prove lacking when applied to a specific individual, but when considering the group as a whole, such simplifications can still be illustrative.

It is with apologies to those who truly do appreciate the difference between the terms 'hacker' and 'cracker' (the latter being the one with malicious intent) that the single term 'hacker' is used in this book. While such distinctions are critical to those in 'white hat' hacker circles, the term 'hacker', as it is commonly used today, is favoured even when 'cracker' is more appropriate. Given that many dictionaries now cite both favourable and unfavourable meanings for the word and since most people in the general public are more familiar with the latter connotation, this more common usage of the term appears here. Rather than trying to fight a high-minded crusade to retrain the world in the use of these terms (a lost cause if there ever was one), this concession has been made.

Products discussed in the book are chosen only to show an example of a particular concept, and many other products on the market may be capable of the same functions. Readers should evaluate products according to the needs of their own unique environment before choosing the one to use.

WARNING: If properly deployed, some of the hacker tools discussed in this book can actually help you identify vulnerabilities in your defence system so that they can be fixed. However, great care should be taken when using such tools as they themselves may create new vulnerabilities. Know the tool that you are using, its source and the reputation of the tool developers, and check scrupulously for embedded viruses, Trojan horses and other malicious software with the latest level of antivirus tools *before* installation. It may make sense to set up a '**sandbox**' environment, which is completely isolated from any production systems, for such testing. This might consist of a standalone LAN along with a few workstations which are separated from all other workstations and networks by an 'air gap'.

part 1

Sizing up the situation

Security concepts

chapter 1

Bringing down the Net

Chapter summary

- The vulnerable nature of the Internet
  - its insecure beginnings
  - DNS and routing system vulnerabilities

'How many bombs would you have to plant to bring down the Internet?' That's the question that Matt Blaze, a network security researcher at AT&T, was asked as a panellist at the *Computers, Freedom, and Privacy Conference* in March 1998. The disconcerting answer he gave was 'None.' In fact, there are any number of ways that an individual could bring the worldwide Internet to its knees and do it all from the comfort of his or her own home.

In fact, two of the most critical components of the Internet are vulnerable. All users of the Internet depend on the **Domain Name System (DNS)**, which is needed to translate those cryptic Web page names like the fictitious 'www.widgets-r-us.com' into the even more cryptic numeric codes that computers actually use. In this regard the DNS works something like a universal telephone directory which, when given a name, will return the corresponding number (in this case an Internet address). Using this numeric code, the Internet's routing mechanism is able to determine where in the world the desired Web page actually resides and begin the process of retrieving its contents.

Normally this process works perfectly well. However, Steven Bellovin, Blaze's colleague, and co-author of *Firewalls and Internet Security*, has pointed out that the DNS is weak because it is *centralized* and the routing system is weak because it is *decentralized*.[1] In other words, the hierarchical structure of the DNS makes it possible for an attack in one critical area to cripple all its subordinates. On the other

1. For more information on these weaknesses see Schneider (1999).

hand, the routing system is vulnerable because of its reliance on its peers. If one of those peers is corrupted, the problem could spread like a disease throughout the entire backbone of the network. Without these two indispensable components (DNS and the routing system) operating as they should, the Internet as we know it would come to a screeching halt.

Blaze and Belovin aren't alone in pointing out the vulnerability of the Net. In May 1998 a group of computer security experts collectively known as L0pht[2] Heavy Industries testified before the US Senate Governmental Affairs Committee that they could bring down the Internet in 30 minutes (Brosnan, 1998).

Why should this matter to you if you're involved in operating a corporate IT infrastructure? The answer lies in the fact that today's networks are becoming more and more dependent upon Internet technologies. In other words, the very life blood of the Internet is also coursing through the veins of your corporate network and with it go some of the same strengths and weaknesses. Even if you never actually connect to the Internet, which is becoming increasingly unlikely with each passing day, you probably still use Internet technology in your internal network. This means that your private network is vulnerable to many of the same ailments as its public counterpart. When the Internet falls sick, it behoves you to take notice, as you could fall victim to the same illness.

1.1   Talking the talk

If you want to communicate with another person you must both be able to speak the same language. Computers are no different in this regard and the language of the Internet and, to an ever-increasing degree, corporate networks is **TCP/IP**

> If you want to communicate with another person you must both be able to speak the same language.

(Transmission Control Protocol/Internet Protocol). To be more precise, TCP/IP is like a set of rules which determine how network devices communicate with each other. When you consider that this networking protocol was never really designed for secure communications over a public network (which is exactly the way it is used today), you realize very quickly that maintaining a secure IT environment is problematic at best.

1.2   Insecure from the start

TCP/IP resulted from work done by the US government as a way to interconnect various geographically dispersed agencies in the event of a catastrophic failure of

2. 'L0pht' (spelled 'L-zero-p-h-t') is hacker slang for 'loft'. The group chose this name because their original meeting place was a loft space in an industrial building in Boston.

traditional communications systems. These developments were motivated by the threat of nuclear war, which grew up during the Cold War era. A curious chain reaction (of a non-nuclear sort) later resulted in the technological infrastructure, known as the Internet, that ties the world together today.

From the beginning, though, this protocol was designed to share information – not hide it. At the time, there seemed to be no need to build in robust security features since it was assumed that all transmissions would be transmitted over private lines. Access to data terminals, which represented the only entry points into the network, was tightly controlled by armed guards – who provided the network's security.

This early effort evolved into what was later known as the ARPAnet – a predecessor of today's Internet. Of course, top-secret military systems are still on private networks, but the basic technology has been given new life in the world's largest public network (the Internet) and in most corporate internal networks. From a security standpoint, however, problems arise from the fact that we have a fundamentally insecure protocol which was designed for *connectivity,* not *security,* running over inherently unsecured public networks where there is a distinct lack of sentries guarding the gates.

chapter 2

Is it safe?

Chapter summary

- The difficulty in proving security

- Security in relative terms

- Learning from past failures

  - root cause analysis

  - defect extinction

- Striking the right balance between security and usability

- The defence-in-depth approach to security

- Death by security

- Information warfare

You're about to open the doors to a new e-business application that has been months in the making. Maybe you're going to start selling your wares over the Web, or maybe you're ready to start collaborating with business partners via the Internet. Your boss walks in and begins to grill you with questions. 'Is it safe? I don't care about business cases and bandwidth, I just want to know one thing ... IS – IT – SAFE?'

Flashback to *Marathon Man* ... suddenly you know how Babe (Dustin Hoffman) felt when former Nazi dentist Dr Szell (Laurence Olivier) had him strapped to a chair, shone bright lights in his eyes, and started drilling a hole in his teeth without the benefit of anaesthetic. Well, maybe not quite that bad, but it might be enough to make you have second thoughts about next week's dental appointment.

How do you even define what it means for a computer system to be safe?

Is it safe? When it comes to IT systems, this may be the toughest question of all to answer. How do you even define what it means for a computer system to be safe? One good operational definition is that 'a computer is secure (safe) if

you can depend on it and its software to behave as you expe.
that it is 'free from risk of loss' (Merriam-Webster Inc., 1996). Eithe
it, it seems like a good question – an important question – but, unfortun.
a virtually unanswerable question.

Dr Hugo Krawczyk, IBM Research, put it into perspective when he saiu
contrast to many other engineering areas, security cannot be verified by experimentation or by simulation. There is nothing on [a] running program that shows that
the program is secure.'[1] When you build a bridge, there are well-known engineering
principles which have been proven both mathematically and through many years
of real-world experience. You can even test the stability of the bridge when you're
done by actually driving over it with a load that exceeds the expected maximum
weight. If it holds up, you can be reasonably sure that the bridge is safe.[2]

Computer security, however, defies such an analogy. It just doesn't fit into the
well-defined structure of an engineering discipline. There are simply too many vari-
ables in terms of hardware, firmware, operating systems, middleware, applications
and networking (not to mention human behaviours) for anyone to account adequately for all the possibilities. Bruce Schneier, a security consultant with
Counterpane Internet Security, Inc., makes this same point. Regarding cryptosystems, which are designed to keep private data safe from prying eyes, he says that 'a
standard security review, even by competent cryptographers, can only prove *insecurity*, it can never prove security' [italics mine] (Schneier, 1999). In other words, the
inability to break into a computer system or penetrate a network doesn't prove it's
safe. It only proves that it isn't vulnerable *at that point in time to a very specific set of
attacks*. More likely, it only proves that you didn't try long enough to break in.

In fact, the only truly secure system is one that is switched off and then, of
course, it's no good to anyone. Any operational system is at risk. If shutting down a
particular system really was a viable alternative, then it probably didn't contain
anything that you really needed anyway. Such a system wouldn't be likely to need
protecting in the first place. Therefore, we are left with a 'catch-22' – the only systems that can be made completely secure are the ones that have no value, and the
systems that contain items of value can never be made totally safe.

Fortunately, the outlook is not as bleak as the previous statement might seem.
There are many things that can be done to lessen the likelihood of loss. Risk is an
inherent aspect of business yet the wheels of commerce roll on. The key is in
coming to terms with what the risks are, doing what you can to minimize them,
and then factoring in the incremental cost of necessary safety measures along with
the cost of potential losses. Finally, you plug all of this into the overall economic
business model. There's really nothing new here. Businesses have been doing this,
consciously or unconsciously, for a few thousand years.

While we all want to know if our systems are safe, a better way to think about
the problem is in relative – rather than absolute – terms. In other words, 'Is

1. Cryptographer's Panel, RSA Data Security Conference & Expo, San Jose, CA, January 1999.
2. Of course, even the best engineering projects must deal with certain unpredictable elements. By
   comparison, however, proving IT security is a considerably more elusive task.

'Is this system *safe enough* given my business model?'

system A *safer* than system B?' or 'Is this system *more secure* or *less secure* than it used to be?' Better still, 'Is this system *safe enough* given my business model?' These still aren't trivial questions to answer, but they come closer to reaching the point where we can get our hands around them and formulate meaningful answers.

2.1 Rising from the ashes

'There is no remembrance of former things; neither shall there be any remembrance of things that are to come with those that shall come after.'

Holy Bible, Ecclesiastes 1:11 (KJV)

Compounding the problem of computer security is the fact that, according to an FBI/CSI study (Computer Security Institute, 1999), nearly 70 per cent of break-ins are not reported. Unlike other industries where critical failures are brought to public attention for thorough analysis, computer break-ins are typically kept as low-key as possible. For instance, if a particular model of automobile experiences repeated failures, incident reporting can alert the manufacturer that an underlying design flaw may be the cause and a recall may be in order. If the manufacturer refuses to acknowledge the failure, repeated public disclosure by affected consumers can eventually apply enough pressure on the company to force them to remedy the situation. Public knowledge of this defect makes it possible for all owners to benefit.

However, if you are a bank eager to sign up new customers to use your new online service, the last thing in the world you want is for word of a breach of your systems to become public. Such an admission could undermine consumer confidence and ravage the company's bottom line. Unfortunately, such an environment makes it nearly impossible for those within the IT industry to learn from their mistakes. As the saying goes, 'Those who fail to learn from history are destined to repeat it.' Therefore, since most attacks go unreported, they are destined to be repeated.

Since it is unlikely that this attitude will change in the near future, the best we can hope for may be that within each organization the principles of *root cause analysis* and *defect extinction,* which have been used in other industries, can be applied on a smaller scale to the security problem. In other words, after the dust has settled from a security incident, representatives from relevant areas of the company should be brought together to determine why this happened in the first place. The focus should be on determining the *root cause* of the problem rather than the after effects and ensuring that it can never happen again. A continuous chain of 'why' questions can help you backtrack to the real source of the problem.

Every attempt should be made to avoid assessing blame in a punitive way. The reason is that to do otherwise allows the whole process to degrade into an unproductive witch-hunt. Since no one wants to be burned at the stake, no one is going to admit their contribution to the problem and, ultimately, nothing is learned.

Once the root cause of the failure has been identified, the team should work together to develop a solution that eliminates the possibility of a repeat occurrence. Defect *extinction*, rather than defect *prevention* or *avoidance,* should be the goal. Installing a new, ancillary process that increases the workload of the staff is rarely the best answer. A more creative solution, is the real goal – one which can be automated and, by its very nature, steers clear of the problem area in the first place.

2.2 You can't have it all

'We're good now, but we can be better still' is the attitude of smart companies. They know that past performance is no guarantee of future success. Continuous winning requires continuous improvement. This is why increased productivity, among other things, is the goal of every competitive business.

One way to make a positive impact in this area is to improve the usability of the business tools. If a task currently takes 30 minutes to complete and a new piece of software can cut that time in half by making the job easier for the operator, then it would benefit the business to implement this improvement (assuming the cost of implementation was less than the value of the resulting benefits, of course). Increased usability, then, can be a means for advancing the business. Usability is a good thing.

Security is a good thing too. Without it, all the productivity gains in the world are meaningless because a hacker can wipe out years of hard work in a matter of minutes. Clearly, the successful business must not only be able to come up with new ideas and improvements, but must also be able to protect its current assets. Without an effective security system, neither is possible.

Unfortunately, when it comes to security, you can't have it all. Usability and security often find themselves locked in mortal combat. In the extreme, the most usable system would be one completely devoid of security measures. There would be no **userids** or passwords to remember, no smart cards to hang on to, and everyone would have access to all the data that they could ever possibly want.

At the other extreme is the system that is completely secure. It can only be operated locally (eliminating the risk of network-based attacks), is housed in a fortified, windowless bunker, and is guarded by a platoon of armed guards and snarling dogs behind barbed wire and overseen by an electronic surveillance system capable of seeing into every conceivable nook and cranny. Very secure, indeed, but who would want to work there? The task of negotiating such an obstacle course just to look up last year's sales figures would clearly hinder productivity to an unreasonable extent because the system had been optimized strictly for security with no thought given to usability.

What we are left with, ultimately, is an uneasy tension with usability and productivity at one end of the spectrum and security at the other (Figure 2.1).

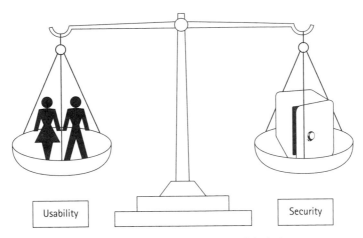

FIGURE 2.1   Usability vs. security: striking the right balance

Since it is rare that optimizing on either extreme is the best decision, the trick is in choosing the right point along the continuum. This point will vary based upon the particular resources involved, their value to the business, their potential value to competitors, and the cost of recovery from loss or compromise. In other words, the needs of the business should dictate the final outcome. Technology can help provide protection but the decision of what to protect and to what extent is ultimately a *business* decision – not a *technology* decision.

One notable exception to this usability vs. security tug-of-war is in the area of Single Sign-On (SSO) tools, which will be discussed later in Section 11.10. In this case we actually can improve both usability and security, but such an example is hardly the norm.

2.3 The hacker's obstacle course

Every security countermeasure is inherently weak. The sooner you come to grips with this unfortunate axiom, the sooner you will be on your way towards building a more secure environment. The fact is that even if you assume that a security tool has been configured perfectly (difficult, but not impossible) and that the software is completely bug-free (virtually impossible), you're still faced with the stark reality that no tool is designed to defend against every possible type of attack. Some tools detect host-based attacks while others focus on the network. Some are designed for detection, others for prevention or recovery.

Every security countermeasure is inherently weak

There's simply no single tool, policy or procedure that will guarantee security. Each has its own unique place within a larger system of defences. Redundancy, which for efficiency's sake is normally something we try to avoid in other areas, is a treasured characteristic of security schemes. Too much stream-lining in a security system creates a fast-track for hackers. A series of barriers, on the other hand, creates a virtual minefield that must be flawlessly navigated before getting to the good stuff.

Think of your defences as an obstacle course for would-be hackers. The more hurdles and hazards you can place between them and the things you are trying to protect, the more likely they will be to fail. Your approach, then, should be to design a *layered system of defences* where various barriers in the form of tools, poli-cies, procedures, etc., work together to make the hacker's job as hard as you reasonably can.

Such an approach is often referred to as **defence-in-depth** because no single mechanism is entrusted with the total responsibility for security. The underlying principle is that even if hackers can break through the first line of defence, they will be thwarted by the second or third (Figure 2.2). In other words, even though each component may have a unique vulnerability, so long as it's not the same vul-nerability throughout the entire defence system, attackers will ultimately be repelled. Some companies even go so far as to choose similar security products such as firewalls from different vendors on the theory that a weakness in one brand is unlikely to occur in another since they were designed and built by differ-ent suppliers. Others, however, feel that the additional complexity of having to maintain multiple platforms, and deal with the idiosyncrasies native to each, increases the likelihood that configuration mistakes will result. Throw in the added cost of acquiring and installing duplicate platforms, along with having to develop the additional skills specific to these competing products, and the disadvantages to this approach quickly mount up.

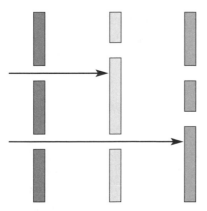

FIGURE 2.2   Defence-in-depth: a layered system of defences

2.4 The lesson of Lord Lovell – or – Too much of a good thing?

If a little bit is good then a lot must be better, right? IT systems and their networks must be secure in order for us to reasonably rely on them for mission-critical operation. More security, then, would surely have to be better than less security, wouldn't it? Not necessarily. In fact, you can get too much of an otherwise good thing if you aren't judicious in the construction of your corporate security policies and defence systems.

Consider the case of Lord Francis Lovell who lived in fifteenth-century England during a time of great upheaval. Lord Lovell supported a man named Lambert Simnel who was attempting to lay claim to the throne. Simnel's dubious claim, however, was eventually exposed. In fear for his own safety, Lovell fled to a village in the country where he planned to ride out the storm in a building now known as Lovell Hall. One description of the events goes as follows:

After Simnel was branded a fraud, Lovell beat a hasty retreat to the Hall where he hid and lived in a secret room which could only be opened from the outside by his manservant, the only person who knew where he was. However, when the servant suddenly died, Lovell's fate was literally sealed. Many years later in 1708, when repairs were being carried out to the Hall a secret chamber was discovered. The chamber contained the skeleton of a man seated at a table with his dog at his feet.

'The Cotswolds – Lovell Hall', Completely-Cotswold, AccoFind.com

Too much security (or poorly implemented security) can starve out a business just as quickly as it did Lord Lovell. The fear of hackers can drive a company into a self-imposed cyber-seclusion. Total withdrawal might have seemed a prudent measure to Lovell at the time, but it ended up being his undoing. Such a strategy, however, is not an option for a business which must be accessible to its customers or risk extinction.

Security measures must be effective without being overbearing. If they are too lax, the result will be the same. Too often, information security is perceived as being all about saying 'no' while business is all about saying 'yes'. When conflicts arise between these two competing objectives, security is bound to lose.

In fact, the real goal of information security is not to say 'no', but rather to say 'yes' to the *right* people. Instead of being an *inhibitor* to business, security should be an *enabler*. If done properly, security will actually *increase* an organization's ability to make a profit by opening new sales channels that would have otherwise been too risky while at the same time protecting the proverbial 'keys to the kingdom' in the process.

The purpose of the 'hacker's obstacle course' described in the previous section must be to keep the bad guys out while simultaneously allowing the good guys to come and go as the needs of the business dictate. Striking the right balance is the challenge of every effective e-business.

2.5 But what's all this going to cost?

The first rule of IT security is that you should never spend more to protect something than that thing is actually worth. Sounds like common sense, doesn't it? In fact, it's not as common as you might hope. Throughout this book we will look at a multitude of vulnerabilities that exist in today's IT systems. We will also examine possible solutions that can improve your odds against serious loss from attack. Such solutions, however, don't come for free. Some will be relatively cheap while others could be prohibitively expensive. Where each one ends up for you is completely dependent upon your own unique business and IT environment. 'One size fits all' might work for T-shirts and baseball caps, but it's a devastatingly poor choice for IT security solutions.

> The first rule of IT security is that you should never spend more to protect something than that thing is actually worth.

The point, then, is to make sure that all security decisions are made within the context of the business objectives. Technology for its own sake belongs in the hallowed halls of the world's great museums and research labs, but it amounts to little more than a costly luxury in the realm of business, where technology is best deployed when it is based upon the value it adds to the organization. Therefore, let this first rule of security be your guide in any subsequent deliberations.

2.6 News from the front

War has been declared. The corporate IT infrastructure is at risk. As an IT professional you are a soldier responsible for defending the enterprise. Your working environment may seem chaotic at times (OK, maybe always) and there may be the occasional (frequent?) verbal sparring match as job responsibilities and egos clash, but this amounts to little more than a few small skirmishes by comparison. The wiring closet and the server room might look peaceful at night when everyone has gone home, but they are actually sitting in the middle of a war zone.

Before you dismiss such statements as being overly dramatic, consider what's at stake. Modern enterprise runs on *information*. Commerce depends upon this elusive resource like never before. With it you can 'build the better mousetrap' and reap the financial benefits from eager consumers overrun by rodents. Without it, your invention may be as welcome as an air conditioner to an Eskimo.

The notorious case of accused hacker Kevin Mitnick provides ample proof. Sun Microsystems, NEC America, Fujitsu and others estimate that collectively they lost

$300 million owing to the exploits of this single individual. Most of these losses were development costs of new products, which were compromised as a result of Mitnick's prying eyes (Poulsen, 1999). Some have argued that these damage claims are exaggerated, but the fact remains that the stakes are enormously high and the risks are real.

Entire industries are springing up around the capture, distillation and targeted distribution of relevant information. Fortunes are made and lost on Wall Street every day based on the quality of information available to investors. Governments rise and fall on the strength of their ability to use information about potential aggressors – both internal and external. One could argue that information is the most valuable commodity on earth. More valuable than time, money, or even power because with information, one can have all of the others. Knowing how to operate efficiently results in more available time. Knowing how to use money properly yields even more money. Having the best information and knowing how to apply it allows one to make the best decisions and, ultimately, wield power over less informed competitors.

If you are an IT professional you are entrusted with the machinery that runs your company's information infrastructure. If a competitor had access to your secrets, you could be out of business and out of a job in no time. Anyone determined to ruin your company could strike with precision if they knew what you already know. In this sense, you are the only thing standing between attackers and their prize. If you consider for just a second the cost of what is at stake, it quickly becomes apparent that the very existence of the enterprise depends upon your ability to defend it from vandals and thieves who would take what is not rightfully theirs – namely, your livelihood.

You are at war. Your desk is stationed on the defensive front. In fact, most companies don't fully appreciate the magnitude of what is going on around them. This ignorance is precisely what can cost them dearly in the long run. Because the battle is one of stealth, it is easy not to realize that it is happening at all. Since it more closely resembles guerrilla warfare than a full frontal assault, its extent may not be fully understood. Because its tactics are so similar to terrorism, defending against it is like shooting at a thousand moving targets all at once.

Adding to the difficulty is the fact that you can't opt out. Companies who decide that the idea of running an e-business connected over a lawless Internet is just too risky could ultimately find themselves downsized out of existence. In 1996 the cover of *Business Week* magazine shouted out the question, 'Can you make money on the Net?' (Figure 2.3). Since that time this question has become moot. Clearly there are people making money on the Net but that's not really the point any more. The inescapable fact is that your competitors are probably

> Companies who decide that the idea of running an e-business connected over a lawless Internet is just too risky could ultimately find themselves downsized out of existence.

FIGURE 2.3   *BusinessWeek*, September 23rd, 1996

already on the Net. If you don't join the fray you risk extinction. It has simply become part of the cost of doing business in the Information Age.

Your attackers know this all too well. They are keenly aware of the vital importance of information technology and feed off the power it possesses. They are counting on the fact that you don't take their threat seriously. Unguarded systems are to them what a waving red flag is to a bull. The unfortunate truth is that there are far more of them than there are of you. They are unbelievably bold and persistent. They may be either ingenious or ignorant but they can hurt you just the same, as we will discuss later. Also, they never sleep. At least that's how it seems. With the entire world interconnected as never before, the sun never sets on the global hacker community.

While you can never declare victory, you can maintain the upper hand through constant vigilance. In fact, your ability to do so could be your company's competitive edge.

chapter 3

What is a hacker?

If you know the enemy and know yourself, you need not fear the result of a hundred battles. If you know yourself but not the enemy, for every victory gained you will also suffer a defeat.

The Art of War, Sun Tzu, c. 500 BC (Giles, 1994)

Chapter summary

- 'Hacker' defined
- The wide range of skills among hackers
    - novice (script kiddie), intermediate and elite
- Why hackers hack ...
    - for fun
    - for power
    - for money
    - for a cause
- How some hackers rationalize their actions
    - Kevin Mitnick
    - Patrick Gregory
- The hacker's persistence

How can you defeat unknown attackers? The answer is, you can't. You don't necessarily have to know their names or what they eat for breakfast, but you must know something – what they want, why, and how they plan to go about getting it – if you are to defend against their attacks. Without at least some basic understanding of the enemy, your defences will be haphazard and your successes few and far between. In order to bring a measure of clarity to the problem you would do well to start with the ancient advice of Sun Tzu and come to 'know your enemy'.[1]

Before we can do that, though, it's important that we settle on some terminology. Some will argue that this is a counterproductive debate, saying 'it's all just semantics, anyway'. How odd. Semantics are all about what a word *means*, and what are words without meanings? Answer: noise.

First, let's examine the term 'hacker'. This is an unusual word since it has many different and distinctly opposite meanings, depending upon the context in which it is used. *Merriam-Webster's Collegiate Dictionary* (Merriam-Webster Inc., 1996) provides the following definitions:

(a) *'one that hacks'* Well, that one isn't much help.

(b) *'a person who is inexperienced or unskilled at a particular activity <a tennis hacker>'* Although a tennis example is cited, the same holds true for golf. You're not going to make many friends on the links if you go around referring to your fellow golfers as 'hackers'. Clearly, this is not the intended connotation when referring to computer hackers, but it is somewhat odd that a derogatory term in one context is worn like a badge of honour in another, as we will soon see. (Maybe if the self-proclaimed computer hackers knew the earlier derivation of the term they might be less inclined to warm up to it. But, then again ...)

(c) *'an expert at programming and solving problems with a computer'* Purists will argue that a hacker is not a villain at all. In fact, one of the original meanings of the term as it applied to computers was as a reference to a programmer who was particularly proficient at dealing with the intricacies of complex software. For this type of 'hacker', the more obscure and difficult the problem, the better. This 'hacker' might be unusually adept at fixing bugs by patching essentially unreadable, executable binaries. Clearly from this perspective, calling someone a 'hacker' was a compliment – not a term of derision.

(d) *'a person who illegally gains access to and sometimes tampers with information in a computer system'* This definition focuses on unauthorized access rather than programming skill, and is what this book is all about.

Many hackers take exception to being lumped together in one group. They are quick to point out that the underlying intent of the break-in needs to be considered. They say that 'real' hackers attack for the purpose of exposing weaknesses rather than doing actual damage. Fuelled by an insatiable curiosity, their exploits are rationalized as actually helping make systems more secure in the long run. To their way of thinking, *they are the good guys.*

---

1. We will deal with the 'know yourself' portion of Sun Tzu's advice in Chapter 4.

Some even fancy themselves as modern-day Robin Hoods striking out against the injustices of the authoritarian overlords of government and industry. A bit mischievous, but on the whole, they argue that they are actually performing a service for the good of all. Some people in the general public may even secretly root for the hackers. They may view the Internet as a contemporary Wild West frontier, which, in some respects, it is. Hackers, then, are likened to high-tech outlaws fighting back against 'the system' as they ride off into the digital sunset. Historical revisionism and selective memory have contributed to the glamorization of the gunslingers of old, but if people really knew what these law-breakers were like, they probably wouldn't admire them. The same might be argued for today's **cyberspace** renegades.

The victims of their break-ins realize this. The hacker's claim of cyber-altruism is lost on these people when they are awakened at 3:00 a.m. to deal with an intruder alert. As Charles Palmer, head of IBM's Global Security Analysis Lab, put it,

> Hacking is a felony in the United States and most other countries. When it is done by request and under a contract between an ethical hacker and an organization, it's OK. The key difference is that the ethical hacker has authorization to probe the target.[2]

Nevertheless, within the hacker community, the term is worn like a badge of honour.

'Crackers', on the other hand, are the bad guys, according to the so-called 'white hat' hackers. Crackers break into systems with the intent of doing damage. Some hackers still take exception to the convergence of these two terms, but the fact of the matter is that language is not static.[3] It adapts to meet the needs of the people who use it. Word meanings change over time no matter how hard one tries to oppose it. Here's the acid test: if you were to ask 100 people at random whether they think the term 'hacker' refers to someone doing good or someone doing bad, probably 99 would go with the latter definition. Quite simply, this is what the term has come to mean for the vast majority, therefore, that *is* what it means.

The point, then, is that while the semantic distinction between hackers and crackers may still be significant to some, the term 'hacker', as it is commonly used, refers to malicious activity and carries a pejorative connotation.

---

2. 'Q&A with IBM's Charles Palmer', *Insurgency on the Internet,* CNN.com, 1999.
3. For a stark example of language evolution, the opening lines of the epic poem, *Beowulf,* in its original Old English dialect reads as follows:
      Hwæt we Gardena in geârdagum
      þeodcyninga þrym gefrûnon
   and doesn't even begin to resemble its modern English translation:
      LO, praise of the prowess of people-kings
      of spear-armed Danes, in the days long sped.

3.1 Homogenized hackers?

Many people make the mistake of lumping all hackers together in one homogeneous group when nothing could be further from the truth. Hacking, like any other skill, involves various levels of proficiency. To assume that all hackers are highly experienced experts is a vast oversimplification that could cost you dearly down the line. It is also important to note that 'hackers are people too'. This is not said in order to gain sympathy for them, but to better understand them. In other words, each hacker is different.

> Hacking, like any other skill, involves various levels of proficiency.

Here, we can only *generalize* certain characteristics that are, more or less, applicable. Hackers, like any other group, don't like to be stereotyped. They want to be seen as *individuals* and not just as nameless clones.

Of course, some don't like such stereotyping because, in fact, it hits a little too close to home. Evidence of this isn't hard to find. Try describing the psychology (pathology?) that leads to a hacker's aberrant behaviour in the presence of hackers or their sympathizers, and you will quickly know if you're on the right track. Miss the mark and you will be dismissed with a yawn. Hackers won't feel compelled to passionately point out the errors in your assertions, because they will be apparent. However, if you start getting close to the ugly truth, you had better be prepared to deal with the hacker's venom, because the vitriolic war of words that follows won't be a pleasant experience. While a brief discussion of such issues will be presented in this book, a thorough treatment is best attempted by the psychologists.

Any classification of hackers into various groups is fraught with problems. Do you use hackers' underlying motivation, their psychological profile, their skills, or the consequences of their actions as the primary criterion? No matter which you choose, you will find that a significant number of cases defy easy segmentation. The motives of two different hackers may be the same, but the type of attack they choose to launch entirely different. Their psychological profiles may have much in common, but their hacking skills may be at opposite ends of the spectrum.

In fact, most hackers have very little idea what they are doing. It is their *ineptness*, not their *ingenuity*, that you should fear. They may download a hacker tool from the Internet and proceed to play around with it using *your* network as their sandbox. While their intentions may be only mildly malevolent, the unintended consequences of their actions can, nevertheless, be catastrophic. What they see as innocent experimentation can, in reality, create a massive migraine for the enterprise.

These **novice hackers** (Rushing, 1998) make up the largest segment of the hacker population (Figure 3.1). Hackers in this group are sometimes referred to as '**script kiddies**' because they often rely on scripts (preprogrammed routines) developed by more knowledgeable hackers to run their attacks. The stereotype for this segment is that they

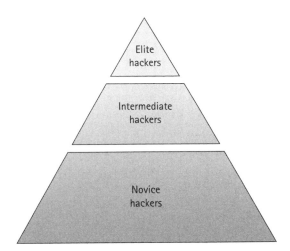

FIGURE 3.1   The hacker pyramid

are most often adolescents (hence 'kiddies') who have little understanding of what they are actually doing. The rise of the script kiddies is a fairly recent phenomenon facilitated by advances in usability, capability and availability of hacker tools along with the ubiquity of the Internet, as will be discussed in Chapter 16. Individually, they may or may not represent a serious threat, but collectively they are a force to be reckoned with.

The results of the 1998 Internet Auditing Project (Siri, 1999) confirmed this. In this survey Internet hosts around the world were tested (usually without the knowledge of their owners) through a series of remotely executed scans, which were automated by software developed for this project. What was learned was that nearly half a million machines suffered from one or more of a common set of well-known, easily exploitable vulnerabilities. The tools needed to attack these systems were, in many cases, readily available and the level of expertise required to run the attack was minimal – two conditions that are tailor-made for script kiddies. The fact that nearly half a million hosts are vulnerable to the lowest-level hacker gives a sense of just how vast the script kiddie threat can be.

Intermediate hackers are fewer in number than their novice counterparts and have a far better understanding of what they are doing. They may possess significant computing skills but lack the experience (and reputation) of the real experts. They are capable of great damage and, since they may aspire to reach the 'next level', they may be highly motivated to strike high-profile targets.

The most skilled group of **elite hackers** is capable of penetrating most systems. They understand the inner workings of major commercial systems and are able to dream up new exploits, whereas novices and intermediates are more likely simply to take advantage of well-known tools and techniques. The elite are on the cutting edge of their 'field' and are capable of devastating results, if sufficiently motivated. Thankfully, they are not always so inclined.

Some estimate that there may be as many as 100,000 'clueless' hackers, 5,000 skilled intermediates, and anywhere from 500 to 1,000 hacker geniuses.[4] The bottom line is that a hacker at any level can potentially do damage – albeit for different reasons. Therefore, you should fear elite hackers because of their *skill* and novices because of their *lack* of it.

3.2 Portrait of a hacker

Another way of classifying hackers is based not upon their skill, as we have discussed, but upon the underlying psychology that drives them. Psychological profiling is messy work, though. No matter how hard you try to take all the factors into account, exceptions to the 'rule' keep popping up. Combine this with the fact that, as some have put it, only the 'stupid and the unlucky' actually get caught and you quickly realize that any study of the hacker psyche is partial at best.

The temptation to rush to widely held stereotypes as a substitute for real research is always present. However, even stereotypes should not automatically be assumed to be completely without merit. Clearly, some stereotypes are based on myth and misunderstanding and should be quickly discounted. On the other hand, some stereotypes derive from trends that can actually be observed for a given population. The real danger comes in trying to apply a stereotype, which might fit reasonably well for a large group, to an individual, who may bear little resemblance to the crowd. In other words, hackers in general do, in fact, share some common characteristics, but as individuals they are 'one of a kind'. With this in mind, consider these two distinctly different 'portraits of a hacker' which deal briefly with only a small cross-section of the hacker community...

The most prevalent hacker stereotype is that of the hard-core *cyberpunk*.[5] It is this group that we normally hear the most about and, therefore, have the most information to base opinions upon. However, this doesn't mean that there aren't other psychological profiles that might fit other groups of hackers far better. For some people, hacking is merely a hobby. Obsession and criminal intent are missing from any accurate description of their activities. They break in just to see if they can, but would never intentionally harm the environment they have targeted. They justify their attacks as harmless pranks or mere curiosity. They believe they have done nothing wrong despite evidence to the contrary. The fact that they have committed the cyberspace equivalent of 'breaking and entering' is lost on them. They are often oblivious to the unintended consequences that they have caused. Like dog owners who allow their pets to chase after strangers and offer up only the hollow reassurance that 'it's OK, he won't bite', this breed of hacker is perfectly willing to let his or her victim assume the risk of whether the incident will be injurious or not. The point is that even this seemingly mischievous behaviour can have grave consequences.

4. Ira Winkler's comments in Loeb (1999).
5. The term 'cyberpunk' has been adapted from the genre of science fiction literature that bears this name.

Cyberpunks, on the other hand, may be quite different. This group tends to be awkward in social settings where close contact is required. Some may even be downright antisocial.[6] At a sentencing hearing in a US District Court, the attorney for a hacker who had admitted to breaking into various US Government Web sites said as much. 'We have a young man ... who is very uncomfortable with any sort of face-to-face interpersonal contact. He gravitated to computers the way others might gravitate to football or the piano.' However, the judge presiding over the case astutely pointed out that 'playing the piano doesn't have consequences for other people' (Masters, 1999).

Behind a keyboard some hackers feel freer to express their feelings. Cyberspace represents an environment that is far less threatening. The consequences of rejection can be more easily deflected or ignored altogether. They can say what they want, to whomever they want, and the worst thing that can happen is that they might start a 'flame war' (a war of words). However, no physical threat is imminent because they can hide behind a 'handle', or pseudonym, which offers protection.

Arrogance is never in short supply when you bring a group of hackers together. Unencumbered by physical or emotional limitations, they can be whatever they want to be in a virtual world. They create alter egos and hide behind imaginary identities. If they want to believe that they are the rulers of the universe, cyberspace gives them a venue where they can escape to that more desirable position.

The best hackers tend to be very cliquish and secretive. They won't talk to just anyone. You have to *earn* the right to gain their 'valuable' attention. You must first have something to offer them such as a new tool, an exploit or stolen password, to gain an audience.

Some believe that these 'cyberpunks' make up the majority of the hacking community. For this reason it is their image that is most often imagined when the term 'hacker' is invoked. Cyberpunks are most often males in their teens and early 20s. However, they can come in all shapes and sizes. Some have grown up (at least in terms of their physiology) and have regular jobs – often in the IT industry. A smaller percentage gravitate to more sinister activities and become **cyberterrorists** or professional computer criminals for hire. In general, they tend to feel disenfranchised by their peers or some segment of society at large but may have bonded strongly with a smaller group of others who share their interests.

Again, these are the general tendencies that describe the hacker community as a whole. However, due to their secretive nature and relative lack of organization, conclusive studies remain elusive. Thus, for any given hacker, 'your mileage may vary'.

---

6. A notable exception to this generalization, however, is that some hackers can be particularly charming and affable when social engineering attacks are involved as will be discussed later in Section 10.1.

3.3 The joy of hacking

Why do hackers do what they do? What makes them tick? You might think that such tangential questions aren't important if your job is simply to repel their attacks, but in doing so you could be making a costly mistake. Knowing what an attacker wants tells you a great deal about what, when and where he or she is likely to attack. Knowledge of this sort can help you bolster your defences appropriately and lessen your risk of exposure.

Most hackers attack just for the sheer fun of it. You might not see how this would provide such enjoyment, but then, that's often why they are able to get away with what they do in the first place. You might be doing the 'reasonable' thing by concentrating on sound business motivations. You try to predict where attacks will occur, based on the monetary advantage that might be gained by attackers. In the meantime, hackers effectively fly below your radar, avoiding detection, because they're not necessarily concerned with the same issues. While your attention is turned toward securing things that directly affect the bottom line, they might be firing away at an unguarded flank.

Consider the comments made by convicted hacker Kevin Mitnick just prior to his release from prison in January 2000, after serving five years for his hacking exploits:

I saw myself as an *electronic joyrider,* having a great time on the Information Superhighway. I felt like I was *James Bond* behind the computer. It was a *big game* to me. I was just *having a blast.*[7] [italics mine]

Unfortunately for Mitnick, his victims, who included Motorola, Sun Microsystems, Qualcomm, Nokia, DEC, Fujitsu, NEC and Novell, didn't share the same enthusiasm for his activities. They figure the price tag for his 'joyriding' to be in the range of hundreds of millions of dollars. Mitnick, however, maintained that he never intended to profit from his hacking, but this was little consolation to those who were damaged in the process.

Did Mitnick know that what he was doing was wrong? Yes. He admitted that 'It was an invasion of privacy. Going in, getting access to other people's information is obviously a gross invasion of privacy, and it is wrong.' Was he bothered by this fact? In his own words, 'At the time I was doing it? No.'

Why did he do it? What compelled him to break in again and again? 'I just wanted to get access to their [Novell's] network because it was a huge company ... Because I was an explorer. And to what end? There was no end. It was a hobby in itself.'

---

7. 'Cyber Thief', *60 Minutes*, CBS News, Ed Bradley, 23 January 2000.

Clearly, the lack of a financial incentive didn't discourage Mitnick from his pursuits. In fact, if anything, it served as a rationale for continuing. Mitnick justified his actions by saying, 'I was an accomplished computer trespasser. I don't consider myself a thief. I didn't deprive these companies out of their software. I merely made a copy without doing anything more with it … I copied it without permission.' When pressed on the issue of stealing, his response was, 'I didn't use it for financial gain nor did I cause any harm.' To his way of thinking, what he did was wrong, but since he didn't make any money doing it, it was somehow justified.

Apparently Mitnick is not alone in this view as 'Free Kevin' messages were often posted to hacked Web sites during the late 1990s as a show of support from kindred spirits (Figure 3.2). Hacker Web sites also frequently bore the slogan which became a popular rallying cry within certain circles.

Some attacks amount to little more than cyber-vandalism and, as such, don't require much in the way of motivation. For hackers, simply seeing what they can get away with is reward enough. Of course, it is imperative that you protect the organization's vital assets, but don't overlook the seemingly less important ones as well. As will be covered in Part 2, even these assets represent a valuable prize for a hacker and could also be a potential stepping stone to an even larger treasure further down the road.

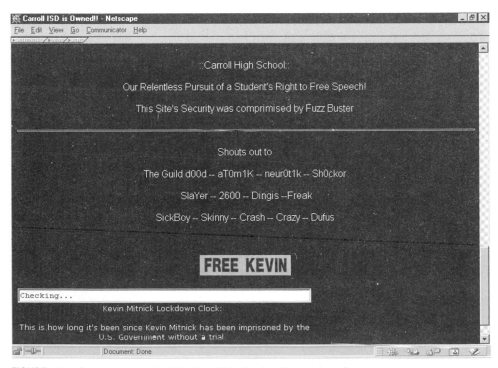

FIGURE 3.2   An expression of solidarity within the hacking community

Many attacks are aimed at making a big splash. The hackers' intention is to feel that they have outsmarted some large corporation or government entity. The enormous ego boost that occurs from such a success creates an almost intoxicating sense of euphoria that can last for days. Hitting high-profile targets can add notoriety to an otherwise unremarkable existence. It can also serve as a means of earning respect by elevating the hackers' status among their peers.

> For hackers, simply seeing what they can get away with is reward enough.

Of course, even this broadbrush attempt to classify the hacker community results in some enormous oversimplifications. The point is that hackers are not all alike. Their skills, motivations and actions vary widely. The reason for even attempting to point out some of these distinctions is to help you to better 'know your enemy', as Sun Tzu put it some 2,500 years ago. By knowing what you're up against, you are less likely to overlook an attack. For instance, if you were to assume that all hackers are of the elite variety, you might not build sufficient defences against the bumbling novice. An effective defence must take into account the full spectrum of threats posed by a wide variety of attackers.

3.4 What do they want?

In the world of investing, 'it takes money to make money'. An analogy in the world of hacking is that 'it takes knowledge to get more knowledge'. To pull off a really great attack requires more knowledge than the average script kiddie has at his or her disposal. Elite hackers, who know the most, tend to hoard what they know, trading 'tricks of the trade' only with a small number of peers. This means that in order to get to the really good stuff, aspiring hackers have to prove that they are deserving. A sort of 'I'll tell you what I know if you tell me what you know' relationship exists within the higher ranks. In order to penetrate this realm, the novice either must acquire some information that is valuable to others or be able to claim responsibility for a particularly noteworthy attack. A sort of cult status within the hacker community awaits those who are successful.

It is important to note, here, that you should not infer from the term 'hacker community' that there exists some sort of well-ordered, hierarchical system. Such relationships can spring up instantly and dissolve just as quickly. In fact, 'hacker communities' might be a more accurate term since small groups or loose confederations of individuals are more the norm. There are some notable exceptions, however, which will be discussed later, but they don't represent the majority.

It is also worth noting that, for the most part, the current generation of hackers grew up with video games all around them. With these games the player is able to wage mortal combat against horrific foes that exist only on a video screen. Entire populations are wiped out through the skilful direction of a joystick or keypad. For some, hacking is not terribly different. Hackers love to swap war stories about how they masterminded this or that attack. A sort of 'who has the highest score?' mentality drives some to push the envelope.

3.5   The real payback

Knowledge for its own sake is not the ultimate aim of the hacker any more than money is the grand prize for the high-stakes Wall Street wheeler-dealer. The real payback is the ego boost that comes from knowing that they have won.

Why is winning important? Because not everyone can do it. In order to have winners there must also be losers. The fact that there are far fewer winners than losers separates the contenders from the pretenders. Hackers figure that if they can do something that others can't, they must be something really special. For those lacking in self-esteem and social skills, the allure of an arena where they can be looked up to, instead of put down, may be simply overwhelming. A virtual world where hackers can instantly be transformed from outcasts who've been branded underachievers to king of all they survey, is a far more gratifying place to be than the mundane 'real world'. Misfits who would be judged irrelevant by mainstream society can suddenly make the entire world take notice of their ingenuity when they rock the very foundations of the corporate world by bringing electronic business to a screeching halt. For them, the distinction between fame and infamy is inconsequential. Either one will suffice.

Of course, such reasoning is rarely this explicit. Usually, it is something that is disguised in a hundred or a thousand other ruses that serve as some more noble justification. They rationalize that by breaking-in they are merely helping to expose existing weaknesses; 'I'm really helping make the world safe by hacking into this classified military system. I'm just exposing the vulnerabilities so that they can be fixed. I'm actually performing a public service by breaking the law. It's just an altruistic act of civil disobedience. I'm not a criminal ... I'm a hero!' They don't seem to be able to grasp that even if someone were to leave their front door unlocked that this is not an invitation to strangers to come inside and take what they like.

The 'inferior beings' that fail to appreciate the hackers' 'wisdom' merely serve as further proof of the hackers' superior intellect. No longer awkward and unsure of themselves, they are addicted to the euphoria that ensues. After a time, the 'ego high' wears off and another 'fix' is needed. Before long, the 'high' becomes too inviting and a *preoccupation* becomes an *obsession*.

Of course, this is the extreme example. Most hackers aren't nearly so unbalanced, but the stereotype did not arise out of thin air. Although exaggerated at times, it has a basis in fact.

Since most hackers lack the requisite skills, endurance, deep-seated insecurity, or other character flaws necessary to progress to this last stage, they are able to keep such impulses in check. However, the ones who do proceed are capable of inflicting incalculable damage on innocent victims.

To them, a disembodied corporation compares favourably to the monsters on the Nintendo screen. When the opponent dies there is no bloodshed and no corpse left to deal with. The illusion is all quite clean and, of course, quite unreal. When these hackers go to war against a huge, faceless organization, they fail to recognize that there are, nevertheless, real people behind those images on the computer screen. Those real people also have real families to support. Jobs are at stake as the result of what a hacker might consider to be playtime.

Attackers' detachment from the real consequences that result from cyber-assaults can essentially short-circuit their conscience. All they know is that the bigger the opponent, the harder it falls. To their way of thinking, a Fortune 500 company is worth more points than a small 'Mom and Pop shop' – an important government organization, such as the military, is worth still more. Hackers never really have to come to terms with the ultimate consequences of their actions because all their victims appear to them as little more than virtual monsters in a video game.

3.6 An eye for an eye

Some attacks are motivated by a perverted sense of justice. One famous case occurred in 1996 when a group of Swedish hackers broke into the Central Intelligence Agency's (CIA) home page and altered it to read 'Welcome to the Central Stupidity Agency'. The vandalism didn't stop there, though. This group had an axe to grind. They felt that one of their comrades was being unfairly targeted by the US government so they proceeded to add the statement 'STOP LYING BO SKARINDER!!!', along with assorted profanities (Figure 3.3). In their minds, it was clear that they felt they were fighting a righteous battle and, therefore, whatever damages resulted were not really their fault but that of the CIA.

Vilification of the victim, a form of 'moral disengagement', is a common aspect of many attacks because, in the hacker's mind, it effectively transfers the guilt that they might otherwise feel away from themselves to their intended target (Rogers, 1999).

Another example is that of the hacker activist or **hacktivist** fighting for a particular social or political cause. One such example is the Electronic Disturbance Theater's FloodNet[8] Web site, which facilitates 'virtual sit-ins' and other acts of 'electronic civil disobedience'. Visitors are told when the next attack will occur, who the victim will be, and why this particular victim was chosen. The 'success' of this type of attack led to other similar approaches by groups such as the Animal Liberation Tactical Internet Response Network (Figure 3.4).

8. FloodNet, www.thing.net/~rdom/ecd/floodnet.html

FIGURE 3.3   Welcome to the Central Stupidity Agency: the CIA hacked

FIGURE 3.4   Hacktivism: hacking on behalf of those that can't

The most novel aspect, though, is that these hactivists actually enlist the help of anyone viewing their page and make it easy for them to join in. To badly paraphrase a famous saying from Shakespeare's *Julius Caesar*, their invitation might be 'Friends, Romans, countrymen, lend me your browsers.' Anyone with Web access can become part of a widespread **Denial-of-Service (DoS)** attack. With a single click of the mouse, you can download a special script which will repeatedly try to access the target's Web page. When taken alone, such an action would be inconsequential. However, when you multiply the effect by thousands or tens of thousands of attackers, the victim's system becomes hopelessly backlogged and, effectively, taken out of service. Defending against such an assault is problematic since attacks are being launched simultaneously from a thousand different directions. Discriminating the attack traffic from the legitimate traffic may be nearly impossible.

As with the attack against the CIA, these hacktivists feel completely justified in their actions. They feel that they are helping to raise public awareness of a case of political persecution. It doesn't take much, though, to imagine how just such an attack could be carried out against a corporation that had offended some group of people. Given the global nature of the Internet and the dearth of international laws to prevent such actions, a foreign attack of this nature could be executed with impunity.

3.7 Cyberterrorism

Perhaps the greatest threat, though, comes from a new breed of terrorists who realize that they may be able to do more damage with computers than with bombs. According to a report in March 1999, a group of hackers actually broke into a British military communications satellite. Early reports stated that the hackers had, in fact, repositioned the satellite and were blackmailing the Ministry of Defence (MoD). The MoD, however, said that the satellite had not actually been moved, but admitted that the group had 'changed the characteristics of channels used to convey military communications, satellite television and telephone calls' (*Daily Telegraph*, 1999).

Whether you believe the original accounts or the government's version, this story highlights the basic insecurity of some of the technology that we have all come to rely on. Some have suggested that in a time of war an effective first offensive would involve seizing control of communications and spy satellites so as to render the enemy blind to incoming attacks. The confusion created by such a disruption could prove decisive. The fact that such attacks are inexpensive and can be directed remotely makes it possible for any country, regardless of size, to create terror in this manner.

Within days of the British satellite attack, US military officials revealed that Pentagon systems were 'being targeted in an organized ongoing attack by unknown hackers trying to get classified data'. It was believed that the attacks were from a 'sophisticated, coordinated assault through computer networks in Canada, Norway, and Thailand' and that systems had been attacked 'up to 100 times daily in the last several months' (Weil, 1999). 'You can basically say we're at war,' said Curt Weldon, chairman of the US House of Representatives Military Research and Development subcommittee. 'It's not a matter of whether America will have an electronic Pearl Harbor, it's a matter of when' (The SANS Institute, 1999).

If you are still tempted to dismiss such attacks as the random effects of a few people working completely on their own, consider the story that broke just a few months earlier in January of that same year. The government of Indonesia was blamed for as many as 18 simultaneous attacks against an Irish Internet Service Provider (ISP). It seems that a resistance movement within East Timor, which was forcibly annexed by Indonesia in 1976, had, in open defiance, applied for and received a top-level domain name (i.e. the letters after the last '.' in a Web site's address or **Uniform Resource Locator** (**URL**). Such a designation is normally reserved only for established nations. As one would expect, this declaration of 'virtual independence' was not received well by Indonesian officials who, it is alleged, ordered the attack on the Irish ISP that hosted the new '.tp' domain (MSNBC, 1999).

If an established nation is willing to declare cyberwar against an adversary, it doesn't take a great leap of faith to believe that some wouldn't hesitate to do likewise in the event of an actual armed conflict. A report from Reuters concerning the NATO military action in Yugoslavia in 1999 made just such an accusation. It asserted that US president Bill Clinton instructed the CIA 'to wage a cyberwar against Milosevic, using computer hackers to tap into the Yugoslav president's foreign bank accounts' (Reuters, 1999a). This report was, of course, denied by administration officials, but it is not hard to imagine how easily the battlefront could shift to cyberspace where not only government agencies but also private businesses could get caught in the crossfire. Throw in the minimal resources needed to launch such an attack and the scenario becomes even more believable. Even the poorest third world country could afford to fight on a virtual battlefield.

Of course, terrorists aren't restricted to attacking only government agencies and military facilities. They may be just as likely to strike other highly visible targets. If terrorists could take over the public electric power grid, civilian telephone systems or air traffic control computers, for example, disruptions of massive proportions would follow. One need look no further than the electrical blackout in New York City in 1977, which resulted in wanton lawlessness, widespread looting and chaos costing the city an estimated $1 billion. Of course, that outage was due to a combination of equipment failure and human error but the results would be the same if it had been instigated by a hacker.

On the other hand, before you, like Chicken Little, conclude that 'the sky is falling', bear in mind that while such things are not *impossible,* there are things that can be done to make them *improbable.* This task begins with knowing your enemies, a subject of which we have only scratched the surface. However, a better understanding of what drives hackers to do what they do should help you design better defences against them. This is, of course, the sort of thing they'd rather you not know, but it's precisely what you need to know to avoid being their next victim.

3.8 Hacking for fun and profit

While most hackers act strictly on their own for their own enjoyment, some are motivated by other factors. We have already discussed how hackers could be used by terrorist organizations or even governments during times of war, but what about hacking as a commercial enterprise? It has been suggested that organized crime syndicates have awakened to the realities of the Information Age and see it as fresh turf to be claimed. It is, of course, hard to verify such assertions, but it doesn't take much to imagine how it might work.

Consider the story of Patrick Gregory (or 'MostHateD' as he was known on the Internet), a member of the gLobaL heLL (gH) hacker group chronicled on the TV news magazine *20/20* in December 1999. In this story it was reported that Gregory penetrated and defaced the Web site of the American Retirement Corporation. Attacks of this sort have become commonplace, but what made this one different was that when Christian Jones, head of computer security for the company, found out who was responsible, he chose not to prosecute him but to *pay* him instead. Even though he knew that a federal crime had been perpetrated, he reasoned, 'The fact that [Gregory] is a member of a gang called gLobaL heLL, if they found out that I had turned him in, then I might incur the wrath of a whole gang of hackers rather than just dealing with one hacker' (Ross, 1999).

Of course, such a justification is fraught with numerous problems. How could Jones know that gH wouldn't later come back for more money? How would he choose to deal with the next bunch of hackers that broke in? Would he pay them as well? Has he, in effect, put a 'Welcome' mat on the doorstep of his Web site inviting all hackers to target his company because there might be fringe benefits for those who succeed? Is he encouraging hackers to break the law by paying them when they do?

Perhaps even more intriguing is Gregory's reaction to it all. When asked, 'If someone went around with rocks and threw them through the front windows of stores and said, I can solve your security problems so that no more rocks come through the window', Gregory admitted that this would not be legal. However, when asked if what he was doing wasn't virtually the same thing, only with computers, his telling response was, 'Yeah, but I mean, I guess for me, it's just on the Internet. It's totally different than the real world.'

Such a revelation might, however, come as a surprise to the company who, estimated that Gregory's initial attack cost them 'several hundred thousand dollars' not counting the 'protection money' they had also paid. To some the Internet might be a game, but to many IT professionals and the organizations that employ them, the Internet *is* the 'real world'.

Another interesting example of extortion came to light a few months after the *20/20* report. In this case a hacker going by the name of 'Maxim' threatened to post to a public Web site the credit card numbers of customers from Internet-based CD music seller CD Universe, unless he was paid $100,000. When the company refused to pay, the hacker released 25,000 numbers to prove his point (Scarponi, 2000).

Clearly, not all hacking has criminal intent, but equally clear is the fact that it can be much more than harmless childish pranks. Even if none of the credit card numbers released were ever used fraudulently, the damage to CD Universe's reputation was incalculable. How many potential customers were scared away from making purchases with that company, or other Internet-based businesses, even if just for a short time?

How much does it cost to repair an organization's brand image?

Compound the impact of lost sales with the additional cost of trying to respond to both the technological and public relations aspects of such a crisis. How much does it cost to repair an organization's brand image? Indeed, these are 'real world' business issues, not merely abstract theoretical concepts.

Evidence also points to the fact that industrial espionage can move into high gear in cyberspace. A company could seriously damage a competitor if it could shut down their systems at critical times. They also could take the edge off any advantage that a competitor might have over them by finding out what unannounced products are under development. Peering into the financial ledger of a commercial adversary could indicate where weak points exist in their strategy as well.

An unethical company willing to steal such information from a competitor could simply hire a group of hackers to do the dirty work for them. In fact, a single individual working for an otherwise legitimate company could pull it off without the knowledge of anyone else in the company. The whole deal could be set up on Internet chat rooms or via anonymous email accounts. The attacking company could hide behind a veil of secrecy so that the hackers wouldn't even know who they were working for. This way, if the attacks were detected, the hackers would bear the brunt of any criminal action and the conspirators remain completely anonymous.

(3.9) Prime-time hacking

But who are these hackers? What do they do when they're not hacking? When are they most likely to strike? The answers to these questions should be of more than just passing interest to you when designing your system of defences.

Who are they? They really could be anybody. Since there's no such thing as a bona fide 'hacker census' we can't know for sure, but all indications are that the vast majority are males in their teens and early 20s. Why this is so is something for the psychologists and sociologists to debate. As such, many are students but some are IT professionals who moonlight on the side.

In either case, you can pretty well guess when they are most likely to attack – and it's not 9–5. During those hours they are more likely to be at school, at work, or asleep (after a long night of hacking, of course!). Unfortunately for you, the times when your staffing and, therefore, your defences are at their lowest ebb is when the hacker is most likely to attack. Add to the mix the fact that the sun (or, in this case, the moon) never sets on the global Internet. This means that the most convenient time for hackers in other time zones may be the worst time for you. In other words, they are most ready to attack when you are most vulnerable – something that hackers don't want you to know.

Of course, you can't control the clock. However, you can control your systems. You can set up a line of defences that alerts you day or night, when intrusions occur. Clearly, you must be able to mobilize a response team at a minute's notice. A '24×7'[9] security operation is required.

Emergency response procedures must already be in place or you risk further damage during the recovery phase. Particular attention should be paid to the forensic evidence that may be scattered across the organization's diverse systems. Admissibility of such evidence is highly dependent upon the laws of the country you are operating in. If you ever hope to catch the intruder, you must ensure that not only the attacked systems but also their supporting infrastructure are left just as they were. Of course, the needs of the business call for immediate restoration of service. In order to balance these two diametrically opposed requirements, a system of backups and a well-defined procedure for making the switch-over is essential.

But what about the cost of such defences? It's really better to ask the question, what about the cost of *not* maintaining around-the-clock vigilance? When you put it in that perspective, the cost of prevention usually pales in comparison. One way to facilitate appropriate emergency preparedness without having to hire a legion of new employees and bankrupting the organization is to outsource it. There are companies with security specialists who make a living at dealing with intrusions and responding to IT emergencies. Their expertise and experience in dealing with similar incidents that have occurred at other client locations can be an invaluable resource. The larger consulting/outsourcing operations can be available to you whenever you need them because they have people stationed all around the world. No matter how late it is where your systems are, it's the middle of the day for them.

(3.10) You've got the money and they've got the time

Another factor working for hackers, and against you, is that they have time on their side. Hacking usually doesn't have to be done on a schedule. Hackers rarely face deadlines. They can simply bang away on a system until they finally get in or get bored trying. Those for whom hacking is an obsession don't mind spending countless hours or even days on end dreaming up new exploits and trying them out on your systems. Since many of them either don't work or have no real life outside cyberspace, they have loads of time on their hands. As a result they can be persistent beyond your wildest imagination. Tenacity and endurance are their greatest assets.

Thomas Edison once said that 'genius is 1 per cent inspiration and 99 per cent perspiration'. Since attacks can be launched from within an air-conditioned room, there's not a lot of sweating going on, but the principle remains the same. You've got what they want and they've got the time needed to get it.

9. 24 hrs/day, 7 days/week.

chapter 4

Analyzing the risks (and counting the costs)

Murphy's Law: 'Anything that can go wrong will go wrong.'
O'Toole's Commentary: 'Murphy was an optimist.'

Chapter summary

- Coping with risk
- The right time to do risk analysis
- Determining acceptable risk
  - striking a balance between overconfidence and paranoia
- The essential elements of risk analysis
- Choosing the right countermeasures
  - calculating the 'bang for your buck'
- Using the numbers as your guide – not your master

We live in a world of seemingly unending risks. When you get out of bed each morning there is a risk that your foot will not plant securely, you lose your balance, and crack your head open on the dresser. You could slip in the shower, cut yourself shaving, get electrocuted by the hair-drier, or break out in a rash from the new cologne you just bought. Then you could fall down the steps, cut your finger slicing a bagel, and burn the house down with the toaster. All this before you've even left the house!

It's enough to make you give up and just stay in bed, although even this option is not without its risks. You could die of starvation, become riddled with bedsores, or just fall into generally poor health from the lack of activity. Of course, unless you're independently wealthy, the fact that you stop showing up for work will surely end in your dismissal. The lack of income will eventually warrant a visit from the bank who will come to take your car away. Finally, you will be evicted because you have fallen so far behind on your mortgage payments. What a pleasant set of choices you have – get out of bed and risk losing life and limb, or stay in bed and end up homeless and destitute.

Of course, this level of pessimism is extreme. The other side of the story is that by getting out of bed each morning you also stand to benefit from all the wonderful things that life has to offer. Today might be the day that you get a promotion at work, soak up the sun on a Caribbean beach, or simply enjoy the company of friends and family. In order to reap the rewards, though, you've got to be willing to take some risks.

E-business is no different. A company that becomes paralyzed by the daunting list of risks it faces by taking its business to the Net will soon find itself extinct as more nimble competitors beat it to new markets. By the same token, a freewheeling organization that is completely unconcerned with the risks of doing business at the speed of light will ultimately meet the same consequences as hackers rob them blind.

Each company must strike an appropriate balance between risk and opportunity.

The key, of course, is balance. Each company must strike an appropriate balance between risk and opportunity. Such a decision-making process is really nothing new. In fact, it's been going on for as long as people have been involved in commercial endeavours. Even our agrarian ancestors dealt with the same fundamental issues. Is the path between my farm and the market safe enough for me to risk loading up my crops, which represent months' worth of labour and investment, onto a cart and undertaking the journey? Along the way, will the horse see a snake, rear up, and topple the cargo into the river? Will the cart lose a wheel and plunge perilously into the canyon? Will thieves hijack the whole works and make off with everything of value?

Obsessive fretting over such risks would deprive the farmer and his family of all the other things available to him at the market. He would have to become entirely self-sufficient and live like a hermit. Any new idea or product that might improve his lifestyle would remain hopelessly out of reach. However, if he knew that the road he travelled was riddled with bandits, he would be a fool not to bring along with him some companions and some means of defending himself and his payload. A healthy understanding of the risks can lead to contingency planning that helps mitigate the negative consequences that might otherwise result.

This is precisely what we are after when we look to make the way secure for e-business. It all starts with a firm grasp of the situation. Only when the risks are understood can they be mitigated. Only when these risks are quantified can we know what types of countermeasures are appropriate.

This is what risk analysis is all about. Of course, too much of even a good thing is still exactly that – too much. It's important to strike just the right balance in this area. A preoccupation with risk and risk analysis activities will undermine the health of the business and induce a climate of 'analysis paralysis' where nothing meaningful ever gets done. On the other hand, failure to pay proper attention to risks inherent in any business endeavour is a prescription for disaster.

Before we go any further, it is worth noting that since this book is focused on IT security, this section will focus on how those issues contribute to a consideration of risk. Clearly, hackers are not the only threat to critical system availability. Other factors such as unanticipated demand, natural disaster, equipment failure, software bugs, etc. all add to the overall risk that key processes will not perform as intended. Therefore, a comprehensive risk analysis should take into account more than just the hacker threat if it is to accurately represent the total picture.

4.1 Risk Analysis or post mortem?

The best time for a Risk Analysis (RA) is *before* you've been hit – not after.

Clearly, the best time for a Risk Analysis (RA) is *before* you've been hit – not after. Unfortunately, it doesn't always pan out that way in the real world. Senior management may be unwilling to expend the necessary resources for a comprehensive risk analysis until they are forced to become believers in its importance the hard way – after they've been hit hard by hackers. 'Better late than never' is OK for some things, but its reverse ('better never late') rings truer when it comes to information security.

RAs that are performed only after an expensive attack are a bit like locking the barn door after all the animals have escaped.

RAs that are performed only after an expensive attack are a bit like locking the barn door after all the animals have escaped. The reason is that an RA done after a security breach tends to be more like an autopsy rather than a real RA (Corby, 1999).

In medical terms a check-up is better than an autopsy. The former gives you a chance to save the patient whereas the latter only tells you what was missed. This is not to say that post mortem analysis is not important – because it is. Only a fool does the same thing again and again and expects a different result. This is why *root cause analysis* (discussed in Section 2.1) should be performed for significant security incidents. The point, though, is that prevention is cheaper than treatment. This axiom holds just as well in the realm of information security as it does in the medical profession.

In fact, if you haven't yet experienced a serious loss, you are in the best position to benefit from an RA. Unfortunately, history tells us that you are also the one least likely to exploit this advantage. This need not be the case, though. It is hoped that in this brief discussion of RA you will get a sense of what is involved, common pitfalls to avoid, and, ultimately, see the importance of such a task.

4.2 Acceptable risk

In short, RA is all about determining the risks that we face and figuring out how we can reduce them to an *acceptable* level. We can't live in a risk-free world, but we can take prudent steps to avoid unnecessary risks and mitigate the damage that might ensue. The trick is in determining what is and is not an acceptable risk within the larger context of the goals of the organization.

'Acceptable risk' may mean different things to different companies depending upon their corporate culture and the business that they are engaged in. Certain industries are naturally more risk averse than others. The same is true of certain companies within a given industry. The legal system that the organization operates under may also dictate a minimum standard of care.

For instance, a court may find that an enterprise is guilty of negligence if they do not take appropriate steps to protect their own operations as well as the interests of their customers. Such an interpretation might also include a requirement to perform due diligence to ensure that your systems aren't used by hackers to harm other organizations. In addition, a legal judgement against someone who attacks your systems might be diminished if you don't do enough to keep your systems secure. A federal judge said as much when he criticized the US Army for failing to 'do its homework' in defending a compromised system. He further indicated that 'the Army's effort, or lack of it, to keep its Web site secure could affect the amount of restitution [the alleged hacker] is ordered to pay'(Associated Press, 2000a).

A common mistake made in assessing risk results from an inability to come to terms with some of these basic issues. The point is that 'acceptable risk' must be defined within the context of the business and legal environments in which the organization operates. An attempt to force artificial, black and white criteria in a world of varying shades of grey, is a certain path towards futility.

Technical people tend to fall into one of two camps on this issue:

(1) Either through naivety or simple arrogance, they have complete and total confidence in the robustness of the technology in question. These modern-day *Titanic* designers are supremely confident in the unsinkability of the ship they have built.

(2) The polar opposites of the first group never miss an episode of *The X-Files*. Their motto is 'be afraid ... be very afraid'. To them, anything less than a concrete bunker defended by nuclear warheads is vulnerable.

Adding to the confusion is the fact that the business people don't have enough information to know which side to believe, so they throw their hands up in disgust and make ill-advised decisions. Since the truth lies somewhere between the two extremes, the ideal approach would be to lay out all the pros and cons and let the needs of the business serve as the final arbiter.

In order to do this, though, a real meeting of the minds must occur. The technical staff need to think more like business people and the business people need to become better informed on the technical issues. Only then can the right answer for the organization be determined.

Implied in the term 'acceptable risk' is the notion that, despite our best efforts, nothing can ever be made completely safe because to do so would render that thing useless. For example, jewellery that is deemed so valuable that it cannot be worn or even displayed for fear of loss is almost good for nothing. It is destined never to see the light of day. Instead of being admired, it can only collect dust in a safe surrounded by armed guards. Unlike jewellery, business resources are more highly valued for their function than their form – but some of the same issues exist. Inherent in functional use is the risk of loss. RA, then, is all about trying to come to terms with this inescapable reality.

4.3 Sizing up the situation

The essential elements of an RA involve answering the following questions:

- *What resources need to be protected*? This question has to be answered at the beginning of any meaningful RA because without it, the entire exercise is completely hypothetical. To provide real protection, real resources must be identified. These resources could range in value from the cost of a single workstation to the *total value of the corporation's brand image*, which, of course, could be immense. It may also include Web servers, mission-critical applications and classified corporate data. Since new resources of value are born into existence each day, any inventory is destined to be incomplete. Nevertheless, some items are persistent and well known. Some of these will deserve special treatment and should, therefore, be listed explicitly. Others will be in a constant state of flux so the best you can do is to categorize them and deal with them as a group.

- *What or whom do they need to be protected from*? Chapter 3 dealt with this question in a general sense, but more specificity is needed for an RA. At this point it is useful to think like a hacker. Remember that hackers can be competitors, script kiddies, social activists ('hacktivists') or even your own employees. Each is motivated by different factors and will, therefore, be drawn more toward certain types of attacks more than others. Clearly, you don't want to make the mistake of assuming that only a competitor would be interested in a critical database and ignore the fact that a disgruntled employee (or former employee, who still has access to internal systems) might execute a very different sort of attack on this same resource. You want to cover all the bases, but it would be wise to double-check the most likely attack scenarios.

● *What is the cost of loss or compromise?* The difficulty here comes from trying to quantify such costs. What is the value of a company's reputation? What is the effect on the bottom line when the corporate Web site is defaced but no classified data is lost? How big is the hit to customer confidence when such attacks occur? Also, it is important to realize that the leakage or compromise of classified data may be just as costly as the actual loss of that data, so both scenarios must be taken into account.

● *What is the cost of protection?* Some well-intended security efforts have succeeded in protecting critical resources but failed to take into account the cost of the countermeasures employed. It might sound like common sense to assert that you never want to spend more to protect something than that thing is actually worth, but such wisdom can be in short supply at times.

● *What is the likelihood of loss or compromise?* This may be the most difficult question of all to answer but it is, nevertheless, important. An error in judgement here can undermine the entire analysis by painting a picture that is too rosy or one that is too bleak. Both extremes could prove costly.

Bear in mind throughout the RA process that the final report needs to be *accurate* but not necessarily *detailed* (Corby, 1999). Don't try to 'boil the ocean'. To answer these RA questions in excruciating detail would ultimately prove counterproductive. Let the needs of the business be your guide.

4.4 Cumulative insecurity

A chain is only as strong as its weakest link, right? IT systems, however, when considered from an end-to-end security perspective, are, in fact, as weak as all their weak links combined. For instance, if a given component is able to repel 99.9 per cent of all the attacks it encounters, this might sound pretty good. However, the flip side of 99.9 per cent security is a 0.1 per cent vulnerability. That might sound like an acceptably low level of risk until you consider that IT systems are comprised of hundreds or even thousands of components ranging from computer hardware and software to networking devices such as routers, switches and hubs. Given that each component contributes its own level of insecurity to the overall mix, you can begin to see how a sort of *reverse synergy* is at work – the system is actually *weaker* than the sum of its parts.

IT systems ... are, in fact, as weak as all their weak links combined.

For example, consider an e-commerce scenario where goods and services are sold via the Web. In order for this business channel to function effectively, all of its underlying components must be up and operational. If transactions are to be meaningful and binding, each of these components must also be secure (otherwise either party could be duped by an impostor). The Web server's hardware platform, operating system, middleware and Web serving application must all perform as expected. Since the Web server may also interact with a separate database server, the database server's hardware and software must be equally solid. The networking components that connect these servers both to each other and to the purchaser's system must be reliable as well.

If a hacker can steal a credit card number through a hole in the database server, he or she doesn't need to try to eavesdrop on the network traffic as it passes by. Either attack would produce the same results if the data is not encrypted sufficiently well. In the latter case the hacker doesn't even need to gain access to the seller's machines in order to undermine the validity of future purchases. Any single vulnerability window can provide just enough daylight for an attacker to slip through, despite the otherwise robust security of all the other components of the system.

Table 4.1 shows how, from a strictly mathematical point of view, the contribution of 10 components, each with a 99.9 per cent security confidence rating, can actually result in a cumulative vulnerability of 1 per cent. This might not seem too bad until you consider that this 1 per cent risk, when carried out over the course of a year, could translate into a window of vulnerability equivalent to just over three and a half days (a hole big enough to drive a truck full of hackers through!). The reverse synergy kicks in when you consider the effect of the increased complexity that each additional component adds to the overall system.

In other words, when you analyze the security of a given IT environment, the cumulative effect of all of the underlying vulnerabilities, no matter how small they may seem in isolation, must be taken into account. Lots of little holes may seem insignificant at first glance, but, when viewed together as part of a larger whole, can represent a substantial risk. It pays to mind the details.

Of course, such reasoning must be taken with a large grain of salt since real-world situations are not so easily quantifiable. The point of this illustration is not that precise vulnerability numbers may be determined – because they can't. Also, since this is merely a *theoretical* discussion, the *practical* ramifications in a real-world environment are likely to differ as other factors come into play. The point is that each piece of the puzzle adds to the cumulative risk. What might seem to be an acceptably small risk when taken alone, can become a completely unacceptable risk when combined with the other pieces that make up the complete system.

TABLE 4.1   Vulnerability window calculation

Component	Confidence of Security	Cum. Probability of Vulnerability	Cum. Vulnerability Window (hrs/year)	Cum. Vulnerability Window (days/year)
1	99.9%	0.1%	8.8	0.4
2	99.9%	0.2%	17.5	0.7
3	99.9%	0.3%	26.3	1.1
4	99.9%	0.4%	35.0	1.5
5	99.9%	0.5%	43.7	1.8
6	99.9%	0.6%	52.4	2.2
7	99.9%	0.7%	61.1	2.5
8	99.9%	0.8%	69.8	2.9
9	99.9%	0.9%	78.5	3.3
10	99.9%	1.0%	87.2	3.6

From the field of statistics we know that the probability (P) that a system is secure is the product of the probabilities that each of its underlying components is secure. Expressed as an equation it looks like this:

$$P_{(system\_secure)} = P_{(component\_1\_secure)} \times \cdots \times P_{(component\_n\_secure)}$$

where

$P_{(system\_secure)}$ = probability that the system is secure
$P_{(component\_1\_secure)}$ = probability that component 1 is secure
$P_{(component\_n\_secure)}$ = probability that component n is secure

Therefore, the probability that a system is not secure and, therefore, vulnerable, is simply 1 minus the probablity that the system is secure or:

$$P_{(system\_vulnerable)} = 1 - P_{(system\_secure)}$$

where

$P_{(system\_vulnerable)}$ = probability that the system is vulnerable (i.e. cumulative probability of vulnerability)
$P_{(system\_secure)}$ = probability that the system is secure

4.5   A meteorite-proof car?

At this very moment millions of objects of various sizes and shapes are hurtling through space. Some are even on a collision course with planet Earth! You could be driving along in your car one day and a meteorite could come crashing through the roof, causing you and your car to go flying off the side of a cliff and explode into a giant fireball. It's not very likely, but it's not completely beyond the realm of possibility.

What if by spending an extra $100,000 you could actually select a 'meteorite-protection package' that would somehow make your vehicle impervious to falling space debris? Assuming such a thing really existed and that it delivered as promised, would you be willing to kick in an extra hundred grand to make your car meteorite-proof? Of course not. Car dealers might like such a feature (after all, they've been adding on all sorts of useless options and overcharging for them for years), but consumers wouldn't go for it.[1]

What if a deadly virus was spreading like wildfire? People in every conceivable corner of the planet were dropping like flies from this killer strain. In fact, every person that had contracted the disease had died within just a few days. There was no known cure once a person had become infected but there was a vaccine that was 100 per cent effective. If that vaccine cost $100,000, would you pay for it? Of course you would. Your life is worth $100,000, isn't it?

So why, then, are you willing to shell out $100 K for a vaccination that would save your life, but not for a meteorite-proofing vehicle option that could do the same thing? Both cost the same amount and the value of the precious commodity (your life) being protected is the same, yet your response to each option is completely opposite.

The answer, of course, lies in the fact that in one case the threat is entirely theoretical and in the other it is entirely real. The likelihood of a meteorite actually falling on your car is so impossibly remote that the value of its protection as compared to its cost is hopelessly skewed. On the other hand, the virus threat described in this hypothetical example is imminent.

No one wants to pay big bucks for protection that will almost surely never be needed, but anyone who could afford to protect against a 'clear and present danger' would be foolish not to do so. IT security is no different. A company that chooses to ignore an obvious and substantial threat to its very existence would be acting with reckless abandon. Eventually, the odds would catch up with such an organization and they would be put out of business. However, a company that squandered scarce capital on exotic mechanisms to protect against dubious threats would surely suffer the same fate. Clearly, striking the right balance between risks and costs is the key.

1. Adapted from Avolio (1997).

4.6 Cost-effective countermeasures

Once you've completed the vulnerability analysis portion of the RA, it's time to figure out what to do with the information that's been gained. Since failing to act upon what you know has the same effect on security as not knowing it in the first place, no RA is complete without an analysis of appropriate countermeasures. The key is in determining which countermeasures make sense within the business context and which ones don't.

Unfortunately, there are no proven, purely mathematical mechanisms that can make this decision for you. Try as you might, you're just never going to be able to come up with a practical way to automate the entire process. Simple formulas are great for dealing with straightforward, objective data, but the effectiveness of security countermeasures will, to one degree or another, defy quantification.

This doesn't mean, however, that you must go it completely alone. There are, in fact, a few calculations that can help *guide* (but not *dictate*) the decision-making process. They can't tell you precisely what you should and should not do, but they can shine a little light on the whole process by illustrating (at least in theory)[2] where the greatest benefit can result from the least expenditure. For example, if you believe that auditing the list of analog lines (which might be used as back doors into the enterprise) at a cost of only a few person-days' effort would have more impact than installing a system to prevent employees from viewing objectionable Web sites (which might cost substantially more and yield only a small improvement), then the choice is obvious. If you had an unlimited budget you could choose to do both, but since the likelihood of that is roughly equivalent to that of finding a diamond mine in your own back yard, we won't spend much time on that scenario.

Unfortunately, in the 'real world' we do have to live with budgetary constraints, so tough choices have to be made. We need to consider things such as the probability of a security breach versus the expense involved in preventing the vulnerability. First, it may help to calculate a '**Bang for the Buck Ratio**' **(BBR)**[3] which can help illustrate the cost-effectiveness of a given countermeasure. To do so, simply divide the cost of loss or compromise by the cost of protection[4] as follows:

Bang for the Buck Ratio = Cost of Compromise / Cost of Protection
    or

BBR = CC / CP
       where   BBR   Bang for the Buck Ratio
                     CC   Cost of Compromise (or loss)
                     CP   Cost of Protection (countermeasure)

2. The practical value of the formulas that will be presented is open for debate. At the risk of oversimplifying, this information is included in order to demonstrate the underlying principles at work. Slavish adherence to the numbers is unlikely to produce optimum results, but failing to think through the issues presented here will, almost certainly, guarantee a poor outcome.
3. Based on Hamilton (1999).
4. The cost of protection should not only include the purchase price of the given countermeasure but also the cost of implementing and maintaining it over time.

This is essentially an ROI (return on investment) calculation. Items with the highest BBR should have the greatest *potential* payback in terms of security. However, this information alone is not enough to make the right decision. The BBR needs to be tempered by the likelihood that such a vulnerability will ever be exploited in the first place. After all, what good is a cost-effective countermeasure that protects perfectly well against a scenario that will never happen?

A **Vulnerability Index** (**VI**) calculation can also help direct the decision-making process. The VI is simply the estimated cost of compromise multiplied by the probability that such a compromise will actually happen. Clearly the probability of compromise will not be exact. An estimate based on past experience or simply your best intuition will have to suffice. This, of course, underscores the need for caution in using these figures.

Vulnerability Index = Cost of Compromise × Probability of Compromise

   or

$VI = CC \times PC$

   where   VI   Vulnerability Index
                CC   Cost of Compromise (or loss)
                PC   Probability of Compromise (or loss)

The VI provides a reality check. It can help show what is at stake and, when taken with the BBR, can provide a level of discipline to the entire process of selecting appropriate countermeasures. One meaningful way of combining some of these factors into a single number that can give insight into the bigger picture is a **Relative Value** (**RV**) calculation. The RV of a given countermeasure is a function of the protection it provides in comparison to its cost and can be expressed in the following way:

Relative Value = Vulnerability Index / Cost of Protection

   or

$RV = VI / CP$

   where   RV   Relative Value
                VI   Vulnerability Index
                CP   Cost of Protection (countermeasure)

From the previous formulas, other expressions of RV can also be derived which might prove useful:

Relative Value = Cost of Compromise × Probability of / Cost of
                                        Compromise / Compromise

   or

$RV = CC \times PC / CP$

From this you can see that RV is a function of the expense that could be incurred from any damages, the cost to prevent those damages, is tempered by the estimated likelihood that damage of this sort might occur. Because the RV gathers up all these important factors into a single expression, it's easy to see why this calculation could be helpful.

In other words, countermeasures with the largest RVs are those whose costs are relatively low compared to the protection that they provide. On the other hand, if costs are high and protection is low, the RV would also be low and the motivation to implement that countermeasure would be lacking.

When taken together, BBR, VI and RV can provide some basis for guiding the discussion of which countermeasures are worth implementing and which are not. These numbers can also help provide the business case that senior management will surely want to see before investing in additional security. These figures aren't magical, though. They are based on *subjective* estimates which will almost surely contain some measure of error. Therefore, it is important not to rely too heavily upon them. Use them as a *guide* but take care not to become their *slave*. The primary reason for including these formulas is not to indicate that the decision-making process can somehow be completely automated – it can't. The real reason is to demonstrate the underlying principles at work. With a better understanding of such issues, more informed decisions can be made.

4.7 Evaluating countermeasures

Let's take a fictitious example to illustrate the points just discussed. Note that the numbers that we will use are completely made up. Don't try to read too much between the lines. Drawing conclusions from this example about what the relative value of these countermeasures might be in your environment could be misleading. The point here is just to show how the calculations work and how they can be used (Table 4.2).

TABLE 4.2   Evaluating countermeasures

Countermeasure	Cost of Compromise	Cost of Protection	Probability of Compromise	BBR	VI	RV
Install firewall	$1,000,000	$25,000	50%	40.0	500,000	20.00
Audit analog lines	$50,000	$2,000	5%	25.0	2,500	1.25
Web surfing filter	$5,000	$1,000	1%	5.0	50	0.05
Smart cards for all logins	$1,000,000	$2,000,000	10%	0.5	100,000	0.05
Smart cards for key logins	$750,000	$20,000	10%	38.0	75,000	3.75
Develop security policy	$1,000,000	$40,000	75%	25.0	750,000	18.75

While it should be possible to come up with a reasonably accurate estimate for the numbers in the Cost of Protection column, the Cost of Compromise and Probability of Compromise figures are by their very nature more elusive. Again, since these are only *estimates*, you need to take care not to give undue credence to the results.

From this analysis we can see that installing a firewall had the greatest BBR. Its moderate cost, as compared to other countermeasures, along with its large Cost of Compromise value (since you could potentially lose everything) give it the greatest bang for the buck. The VI leader, though, is the development of a security policy. The cost of bringing in a consultant and the time it will require from a larger number of employees (whereas the firewall could be installed by one person) drive its costs up a bit, but the higher probability that it will impact security in a positive way makes it the winner in the VI column. Since firewalls essentially implement only a portion of the security policy and, therefore, depend upon good policies in order to be effective, it makes some sense that the policy item would do better in the VI owing to its broader scope of influence.

Another way of looking at these calculations is to focus on the RV results. Here, again, installing a firewall and developing a security policy are the winners. Notice also how the RVs differ dramatically when comparing a smart card deployment for all logins versus just for selected, high-priority accounts. As you might expect, the cost of rolling out smart cards and smart card readers to all users (instead of just a few) can dilute the ROI numbers. The higher RV for the limited rollout indicates as much. In other words, more technology is not always the best answer.

Again, these calculations aren't foolproof. In fact, over-reliance on them can be just as damaging as not using them at all. Since they are based on subjective estimates, their inherent accuracy can never be more than an educated guess. But an educated guess beats a wild guess more often than not, so the exercise *is* useful. The key is to let these numbers be your *guide* – not your *dictator* (Corby, 1999). Numbers don't make decisions, people do. Stand back after the tallying is complete and use your own intuition as well.

chapter 5

The role of policy

Chapter summary

- Why a security policy is important

- Common pitfalls in security policies

- The importance of keeping policies simple

- Using policy as a tool

- Policy as a positive rather than a negative

- Important elements of an effective security policy

The surest way to fail is never to set a goal in the first place. After all, if you don't know where the finish line is or what it even looks like, it's highly unlikely that you will ever find it, much less cross it.

The same is true for computer security, where a good security policy illuminates the path to the finish line – an environment of secure, trusted e-business. The unfortunate reality, however, is that anywhere from roughly one-half to one-third of companies worldwide have no security policy in place (Duncan and Ahsan, 1999) and, therefore, essentially have no idea what the goal is or how to reach it. Furthermore, it is quite likely, even for those companies that have gone to the trouble of establishing a security policy, that fewer still actually have one that is understood by their employees.

For a security policy to be effective, it must be customized to the unique business culture and computing environment it will serve. There's simply no such thing as a 'one size fits all' security policy. A comprehensive discussion of security policy is beyond the scope of this book, but one excellent resource for this sort of information is British Standard (BS) 7799, a *Code of Practice for Information Security Management* (British Standards

There's simply no such thing as a 'one size fits all' security policy.

Institute, 1995). BS 7799 does a great job of summarizing in a very concise form the issues that need to be considered when designing a corporate security policy.

The US National Institute of Standards and Technology (NIST) also has a couple of great resources that can help. In particular, *Generally Accepted Principles and Practices for Securing Information Technology Systems* (Swanson and Guttman, 1996), which is based, at least in part, on BS 7799, goes a step further by providing a discussion of key security topics and useful checklists. *An Introduction to Computer Security: The NIST Handbook* (National Institute of Standards and Technology, 1995) gives an even more in-depth look at security policy along with a wide range of IT security issues.

These documents are a good place to start, but just because you've read them doesn't make you an expert. It is highly recommended that you seek out the assistance of someone who *is* when approaching this subject. Fortunately, there are plenty of security consultants who have experience in this area and are willing, ready and able to help you develop or improve your own security policy.

Of course, the standard guidelines for selecting a consultant apply. You will want to consider their experience in this area, find out what sort of methodology they use, check references, and so forth. Also, you should avoid the oxymoronic 'reformed hackers'. Anyone who would break into an organization's IT systems without prior authorization is, quite simply, unfit for the task of legitimate computer security. Think of it this way – if you were awakened in the middle of the night by a burglar who had successfully entered your home while you and your family slept, how likely would you be to hire him the next morning to design and install a new security system for your home?

(5.1) How to mess up a security policy without even trying

The challenge with corporate security policies is that while there is no single right way to design one, there are a million ways to mess one up. Fortunately, there is an identifiable set of common pitfalls which, when understood, can be avoided. Some common characteristics of bad policies are that they are:

● *Out of touch with reality.* Too many security policies appear to emanate from deep within the hallowed, windowless halls of the data centre and, as a result, bear no resemblance to the real-world work environment. For a policy to be effective it must be perceived as being relevant by the vast majority.

● *Inaccessible.* If employees are unable to quickly locate the portions of the security policy that are relevant to them, the policy will effectively cease to exist. If it can't be found within about three mouse clicks of the corporate intranet home page, it is essentially hidden.

Many external Web pages contain counters that reveal the number of visits or hits to that particular page. Marketing departments use this information to determine the effectiveness of their Web presence. The same technique could help a company gauge the accessibility of their security policy. If the page appears to be gathering dust, you know you've got a problem.

- *Poorly marketed.* Security specialists would do well to take a page from their marketing counterparts. Just because you're the only security group within the company doesn't mean you have no competition. Your competition comes in more insidious forms. Apathy, ignorance, and failure to comprehend the magnitude of the situation are just a few examples. Security groups are notoriously poor at marketing the value they bring to the business and, as a result, suffer from a chronic lack of funding and debilitating lack of respect. An internal marketing program for the organization's security policy which emphasizes the importance of each employee's participation and spells out what the cost of failure means to them as a company and as individuals could pay big dividends.

- *Draconian.* Policies that are overly punitive are likely to be feared and avoided. No one wants to read about all the thousands of ways that they can mess up. People naturally cringe at the thought that the company is acting like some sort of Orwellian 'Big Brother' looking over their shoulders just waiting to catch them in the act. Of course, employees should clearly understand that computer security is serious business because the stakes are high, but the policy should make everyone feel like they are on the same side. When battle lines are drawn, security falls by the wayside.

- *Not informative.* No one likes to be lectured on what they aren't allowed to do. With children we have to set down specific behavioural ground rules for which they may not fully understand the justification. Adults are far less likely to respond positively in such an environment, though. If you want cooperation and adherence, you've got tell them *why* something is the way it is or they will probably find a way to subvert it or ignore it altogether. Good policies *educate* their intended audience as they lay down rules.

- *Too long.* Policies that attempt to enumerate every possible threat will ultimately fall under the weight of their own bureaucracy. Another common mistake occurs when high-level policy statements, detailed security standards and enumerated security procedures are all intertwined into a single, rambling document. The policy statement should be a concise statement of the organization's security goals. On the other hand, security standards documentation should deal with more specific details such as password rules, encryption specifications and firewall filtering guidelines, for example. Security procedures, then, fill in the remaining holes by stating step-by-step instructions for certain key security tasks. Providing a series of meaningful links among these various documents is a great idea, but interleaving broad objectives with detailed instructions makes for an incomprehensible hodgepodge of seemingly unrelated concepts. The bottom line is that if the essential components are too long, no one will read them. If no one reads them, it's no different than if they didn't exist in the first place.

- *Not targeted.* The security policy should be segmented so that people can easily find the portion that is relevant to them. There's no point in requiring the secretarial staff to read the section on corporate Web-site security standards. A security policy divided into meaningful subsets can better address the competing requirements of brevity and completeness.

- *Too narrow.* Some policies are simply too specific. They discuss, in very narrow terms, the consequences of particular vulnerabilities while ignoring the underlying principles involved. Hackers are dreaming up newer and better attacks every day, but most vulnerabilities still revolve around well-known security *faux pas*. In some cases, specific attack details could be relevant, but, in general, it's best for a policy to be based on key principles that have proven their worth over time.

- *Out of date.* No security policy, no matter how good it is, will be able to anticipate all the issues that will arise in the future. For instance, how good would a security policy written before the days of ubiquitous Internet access be today? Clearly, the Internet has introduced an enormous number of new situations that an old policy could not possibly have envisioned. The point, then, is that once you think you've got it right, do it again. Of course, you don't want to spend every waking moment revising the policy, but it should be revisited and revised as necessary at regular intervals. However, if the policy needs to be changed frequently, then it ceases to be effective because the end-user community can't keep up with it. On the other hand, if the policy reads like an exhibit in a technology museum then it has outlived its usefulness.

- *Not supported by management.* Even if everything else on this list is covered, a surefire way to ensure that a security policy will end up on the rubbish heap is to fail to get the necessary buy-in from corporate management. Management support can't guarantee success, but not having it will surely guarantee failure. Uneducated or unmotivated managers will, either through their actions or lack thereof, communicate to employees that security is not important. They may even go so far as to undermine security by overtly approving risky exceptions to the policy or simply ignoring it altogether.

(5.2) KISS that policy goodbye

A policy that is overly complicated will never succeed. This sounds obvious, but judging from some of the security policies in place some policy developers don't believe it's true. To be fair, though, policy creation is not an easy job. On one hand there is the need to be thorough while on the other there is a mandate to be brief. We live in an age of instant gratification and short attention spans. Failing to take this into account when creating a corporating security policy is one of the best ways to ensure that almost no one will ever hear your message, regardless of how important it may be.

A key concept which, when utilized properly, will go a long way toward making a security policy acceptable to the people that, ultimately, will implement it is the

Not all simple policies are good but all *good* policies are *simple*.

KISS principle. KISS stands for 'Keep It Simple, Stupid' and it pretty much sums up the feedback that people who have had to wade through a pile of policy pages would like to give to its authors. Clearly, not all simple policies are good but all good policies are simple – at least as simple as they can practically be. Portions that need to go into greater depth should be separated from the mainline directives everyone needs to see. This way, readers can choose the level of detail appropriate to their own background and needs. An example of how this can be done will be discussed in the next section.

5.3 Policy that teaches

As you can see from the previous list of pitfalls, at least one common theme emerges – education. The people making the security and Internet access policies need to be sufficiently familiar with the technologies involved so that they make intelligent decisions. Too many times IT staff have taken the short-term view of trying to simplify their lives by 'just saying no' to any and all requests for access. They view the Internet with suspicion largely because they don't understand it and are, therefore, incapable of appreciating its value.

In addition to educating the policy-makers, it is critical to educate the user community. They need to understand how their seemingly innocent behaviours can have catastrophic effects. The typical approach has been to pass down the security policy as if it were some infallible, unchanging edict from the corporate ivory tower. Such an approach causes these policies to die a slow and painful death. They end up being nothing more than an artefact that is occasionally taken out and examined as some irrelevant curiosity bearing no resemblance to the real world. Threats are unlikely to ensure compliance (although they do tend to make the policy-makers happy).

The key to success is an educated user community that understands not only the *do's* and *don'ts* but also has a sense of the *why's*. Since no policy can cover every situation that might potentially arise in the future, it is important that there be a widespread realization of the underlying principles. Such knowledge can serve as a guide in the grey areas of new frontiers not envisioned by policy developers.

One way to achieve this is to use the familiar hypertext technology of the Web to make the whole thing manageable. You might start with a brief statement of important security principles and corporate security standards which would fill no more than a couple of screens. Interspersed throughout this overview would be 'hot' links to more detailed explanations of each key concept and unfamiliar term. See Figure 5.1 for an example of this approach.

This way, employees can get as little or as much as they want. Policies presented in the traditional linear form employed by books tend to put people off by their sheer volume. They also fail to take into account the existing knowledge of the reader, forcing even the most savvy user to dig through seemingly endless streams of basic information. Hypertext format lets the reader, rather than the author, guide the learning experience. This flexibility makes for a more conducive learning environment by meeting the needs of each student rather than catering to the rigidity of the bureaucrats who insist upon conformity.

The security policy must be understood in order to be followed. It must also be distributed and explained in order to be understood. Companies that actually have

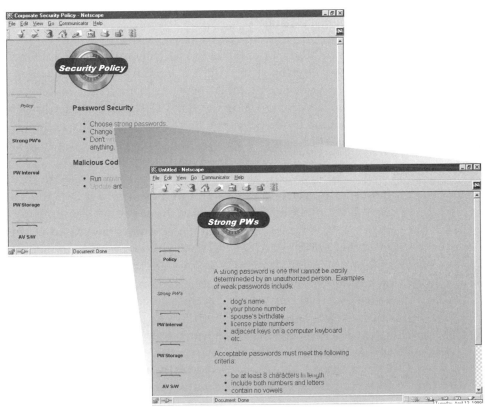

FIGURE 5.1   Leveraging hypertext to navigate the corporate security policy

policies should be able to do an adequate job of disseminating this information as this can be, more or less, automated. It's the education part that most ignore – at their own peril.

5.4 Getting it right

Now that we've covered what a policy should not be like, what sort of things should a good policy include? There are, as you might imagine, many schools of thought on this subject. The ultimate answer lies within the uniqueness of your own environment, but some areas that you might want to consider covering in your corporate security policy are discussed below.[1]

5.4.1 Acceptable use statement

It should be abundantly clear to all employees that the IT systems they use belong to the company and are, therefore, to be used to further the legitimate interests of the organization. Without this baseline firmly established, the remainder of the policy will have no teeth. Also, the absence of a definitive statement in this area could come back to haunt you if an employee causes damage to your systems (or those of another organizat3ion) and you end up looking to the legal system for justice.

5.4.2 Single point of incident reporting

Just as important as the existence of a meaningful security policy that is accessible and understandable by all is the establishment of a single, well-known focal point for security incident reporting.

The simple fact of the matter is that despite our best efforts, there is no way to guarantee that a system won't be penetrated. Even though a well-designed system of defences and intrusion detection monitors may be in place, an end user may still be the first to discover a break-in. If this incident is not reported promptly, any hope of containment may slip through your fingers. From a centralized vantage point, an emergency response team can size up the threat and pinpoint their actions to the areas where they will be most effective.

5.4.3 Crime scene preservation

Once a break-in has been discovered, it is critical that all available evidence be preserved. The compromised system should be treated as a crime scene that no one is allowed to disturb. Precise records should be kept as to the events that transpired before, during, and after the breach. This might sound like an overreaction but

---

1. Only a brief summary is included here as most of these areas will be covered in greater detail in Part 2.

without the information on the machine in question it may be impossible to learn from the mistakes that were made and could, therefore, increase the likelihood of a repeat performance. Also, if disciplinary action or even criminal prosecution are deemed appropriate, the current state of any compromised systems could be critical both in isolating the source of the attack as well as proving 'who did what to whom and when'. Courts aren't likely to simply take your word for it, after all.

The sales manager's first reaction may be to get the system back online as quickly as possible in order to minimize the short-term impact to the business. However, this might leave the company open to even more damaging attacks in the future. The best course of action may be simply to kill the power to the system, since an orderly shutdown procedure may help cover the hacker's tracks. An experienced computer forensics expert can use the disk drive from a compromised system to re-create the crime scene and gather any available evidence. In any case, the organization should consult both legal counsel and law enforcement officials to determine the best course of action *before* a break-in occurs.

5.4.4 Single point for warning issuance

This same focal point for incident reporting should also be the *only* group that issues vulnerability warnings. It has been said that 'the penalty for telling a lie is that no one believes you when you tell the truth'. The same principle applies to security warnings. If everyone in the company takes it upon themsleves to forward virus warnings to everyone they work with, and such warnings prove to be hoaxes, then eventually no one will believe even the bona fide advisories. 'Crying wolf', no matter how well intentioned it might be, is bad for security and, therefore, bad for business.

5.4.5 Backup and recovery

If you knew that a hacker was going to break into your system and that there was nothing you could do to prevent it, what would you do? You could sit around and fret endlessly, which would do no good whatsoever, or you could make sure that you can recover quickly from any loss that might be incurred. For IT systems this means ensuring that your data is backed up frequently so that downtime is minimized. Since computer security can never be guaranteed, it must be assumed that every system will one day be compromised. Without a uniform[2] corporate policy for data backup and recovery, you leave to chance the health and reliability of your critical business systems. The alternative is not unlike performing a high-wire act without a net. It makes for great drama but bad business.

> Since computer security can never be guaranteed, it must be assumed that every system will one day be compromised.

2. In this context uniformity does not imply that the policy will be identical for every system but that all systems of a given type are treated the same way.

A good policy might include details such as which systems require backup (it may not be cost-effective to back up all of them), how often backups should occur, will backups be performed manually or automatically, will backup files be stored locally or in a more secure location, and so forth. An important point to consider after these details have been decided is which tools can implement the policy across the entire enterprise with its variety of operating platforms. Allowing each platform support specialist to pick their own favourite backup/recovery tool might sound like a good idea at first, but a uniform, multi-platform system would go a long way toward alleviating the chaos that otherwise normally ensues.

5.4.6   Malicious code

Malicious code (sometimes called '**malware**') can take many different forms. It may be in the form of a computer virus, a Trojan horse (a program that purports to do one thing, which may be useful and benign, while also creating an unintended security vulnerability), or active content such as Java, JavaScript and ActiveX programs. Excellent antivirus tools exist on the market today. Given the tremendous threat that viruses present, there is simply no excuse for not having every PC protected.[3] Not only should the policy require such protection but it should also spell out how and when virus signature files should be updated and, if possible, provide for a means for automating this process.

Employees should also be informed about the risks of detaching and executing email attachments (a common source of viruses) and running active content in browsers. In theory Java's sandbox implementation should provide a robust security environment that keeps malicious applets in check. However, practical experience teaches us that until we have error-free Java Virtual Machine implementations (when was the last time you saw a bug-free browser?), running Java code will not be without its risks. JavaScript and ActiveX are even more vulnerable as we will discuss in Chapter 18.

As a result, you might consider a policy that encourages users to turn off these features in their browsers except in cases where they are truly necessary. Active content can be used to provide essential business functions in exciting new ways. Unfortunately, it can also chew up bandwidth and CPU cycles, leaving you with meaningless 'eye candy' at best or even a compromised system in the worst case. Therefore, it pays to be judicious in your use of this technology.

Finally, you can improve your protection against malicious code by running one of the commercially available active content screening tools which can block suspicious programs as they enter your network.

---

3. At the time of this writing, the number of antivirus tools for other platforms such as UNIX is sparse, but this could change over time.

5.4.7   Permissible network traffic

A complete security policy should spell out what types of network traffic should and should not be allowed to enter and exit your network. This policy can be enforced through the deployment of firewalls but the decision as to its permissibility should not be left to the implementation phase.

5.4.8   Authentication

The most common form of user authentication (the way users prove to the system that they are who they claim to be) is through the use of passwords. As a matter of policy you should consider whether stronger authentication methods (smart cards, security tokens, biometric readers, etc.) should be deployed on a limited basis or even across the board. Where passwords will be used, there should be a clear policy prohibiting the selection of weak passwords that can be easily guessed or cracked. Password rules enforced on each system when new passwords are chosen are a good starting point. The length of time a password should be allowed to remain in effect and where passwords are stored on systems and in the employee's work space should be spelled out. Chapter 11 discusses these issues in greater detail.

5.4.9   Modems

Since modems attached to PCs can be exploited by hackers as a means of bypassing mainline defences, the organization should carefully consider who should have them and what the valid business justification would need to be. Instructions on how and why auto-answer mode should be disabled might also be useful. Also, if it is possible to disable analog lines outside of normal working hours, this may help reduce vulnerability from war-dialler attacks, which are discussed in Section 20.4.

5.4.10   Waste disposal

Hackers can learn a lot about your people and the systems they use by going through your garbage. 'Dumpster diving' might sound like an inglorious means of attack, but it is, nevertheless, effective. Classified information should be separated from other garbage and handled appropriately. Since passwords are often written down on paper (even though they shouldn't be), it is important that this paper be handled in the same way as the classified garbage (shredded, stored in locked bins until recycled, etc.).

5.4.11   Social engineering

Employees need to understand that hackers may attempt to exploit their good nature and coax information out of them. This information may seem harmless but when combined with other bits could reveal far too much. Tips on what should and should not be done on behalf of an unknown person, no matter how nice they may sound or how urgent the situation they describe may seem, should be considered for inclusion in the security policy.

5.4.12   Cryptography

What sort of information should and should not be encrypted to protect it from prying eyes? How strong (key length) should the encryption be?[4] What is the plan for recovering encrypted data for which the keys have been lost or are temporarily unavailable (key recovery plan[5])? A security policy would do well to deal with these issues.

5.4.13   Downlevel software

Since an astounding number of attacks depend upon the fact that you are running downlevel software (which contain vulnerabilities that have since been fixed in more recent versions), a uniform policy regarding upgrades on key systems is in order. Someone (or group) should be assigned the responsibility of monitoring security bulletins from vendors and other advisory services.

Again, this is only a short list of items that you might consider. The key is to strike the right balance between covering all the important areas and not going overboard by creating a policy that is too big for anyone to actually read. Segmentation by employee job function and presentation through a well-conceived set of hypertext links can go a long way toward helping you reach this goal.

---

4. Cryptographic strength is an especially important issue when dealing with data that may be sent to or received from other countries as import/export laws differ around the world.
5. While government requirements for key recovery/escrow on private citizens and corporations alike are almost certainly a bad idea, this technology can be indispensable when used by a corporation to recover its own data that might otherwise be lost.

chapter 6

Putting all the pieces together

- The three essential elements of effective security
  - people
  - policy
  - tools

As we saw in Chapter 4 on risk analysis, the point is that you shouldn't immediately look for the hottest new security product when a low-tech (or even no-tech) answer will suffice. This is not to say that technology can't help increase the security of your IT systems because it most definitely can, but it should be viewed as a *tool* which, in the right hands, can provide a great deal of protection. Like any tool, however, it must fit within the larger context. A total security solution involves three essential elements:

(1) *people*, properly motivated and educated;

(2) *policy*, well stated and easily accessible; and

(3) *tools*, suited to the task at hand.

It starts with people because they are the ones who drive the other components. They are the ones who possess in their collective experiences the knowledge of the business and its essential systems. Only from this basis can meaningful policy be defined and only from good policies can effective defences be built. Technology can assist in marvellous ways, but by itself it will never be adequate to get the job done.

In fact, the beginning, middle and end of the entire process revolve around people. Ultimately it is their behaviour that enhances or detracts from the security of the IT systems. If they don't understand (or care) how they impact the security scheme, they will, in the end, contribute to its undoing.

part 2

The hacker's edge

Internet security vulnerabilities

chapter **7**

What you don't know *can* hurt you

Chapter summary

- The hacker's edge

- Your response

  - levelling the playing field

- An overview of subsequent chapters

Ignorance may be bliss for some but if it's your job to protect your organization's IT resources, nothing could be further from the truth.

Simply stated, hackers know things that you don't. That's their edge. In the 'Information Age' it is *information* and its successful use, rather than military might or wealth, that results in power. If you want to storm the enterprise, you don't need a battering ram or a tank because a few freely available software tools will suffice. Whether they like it (or are even aware of it) or not, IT staffers are at war against a faceless, unknown enemy that can appear out of nowhere and vanish instantly – only to repeat the cycle again and again. The term 'information warfare' might sound overly dramatic, but when you consider what is at stake (the very existence of the enterprise), you quickly begin to understand that the consequences of failing to mount an effective defence are potentially catastrophic.

Hackers know things that you don't.

So, if hackers know things that you don't, what's the best way to even the score? An obvious answer would be to learn what they know. That is, of course, the purpose of this section – taking the hacker's edge and turning it to your advantage.

7.1 Gotcha!

Successful attacks involve an element of surprise. If you knew when an attack would occur, which systems would be targeted, how the attack would be launched and what the cost of the casualties would be, you would surely thwart the attack before it ever started. However, since no one's crystal ball is that good, the best approach is to strengthen all the expected attack points. It turns out that information concerning well-known attack points is readily available to hackers. In this section we will endeavour to explore some of these areas. In an effort to make this same knowledge available we will discuss:

● common misconceptions regarding IT security that pervade the industry,

● tried and true hacking techniques, and

● well-known security holes that continue to be exploited by hackers.

By 'levelling the playing field' your adversaries will no longer have the upper hand. But knowledge, alone, isn't going to protect your systems. You have to *act* on that knowledge and implement an end-to-end security infrastructure that can withstand the assaults of unauthorized entities as well.

The remainder of this book will deal with these issues. The approach taken is to state in simple (sometimes oversimplified) terms a key concept around which a number of important vulnerabilities revolve. These vulnerabilities are not really new, as hackers have successfully exploited them for years. Unfortunately, they seem to be unfamiliar to their victims who continue to be exploited in much the same ways time after time. Each major concept is presented along with a discussion of that area.

Hackers don't want you to know that ...

firewalls are just the beginning

Too many times a discussion of network security consists of little more than a discussion of firewalls. Firewalls are a critical component of an effective defence system, but they are significantly limited in terms of the types of attacks they can detect and repel.

not all the bad guys are 'out there'

The assumption that all the 'bad guys' are out there and the 'good guys' are in here might sound reasonable, but that doesn't make it true. In fact, roughly half of all attacks are engineered by insiders who, through their extensive knowledge of the target environment and greater access, can potentially do more damage than hackers coming in from the outside.

humans are the weakest link

A chain is only as strong as its weakest link, and human fallibility, rather than technology, is likely to be the link that breaks in the IT security defence system. Well-intentioned but uninformed employees are easily exploited by hackers who know which strings to pull.

passwords aren't secure

The most common form of user authentication on IT systems is a 'secret' password. Unfortunately, this also happens to be one of the most vulnerable for a variety of reasons.

they can see you but you can't see them

Eavesdropping on network transmissions can reveal more than enough information to a hacker looking to gain higher levels of access. The bad news is that attacks of this nature are generally passive and, therefore, hard to detect. The good news is that there are, in fact, some things you can do to snoop on the snoopers as well as limit what they are able to intercept.

downlevel software is vulnerable

Wine might get better with age but software usually doesn't. In fact, just the opposite generally occurs. Old software has been around long enough for hackers to probe its weaknesses and publish information on how to exploit it. Organizations that fail to realize this are setting themselves up to be victims of any of a number of well-known attacks – attacks that might have easily been prevented.

defaults are dangerous

A vendor's choice of defaults for their product might meet *their* needs perfectly well but might, on the other hand, spell disaster for you. From the standpoint of security, it is best to turn off all services that are not essential to the operation of the organization or you run the risk of having them exploited by attackers and used against you.

it takes a thief to catch a thief

If you want to catch hackers – or merely repel their attacks – it helps to think as they do. Your ability to anticipate their moves could mean the difference between costly reactive efforts and more effective proactive defences. The good news is that you can learn the tricks of the hacker trade from the same sources that they do – namely, the Internet.

attacks are getting easier

You don't have to be a genius to be a hacker. In fact, all you really need are a few tools, which can be downloaded for free, and enough audacity to use them. Some of the latest hacker tools support easy-to-use graphical user interfaces which make attacks as simple as 'point and hack'.

virus defences are inadequate

Clearly, some people are doing a great job of protecting their systems against malicious software but many aren't. Outdated antivirus tools and risky end-user behaviours help to ensure 'success' for virus creators.

active content is more active than you think

Java, Javascript and ActiveX can change a customer's reaction to your Web page from a yawn to a yell. If the dynamic content being delivered performs properly and truly adds value, the sounds you hear will be shouts of joy. If it leaves a system open to attackers, victims will be significantly less enthusiastic.

yesterday's strong crypto is today's weak crypto

Just because you've encrypted a message is no guarantee that only authorized personnel will be able to read it. As computer processing power increases, a hacker's ability to 'crack the code' increases as well. Judicious use of appropriately strong cryptography can lessen the likelihood, though.

the back door is open

Putting in a good firewall at the perimeter of your network is somewhat like putting a security guard at the front entrance of a building. Failing to secure phone lines coming into the organization is akin to leaving the back door wide open for hackers.

there's no such thing as a harmless attack

What is the value of your company's brand? What would it cost to recover from a major public relations *faux pas*? Just because a hacker didn't steal corporate secrets or drain the payroll account doesn't mean that an attack didn't cost the organization a ton of money.

information is your best defence

In the realm of 'information warfare', information is both the hacker's prize and your best means of defending it. Too often, important security information is known only by hackers or their adversaries in the corporate IT security group. Getting the relevant details to the end-user community and ensuring that awareness of attacks is communicated to the right people can mean the difference between winning and losing the war.

the future of hacking is bright

Unfortunately, hackers aren't going away any time soon. In fact, their numbers seem to be growing. Emerging trends in the IT arena point to a brighter day when computers will do even more for us than they do now. These same changes may also usher in a host of new vulnerabilities for the next generation of hackers to exploit.

chapter 8

Hackers don't want you to know that ... *firewalls are just the beginning*

Chapter summary

- Firewall defined
- The importance of a firewall
- The basic functions of a firewall
  - packet filtering
  - stateful packet inspection (SPI)
  - application-level proxies
  - circuit-level proxies (SOCKS)
  - network address translation (NAT)
- What a firewall can be expected to do
- What a firewall cannot be expected to do
- The critical relationship between firewalls and policy
- How firewalls become weak
- Various firewall platforms
  - software-based
  - hardware-based
  - embedded
- The value of personal firewalls
- The dangers of overdependence on firewalls

When you ask a networking specialist if their network is protected you're likely to get the answer: 'Yes, we have a firewall from vendor X.' Unfortunately, this answers a different question than the one that was asked. Having a *well-configured* firewall is an essential component of any network security infrastructure, but even it can't guarantee that your systems are completely safe.

Credit card giant Visa received a less than gentle reminder of this fact in July 1999 when their systems were broken into. A company spokesman commented that, 'We have firewalls upon firewalls, but are concerned that anyone got in.' The attackers threatened that if they weren't paid £10 million (approx. $15 million at the time) in ransom, they would crash the company's systems. Presumably these hackers figured their offer was reasonable since Visa stood to lose that much or more for just a single day's outage (Ungoed-Thomas and Arnaud, 2000).

Firewalls alone simply aren't enough. It is the widespread ignorance of this basic fact that, in many cases, allows hackers to perform their misdeeds. Therefore, hackers don't want you to know that firewalls are just the beginning.

8.1 What is a firewall?

A **firewall**, quite simply, is a device that acts as a buffer between a trusted (and presumably secure) network and an untrusted (and, therefore, potentially insecure) network (Figure 8.1). The term 'firewall' is borrowed from the construction industry. To a builder, a firewall is a wall built of fire-retardant materials which is designed to prevent or, at the very least, slow down the spread of fire from one room to another. As such, a firewall acts as a *containment barrier* which protects against disaster.

Network firewalls perform a similar function by acting as a barrier between your network and potentially harmful traffic emanating from an adjacent network.[1] Typically, firewalls are positioned at the perimeter of a corporate network

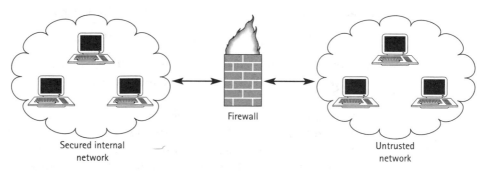

Firewall

Secured internal network

Untrusted network

FIGURE 8.1   Keeping the bad stuff out: a basic firewall configuration

1. Or even another portion of your own internal network as will be discussed in Section 9.2.

in order to guard against attacks from other networks. Those other networks could be public networks such as the Internet or other private networks belonging to business partners.[2]

8.2 Under the hood

How do firewalls do what they do? The answer depends upon which firewall you're using and which of its features you've turned on. The four main categories of firewall technologies are:

(1) packet filtering,

(2) stateful packet inspection,

(3) application-level proxies, and

(4) circuit-level proxies.

Let's take a brief look at each ...

8.2.1 Packet filtering

The most basic of firewall technologies is that of **packet filtering**. A packet filtering firewall simply examines the header of each packet it encounters and decides whether to let that packet proceed or stop it dead in its tracks. This decision is made in accordance with a set of rules defined by the firewall administrator. These rules can be based upon information such as:

- where the packet came from (e.g. source IP address or range of addresses),
- where it is headed to (e.g. destination IP address or range of addresses),
- the network protocol involved (e.g. TCP, UDP, **ICMP**, etc.), or
- the port number being used, which can indicate the type of traffic encountered (e.g. Web browsing, file transfer, streaming audio/video, etc.).

Packet filters are the simplest to implement and are, therefore, reasonably inexpensive to buy. In fact, packet filtering capabilities are often built directly into routers and other networking gear as a standard feature. Because they concern themselves only with the first part of the packet being inspected, they are also relatively fast as

---

2. A comprehensive treatment of firewalls is beyond the scope of this book. One excellent resource, however, is Cheswick and Bellovin (1994).

compared to other firewall technologies. However, their inability to dig deeper into the packet also limits their ability to spot certain types of vulnerabilities such as those that are targeted at a particular application (Sample, 1998).

8.2.2   Stateful packet inspection (SPI)

Stateful packet inspection (**SPI**) takes the concept of packet filtering to the next level. In addition to selectively allowing or denying access based on information in a packet's header, SPI firewalls keep track of the larger context, or 'state', of the specific transmission. By maintaining a table of current connections and their most recent events, these firewalls are able to spot abnormal sequences which might represent a threat. An SPI firewall may also take into account certain aspects of the application data included in the packet, thereby extending its reach beyond just the networking layer.

8.2.3   Application–level proxies

Application-level proxy firewalls (often called simply 'proxies', for short) take a very different approach. As their name implies, they inspect packets at the application level through the use of a specially designed 'proxy'. This proxy essentially executes a stripped-down version of the application in question to determine whether the behaviour of the packet is acceptable. Proponents of this approach assert that proxies provide tighter security for this reason (Sample, 1998).

Another key feature of this type of firewall is that they actually 'break' the networking session between the two endpoints at the proxy (Figure 8.2). The proxy maintains one session with the host in the trusted network and another session with the host in the untrusted network. Both hosts believe that they are communicating directly with each other when, in fact, they are really only talking to the proxy between them. This isolation helps hide internal network details from outsiders that don't need to know them while still allowing permissible traffic to flow as needed. Proxy vendors often point out that this arrangement makes their solution more

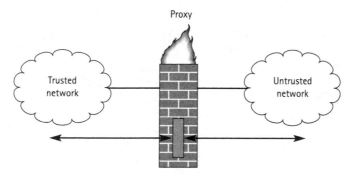

FIGURE 8.2   Breaking sessions at the proxy

secure than other alternatives. What they are less likely to point out is that the proxy mechanism may add additional overhead, which can hurt perform-ance. Add to this the fact that proxies must be written for each application to be protected, and other alternatives might start looking better for some environments.

8.2.4   Circuit-level proxies

Circuit-level proxy firewalls fit somewhere between application-level proxies and SPI/ filtering firewalls. The most common example is that of **SOCKS**, an IETF specification. SOCKS works at the session level, which means that it lacks the application-level checking of other proxies, but is more adaptable to new types of network traffic.[3] Since SOCKS offloads much of its checking to the client platform (IBM, 1997), it requires that special functionality be added to each system (a process known as 'socksification'). In exchange for this additional setup work, SOCKS is able to distribute the workload, thereby reducing the likelihood that the firewall will become overloaded.

Like application-level proxies, SOCKS can also hide internal network addresses from outsiders because it sets up two distinct sessions – one to the remote server and another to the client. The SOCKS server, then, relays data between the two sessions. Since only the SOCKS server knows the precise correlation between the two, insiders are insulated from certain types of network-based attacks.

Although its initial rollout was slowed to some degree owing to its inability to authenticate users and lack of (**UDP**) **User Datagram Protocol** support, these issues have been addressed in version 5 of the spec.[4]

In the early days of these various firewall technologies, the differences among them were easily delineated. Now, however, much of the debate as to which approach is best has lost a lot of steam. One reason for this is that both SPI firewalls and proxy firewalls have improved to the point that the chasm which once separated them years ago has diminished (Morrissey, 1998). Another reason is the fact that many commercial implementations have chosen to stake their claim in the middle by offering **hybrid firewalls** which combine multiple technologies into one product (Skoudis, 1998).

3. 'SOCKS v5 White Paper', Aventail Corporation, www.aventail.com.
4. RFC 1928 'SOCKS Protocol Version 5', Internet Engineering Task Force, www.ietf.org.
5. Adapted from Scott (1998).

8.3 What a firewall *can* do ...

Like any technology, firewalls have their strengths and weaknesses. Failing to recognize this could result in weakened defences and subsequent break-ins. Here's a brief list of what properly implemented firewalls *can* reasonably be expected to do.

8.3.1 Isolate your corporate network from an untrusted (or partially trusted) network

Firewalls *can,* for example, provide a degree of isolation between your internal network and the Internet. They are, in fact, most often used as a means of controlling which traffic is allowed to enter and exit your network. The fact that you can select the degree of isolation you want is the key. The goal, of course, is to stay away from the bad stuff while not impeding the flow of legitimate network traffic.

For example, you might want to allow **File Transfer Protocols (FTPs)**[6] to a public server containing unclassified information you wish to share with others outside your network. If these files are stored in a read-only directory you might feel confident in allowing open access to it. However, you may want to reject any attempts by outsiders to telnet into this box because there may be no legitimate reason for providing such access. This could be implemented easily with a few simple packet filtering rules in the firewall.[7]

What a Firewall *Can* Do...[5]

- Isolate your corporate network from an untrusted (or partially trusted) network

- Isolate portions of your own intranet

- Limit (but not eliminate) your exposure

- Provide a single point into and out of your network where your security policies may be imposed

- Provide a single point of logging/monitoring of activities

8.3.2 Isolate portions of your own intranet

Firewalls *can* subdivide your internal network into various security zones as will be discussed later in Section 9.2.

8.3.3 Limit (but not eliminate) your exposure

Firewalls *can* substantially reduce the risk from certain types of attacks as we will soon see, but such improvements are not without their limitations.

6. FTP provides a means for transferring files over an IP network such as the Internet.
7. In addition to disallowing telnet traffic at the firewall, security could be bolstered by also disabling the telnet service on the target machine.

8.3.4   Provide a single point into and out of your network where your security policies may be imposed

Firewalls *can* act as a 'traffic cop' deciding what is and is not allowed to pass through your network. When strategically positioned, they can bring a great deal of order to what would otherwise be a chaotic security nightmare. However, if performance considerations are not adequately taken into account, the firewall can also become the prime 'choke point' for the network.

8.3.5   Provide a single point of logging/monitoring of activities

Firewalls *can* provide a means for recording network activity. This is important because, in the event of attack, the information in this log can potentially be used to pinpoint the source of the attack. By documenting the originating address of the attacker, the systems that were targeted, and the frequency and duration of the attacks, the firewall's log can help track down the hacker as well as assist in the design of appropriate countermeasures to fend off future attacks. Once attack points have been strengthened, this same information may be needed as evidence in subsequent criminal prosecution, should you choose to go that route.

8.4   Drawing the battle lines

In many cases, companies have elected to use the packet filtering functions in network routers instead of full-function firewalls. This approach may be appropriate as an initial line of defence, but since simple packet filters often lack an effective logging and alerting function, they may be insufficient to guard critical resources. Using so-called **screening routers** to complement rather than replace full-function firewalls is consistent with the defence-in-depth approach discussed earlier in Section 2.3. In combination, these two technologies can be used to construct a demilitarized zone (DMZ), which buffers an internal network from external traffic while still allowing outsiders to access corporate resources such as the company's Web site. Figure 8.3 is a simple illustration of a **dual-homed** (that is, it resides in both the trusted and untrusted networks simultaneously) **firewall** and a screening router used together.

This configuration is rather basic and, therefore, insufficient to meet the needs of every environment. More complex arrangements involving multiple DMZs separated by additional firewalls can provide greater granularity and, therefore, greater security, but this architecture is a good starting point.

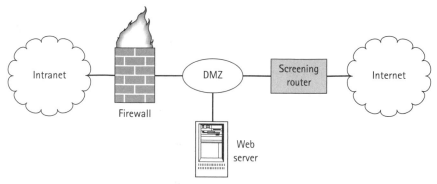

FIGURE 8.3   A basic DMZ configuration

8.5 What a firewall should *not* do ...

Just as important as knowing what a good firewall *should* do is knowing what a good firewall *should not* do. Of course, there may be some cases where you can get away with some of the things discussed here, but, in general, they aren't considered a great idea. Here are a few examples.

8.5.1 ... reside on a shared platform

There is a temptation to economize by combining firewall and non-firewall functions onto the same computing platform. An example of this might be consolidating a firewall along with a Web server, network traffic load balancer, or network router on the same box. The idea being that it is cheaper to add memory and other resources to an existing box than it would be to buy a new one.

However, most security experts will tell you that a firewall you're going to depend upon to any great extent should be on a dedicated platform. The reason is that a failure in one of these additional programs could either disable the firewall and shut down communications or, even worse from a security standpoint, open a hole in the firewall allowing unsecured traffic into your network. There are some exceptions to this fundamental rule of firewall implementation which will be discussed later, but, for the most part, it is best to look to other areas to economize as this one is simply too important to mess up.

8.5.2 ... be permissive by default

Vendors are, as you would expect, motivated to show off the capabilities of their products. It's in their best interest to have you duly impressed with all the bells and whistles that they've worked so hard to develop. As a result, they may be inclined to ship their product so that a default installation will have lots of features turned on.

Firewalls should do just the opposite. For maximum security the default installation should have essentially everything turned off, thereby denying all traffic not *explicitly* permitted by you. This approach may seem draconian at first, but the reason is to ensure that anything that is, in fact, allowed should result from a careful analysis and not be left to chance (or the firewall vendor's best guess as to what is best for you).

8.5.3   ... reveal internal network details

If knowledge is power then a lack of information about your internal network can leave would-be attackers powerless. The less they know, the better off you are. The reason is simple. Hackers need to know, at least to some extent, what they are dealing with in order to formulate their attack. In order to learn what they need to know, they must do a certain amount of fumbling around in the dark during their reconnaissance phase. The darker you make it, the more likely they will be to trip over something that alerts you to their presence, assuming you're paying attention. You can turn down the lights on their understanding of your environment by cutting off their sources of information.

One such source is the network addresses that are used within your network. Knowledge of your addressing scheme and the layout of your network is valuable to a hacker. Technologies such as application proxies, SOCKS and **Network Address Translation (NAT)**, which are included in many full-function firewalls, can be used to hide this information from outsiders. These facilities operate differently but all effectively translate internal addresses to new, external addresses before allowing packets to leave your network. This way, outsiders see only the external addresses, which you have chosen to expose. Since these addresses all point back to the firewall and since only the firewall knows how to translate these external addresses back to their internal counterparts, the hacker's view is obscured (Figure 8.4).

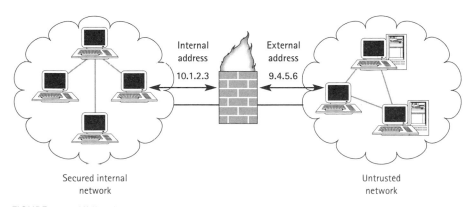

FIGURE 8.4   Hiding internal network addresses

8.5.4   ...tell anything about itself

Now that 'all roads lead to the firewall' you may be wondering if this exposes the firewall to attack. The answer to that question is 'yes and no'. Of course, the mere fact that the hacker can see only your firewall will effectively paint a big bull's eye on this critical component.

However, if properly implemented, the firewall will appear to be a huge black hole to potential intruders. This is because the firewall should only respond to required network traffic that is relevant to it. By ignoring PING, WHOIS and other nosy requests for information, the firewall will stand as a 'silent sentry' maintaining the perimeter. Good firewalls aren't much interested in chit-chat. They speak only when spoken to and often it is only to someone they know. When they do, in fact, respond it is with the kind of scarcity and precision that would make Captain Joe 'just the facts ma'am' Friday, of *Dragnet* fame, proud. This approach helps maintain a veil of secrecy around your network that frustrates the hacker's attempts to glean useful information.

8.6   Firewalls and policy

According to Marcus Ranum, president and CEO of Network Flight Recorder Inc., a firewall is 'the implementation of your Internet security policy' (Rothke, 1999). As you will see shortly, there's much more to a security policy and its implementation than just a firewall, but the basic sentiment of this statement hits the nail precisely on the head.

A good firewall will faithfully do exactly what you've told it to do through its filter rules. But how do you know what the rules should be in the first place? Which traffic should be allowed and which should be rejected? The answer lies in the corporate security policy which should spell out such things.

Unfortunately, this answer puts us squarely in the face of one of the industry's dirty little secrets – most enterprises don't have one. As we discussed in Chapter 5, most businesses worldwide don't have a definitive, well-known security policy. This means that critical decisions regarding what should and should not enter the corporate network are far too often left to lower-level technicians responsible for installing firewalls. Without a consistent policy to guide them in their work, the chances of actually getting the job done right the first time are, at best, remote.

'If you haven't got a security policy, you haven't got a firewall'.

Ranum sums it up perfectly in saying, 'if you haven't got a security policy, you haven't got a firewall'. And if you haven't got a firewall, you have essentially left the front door wide open.

8.7 Holes in the firewall filter

But let's say you're one of the diligent minority that actually have a good, well-thought-out security policy to start from. Will the rest of the firewall implementation fall into place? Not necessarily. It turns out that even the best policy may result in an almost incomprehensible stream of filter rules. Throw in the fact that humans have an astonishingly poor track record in dealing with the daunting task of trying to reduce conceptual rules down to discrete, precise, unambiguous instructions and you've really got a mess on your hands. If you have any doubts about this assertion, then you haven't tried running any of the latest shrink-wrapped software available these days. Buggy programs are the norm rather than the exception.

Unfortunately, coding firewall filter rules is a lot like programming and, as such, is subject to some of the same pitfalls. In other words, filter rule definition is a tedious task that can be unsettlingly error-prone. The disturbing part, though, is that unlike a bug in your favourite word processor or spreadsheet, firewall bugs can result in gaping holes in the IT infrastructure and ultimately in the enterprise. What may begin as a few simple rules can snowball into an avalanche of exceptions over time.

What a Firewall _Cannot_ Do...[8]

● Protect against attacks not made through the firewall

● Protect against an authorized user's malicious behaviour

● Protect against viruses and Trojan horse programs[9]

● Protect against completely new threats

● Protect against bad or nonexistent policies

● Protect against your own errors (e.g. incorrect filter setup)

● Act as an effective single point of defence

What if you are one of the fortunate ones that not only has a great policy in place but also has faithfully captured this in your firewall configuration? Surely, you don't have anything to worry about, right? Wrong. The simple fact of the matter is that even the best firewall implementations have their limits. With some exceptions, firewalls are mostly only able to analyze the type of network traffic they see at a very broad level. They really can't tell exactly _what_ the packets will do. Is a given packet acceptable or malicious? The firewall may not be able to tell.

For example, a firewall can recognize that it's dealing with telnet traffic but it can't tell whether the session is being used for legitimate purposes or an attack.

8. Adapted from Scott (1998).
9. Strictly speaking, virus/Trojan horse protection and other content security issues are not the responsibility of a firewall since this involves actually examining the payload contents of the packet being inspected. However, newer product packaging arrangements which seek to integrate content security and antivirus tools with firewalls are causing this line to become blurred.

A knee-jerk reaction might be to turn off all telnet access, but this approach may represent an unacceptable impediment to the needs of the business.

8.8 Traditional firewall options

Most full-function firewalls on the market at the of writing are implemented in software, although some hardware-based options do exist. Software-based firewalls run either on a proprietary operating system (OS) from the firewall vendor or on a commercially available OS. In the latter case it is strongly recommended that the OS be *hardened* by disabling all non-essential services, userids and privileges.

The advantages of software-based firewalls are that they can be easily upgraded with new features and bug fixes and can be scaled up for increased capacity by moving the firewall to a larger hardware platform. This flexibility is not without its costs, though. As you might expect, implementing firewall functions in hardware offers the potential for greater throughput, but these platforms tend to be less flexible by comparison.

8.9 Firewalls, firewalls, everywhere ...

An alternative to a traditional, dedicated firewall is that of the embedded firewall. These reduced-function firewalls may be implemented in a variety of ways. For instance, many network routers are able to perform the basic packet filtering function on their own. Since this capability is already built in, there's no reason not to go ahead and make use of it. The router's filter can serve as a first line of defence against attack by discarding some of the clearly errant or dangerous packets before they even reach the firewall or your network. The advantages to this approach are that:

(1) the workload on the firewall is reduced,[10] which allows it to spend its time concentrating on more subtle attacks, and

(2) by creating an additional barrier for hackers to overcome, you make their job harder and, therefore, your network safer.

Of course, there could be a downside to taking the firewall out of the loop for some of this traffic. Since firewalls are typically capable of logging traffic and routers aren't, the ability to go back and learn from the erroneous or even threatening traffic

---

10. At the time of this writing, most firewalls are capable of keeping up with commonly available network speeds and, therefore, are infrequently the cause of network traffic bottlenecks. However, increased dependence upon network-based services in the future could cause this to change. The result will be a need for improved firewall efficiency as well as spreading the workload out among a bank of firewalls.

that has been discarded is forfeited. Also, you may lose a sense of the value that the screening router and the firewall are providing as this data can be used to justify to management the need for such protections.

In addition, some systems offer integrated firewalls that can be sufficiently isolated from other operations on that platform. For instance, the OS/390 operating system which runs on mainframe systems provides a very robust mechanism for isolating programs into discrete, logical partitions (LPARs). The firewall included with OS/390 can be run in its own dedicated LPAR, thereby creating the necessary buffer between firewall and non-firewall functions. Also, the AS/400 midrange system offers an optional integrated firewall which, even though it runs in the same hardware box, is actually contained on a separate coprocessor card with its own, unique OS. In effect, this firewall is running on a different platform that happens to reside within the same housing as the AS/400 system. Purists still may argue that a separate firewall running on a dedicated platform is needed between this system and the public Internet, but the point is that such integrated firewalls can, at the very least, provide a valuable backup defence system.

Some have suggested that rudimentary firewall functions should be integrated into Web servers and even client systems. One example of this approach is the 'personal firewall' product, AtGuard, from WRQ Inc.[11] AtGuard software runs on client workstations and not only includes the basic firewall filtering functions but also adds privacy management and active content blocking on a Web site by Web site basis (Figure 8.5). As such, it can empower end users, who once had to fill the role of the helpless victim, with the tools to better control their own destiny from a security standpoint. Of course, you wouldn't want to rely on client software as the only means of defence for the corporate network, but when deployed within the context of a *series*

FIGURE 8.5   Using a personal firewall to control network traffic

11. In November 1999, AtGuard was integrated into Symantec's Norton Internet Security product and offered only in that packaging.

of firewalls between the user and the Internet, it can be quite effective.[12] Since a personal firewall runs on the user's system, it can be more finely tuned to weed out unwanted traffic that shared firewalls can't afford to block because its appropriateness can't be determined.

This sort of 'if a little bit is good, then a lot must be better' philosophy, though, is not without its problems. The management task involved with such a proliferation of firewalls could be daunting, to say the least.

- How could you ensure that all of your various embedded firewalls had a rule set that was appropriate for their unique roles within the enterprise?

- How would you deal with the different GUIs (graphical user interfaces), CLIs (command line interfaces), and config file formats that would be used in the various vendor implementations?

- How would you overcome the fact that one of the fundamental rules of firewall implementation (running more than one function on the same platform with the firewall) has been violated? (Note: This is, of course, of less concern as long as you maintain an effective system of full-function perimeter firewalls and avoid the trap discussed in the next point ...)

- Would you end up creating a false sense of security that could result in IT staffers and end users 'letting their guard down'?

8.10 Keeping the firewall in its place

The point is that firewalls come in all shapes and sizes with varying degrees of capability. Since there is no 'one size fits all' alternative when it comes to IT security, you can use this diversity to your advantage, if you are careful to keep the firewall in its place.

In all cases firewalls should be viewed as a *first line of defence* and not the total solution. They are an indispensable component of any secure IT infrastructure, but if they are the only thing standing between hackers and your enterprise, they are likely to be found sorely lacking. Bear in mind that *a single point of defence can become a single point of failure.*

> Firewalls should be viewed as a *first line of defence* and not the total solution.

All too often firewalls become the beginning and the end of the network security discussion. Firewalls should not be considered the definitive word, but a part of the larger whole. Policy is the place where the security discussion should begin. Some of that policy should manifest itself in the form of a firewall (or even multiple firewalls). As you will see, there's still plenty more heavy lifting to be done in order to secure the enterprise.

12. Another important application for personal firewalls is on end-user systems that are either dialled into the corporate network or linked via high-speed connections such as cable modems or DSL (as will be discussed in Section 23.3).

chapter 9

Hackers don't want you to know that ... *not all the bad guys are 'out there'*

... we have met the enemy and he is us.

Pogo (comic strip character), *Pogo* by Walt Kelly, Earth Day poster, 1971

Chapter summary

- The enemy within
  - the often overlooked insider hacker
- The value of internal firewalls
- The disgruntled ex-employee threat
- The critical importance of the efficient security administration

Firewalls are traditionally used only on the perimeter of the corporate network. Implicit in this placement decision is the notion that the bad guys are 'out there' and that the people inside the organization's network are all good guys. Is this a reasonable assumption? Do you need to be concerned about 'insider attacks' as well? Surely, you can trust the people that work with you each day, can't you?

Nearly half of all such attacks started from *within* the enterprise.

According to a study sponsored by the FBI and the Computer Security Institute (CSI) (1999), you can't. They found that *nearly half* of all such attacks started from *within* the enterprise. In previous years this annual survey has, in fact, indicated that *most* attacks were the result of an 'inside job'. Some may be tempted to conclude that since the outsider attacks have now caught up, the threat from insider attacks has diminished. However, Richard Power, CSI's Editorial Director, disagrees. 'The old rule that we would see 80% of the penetration coming from the inside, 20% from the outside, is out-moded. This isn't to say the threat from the inside has diminished – it hasn't. It is just showing that the threat from outside is now co-equal to it' (Larsen, 1999).

Surveys and statistics are one thing, but the problem isn't really that bad after all, is it? Besides, that stuff always happens to someone else. We've never had any-thing like that happen to us. That's probably what Omega Engineering, Inc., used to think – until, as they claim, their systems were sabotaged by a former employee who left on unfavourable terms. An indictment[1] filed in District Court by the US Attorney's office alleges that a 'chief network program designer' for Omega 'caused the transmission of a computer command that permanently deleted all the design and production programs that Omega needed to operate'. Omega says that the dis-gruntled worker essentially planted a software time bomb that was detonated a few weeks after his dismissal (Chen, 1998). This company learned the hard way that not all the bad guys are 'out there'. The cost of this lesson? *Ten million dollars* in lost revenue according to the indictment.

9.1 Model employee or spy?

Further complicating the situation is the fact that insider hackers can be very diffi-cult to spot. Ira Winkler, author of *Computer Espionage,* said that during his time at the US's National Security Agency (NSA), he was shown 'two documents, each characterizing a person who:

- volunteers for extra assignments;
- works late hours;
- never takes a vacation, and;
- seems interested in what their co-workers are doing.

The first document was from the Personnel Office, and was telling how to get pro-moted. The second document was from the Office of Security and was describing how to tell if a coworker is a spy' (Winkler, 1999). Of course, not all dedicated workers are corporate spies, but you can see how it might be hard to tell the differ-ence between the two.

---

1. 'United States of America v. Timothy Lloyd', US District Court, District of New Jersey, 28 January, 1998.

Add to this the fact that inside hackers have an advantage over outsiders in that they probably:

- know which systems contain mission-critical data and which ones don't;

- know the company's security policy and where it might be weak;

- know the undocumented realities of how other employees may not actually adhere to the company's security policy (e.g. shared passwords that are never changed);

- have physical access to critical servers;

- are inside the perimeter firewall and, therefore, beyond its scope of control.

In fact, an insider is in a better position to do harm and do it more quickly and more stealthily than an outsider and must, therefore, be considered a viable threat. Insiders may also be dissatisfied with their current work situation and, hence, may have additional motivation to strike back against the company.

Does all this mean that we should never trust anyone? Clearly not, but a certain sense of 'healthy paranoia' can be a great asset when designing defences (as long as it doesn't get out of hand, of course).

9.2 Good firewalls make good neighbours

The bottom line is that it doesn't matter how strong the walls are if the attacker is already inside the compound. By the same token, no matter how good your perimeter firewalls are, they can't protect you against attacks that don't pass through them. Clearly, a firewall positioned on the outer edge of the network would never even see an insider-initiated attack, much less be able to defend against it.

A simple, yet often overlooked answer to this problem is to deploy additional firewalls *within* the corporate intranet. This approach allows you to identify critical *security zones* that need extra protection (even from insiders), such as Personnel Accounting, and R&D (Figure 9.1) – information that is not needed by the majority of users within the enterprise. This way, for example, only the people in the Human Resources department will be able to get into the portion of the network that contains sensitive personnel data.

Some might argue that since these systems are protected by a userid/password checking defence, additional measures are unnecessary. But how much safer could these systems be if people lacking a 'need to know' were never given access to the logon screen in the first place? How much safer would your home be if only well-known (and presumably well-liked) family and friends were afforded access to your property? Of course, you would probably give up any hopes you

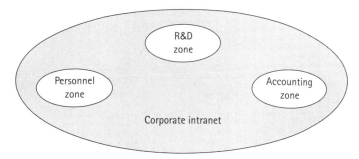

FIGURE 9.1   Protecting the internal network with intranet firewalls

might have had of winning the 'most congenial neighbour award', but security would certainly be increased. Since internal IT systems should be more interested in conducting critical business functions than in conducting idle chit-chat with unauthorized users, this trade-off is an easy one to make.

Another advantage of *intranet* firewalls is that they provide yet another hurdle for an external intruder, who might have slipped past the first line of defence. Let's say, for instance, that a hacker finds his way into your network. Without additional firewalls within the intranet, he can freely move about, wreaking havoc all along the way. Intranet firewalls, however, would help mitigate the risk of further damage by containing a security breach to a specific portion of the corporate network.

Not every organization will conclude that intranet firewalls are necessary. This is not inherently good or bad. It goes back to the subject of risk analysis as was discussed in Chapter 4. In any case, the corporate security policy should provide definitive guidance as to when and where firewalls – be they Internet or intranet based – should be placed.

Intranet firewalls alone are not the total solution, but they can make life more difficult for a hacker – and if it's your responsibility to protect the corporate network, then your job is, in part, to make life as difficult for hackers as you can. (If this sounds mean-spirited, don't worry. Just remember that they are out to do the same to you!)

9.3   Managing the revolving door

Employees come and employees go. It's a fact of life in any organization. Sometimes the parting is bittersweet and sometimes it's just plain bitter. In any case the revolving door of hiring, firing and retiring presents some daunting security challenges.

Let's say, for example, that a new employee is brought on board and this person's job requires that they access certain applications on an NT server, some on a UNIX server, and some on a mainframe. This means that we will need to work with the NT server administrator to create a new account, figure out what access rights this employee should have based on the job assignment, and assign these attributes to the new account. Of course, the NT administrator will know how to do all of this since he or she is well acquainted with the intricacies of the NT administration interface.

Next, we will need to repeat this exercise with the UNIX administrator, who almost certainly will be a different person from the one we just worked with for NT. Finally, we'll get to do it all over again with the mainframe administrator who is, again, bound to be yet a different person still.

The inherent inefficiency of such a procedure should be readily obvious. Wouldn't it be simpler if we could talk to one administrator who was capable of dealing with all of these platforms? Owing to the vast differences in each of these systems, however, it is highly unlikely that any single person would have the necessary skills on all of these platforms to get the job done. (Even if we could find such a rare guru, we would probably have to pay them the better part of the IT budget just to keep them working for us.)

A better approach would be to leverage technology to forge a solution. Tools such as those from IBMs Tivoli Systems would allow this sort of coordinated, centralized user administration without requiring deep (and, therefore, expensive) technical skills to do the job.[2] Also, by pre-assigning access rights based on job roles such as Teller, Loan Officer, and Branch Manager (assuming you work for a bank), you could ensure that new employees automatically have the capabilities they need while uniformly following the corporate security policy. This sort of automation not only represents a significant improvement in efficiency, which will surely please IT managers, but also has the advantage of providing greater security by reducing the likelihood of errors that could result in security breaches later on.

That should be justification enough, but if you're looking for a really big security pay-off, consider what happens when employees leave the company 5, 10, or 15 years after they joined it. What are the chances that we will still have a record of all the accounts and privileges that they have accumulated throughout the years? Even if we've been careful to keep such records, what is the likelihood that we never made any errors along the way? How long after employees leave will it take us to remove all these doors into the enterprise? If, for instance, they left on less than friendly terms, they might be inclined to strike back by taking out their frustrations on the IT systems to which they still have access.

What is needed is a system that closes all the doors at least as efficiently as they were opened. (In fact, it needs to be even more efficient than the earlier process because the cost of failure is greater and time is of the essence.) Again, systems

---

2. Tivoli SecureWay User Administation and Security Manager can be used in conjunction with other systems, to provide this capability.

management tools that provide 'single action management' would allow immediate removal of all of an individual's privileges in one fell swoop. With a few mouse clicks from a graphical user interface, all the accounts anywhere in the company that belong to the employee in question can be removed. Closing the loop by integrating this process with the Human Resources system which manages employee hiring and termination would provide even greater efficiency.

In case you aren't convinced of the value of such a tool, consider the fact that in the FBI/CSI study mentioned earlier, survey respondents pegged disgruntled employees as *the* most likely source of attack (Computer Security Institute, 1999). Independent hackers, competitors and foreign governments were all considered less likely. Given that the cost of a single security incident can run well into the millions, it's not hard to see how the cost of good security administration tools could easily be justified by the avoidance of just one such incident.

chapter 10

Hackers don't want you to know that ... *humans are the weakest link*

As the old saying goes, 'a chain is only as strong as its weakest link'. This truism applies just as well in the realm of network security. You can install all the latest, state-of-the-art security tools you can get your hands on but all it takes is one small crack in your defences to allow hackers free reign over your systems. The often surprising reality of today's high-tech environments, however, is that it is the carbon-based life forms (that's you and me) and not the silicon or the software that represent the weakest link in the security chain. This fact shouldn't come as a big surprise when you stop to think about it, but it may be the single most overlooked aspect in IT security.

One such high-profile case involved John Deutch, the former head of the US's Central Intelligence Agency (CIA). You would surely think that the person who directs the official spy organization of a global superpower would know better than to transfer top secret documents to his unclassified home computer, wouldn't you? Certainly a person whose job it is to gather sensitive information regarding things that might threaten the security and welfare of an entire nation would fully appreciate the dangerous ramifications of careless data handling, right? Wouldn't such a person know better than to put classified documents on a vulnerable home computer with an unsecured connection to the Internet? Evidently not, according to a CIA Inspector General report which found that Deutch committed just this sort of risky behaviour (Reuters, 2000).

Unlike machines, people aren't completely predictable. While it is true that on a larger, macro level, certain trends in human behaviour can be readily observed and outcomes predicted with reasonable accuracy, the actions of a given individual are something of a wild card. It may sound like a daunting task to get 1,000 PCs working in harmony but try to get 1,000 people to walk in lock-step to solve a complex problem and you'll quickly find that getting the machines to cooperate is child's play by comparison. We will never be able to completely control the actions of every employee in the company, but we do have a chance to get our arms around some of the most basic, common behaviours that increase the risk of successful attack.

10.1 Hacker or con man?

One of the more predictable aspects of human behaviour is that if you try hard enough you can usually find someone who will believe nearly anything. P.T. Barnum, of Barnum and Bailey Circus fame, put it less delicately when he said 'there's a sucker born every minute'.

Hackers know this too. In fact, they exploit this basic human quality (or flaw, depending upon your perspective) in many attacks. If hackers can contrive a somewhat plausible story, it is likely that they can talk someone out of the information that they want. The term applied to this act of preying on human nature is called *social engineering*.

Even if hackers fail initially (as they often do), they can simply try again with another unsuspecting victim. The fact that hackers may have:

● an abundance of spare time,

● persistence beyond belief, and

● a complete lack of shame

all work to their advantage. And since the enterprise is busy doing productive work, such activity often goes unnoticed. They're counting on this as well.

Also, the element of surprise and, in some cases, even urgency can increase their odds of success. A simple example might involve a hacker placing a call to the IT help desk of the company he wants to attack. The following conversation transpires:

Hacker: 'This is I.M. Bigshot, Director of Finance. I'm working on the fourth-quarter financial statement, which must be presented to the CEO first thing tomorrow morning, and I'm really in a jam. I just got a new userid last week and I can't for the life of me remember what it is. Could you look it up quickly and tell it to me so that I can get this thing finished up? I'll make sure your manager gives you a raise if you can just rescue me on this one.'

Help Desk: 'Sure, Mr Bigshot. I'd be glad to help. Your userid is ...'

After all, the help desk attendant figures no real harm can come just from giving out a userid. An intruder still wouldn't be able to get into the system, right? A second call to the help desk gets a different attendant and the following exchange takes place:

Hacker: 'This is I.M. Bigshot, Director of Finance. I'm working on the fourth-quarter financial statement, which must be presented to the CEO first thing tomorrow morning and I'm really in a jam. I seem to have forgotten my password. Could you look it up quickly so that I can get this thing finished up? I'll make sure your manager gives you a raise if you can just rescue me on this one.'

Help Desk: 'But how do I know you're really Mr Bigshot and not some impostor?'

Hacker: 'Look, I don't have time for this foolishness. You can either give me that password or you *and* your boss can explain to the Board of Directors on Monday why the financial statement isn't ready! Then you can explain to the CEO why we shouldn't fire you right on the spot!!'

Help Desk: 'I'm sorry, Mr Bigshot. Your password is ...'

Hacker: 'That's quite all right. You were only doing your job. You can never be too careful these days, what with all those hackers out there ...'

In the second call you can see that the attendant was more leery of giving out a password (as he or she should be), so the hacker proceeded quickly to Plan B by pretending to throw his weight around and bully the attendant. Since the attendant may be a temporary or entry-level employee (a common practice in the industry), the last thing he or she wants to do is rock the boat.

For an added appearance of legitimacy, the hacker could make it appear as if he is calling from inside the company's premises via an internal phone line. He could pull this off by first calling the company's main number and conducting this exchange:

Operator: 'Widgets –R–Us – how may I direct your call?'

Hacker: 'I.M. Bigshot, please.'

Operator: 'Thank you. I'll transfer your call ...'

Secretary: 'I.M. Bigshot's office. How can I help?'

Hacker: 'Could I speak to Mr Bigshot?'

Secretary: 'I'm sorry, he is in a meeting. Can I take a message?'

Hacker: 'No, that's all right but you could do me a huge favour if you would transfer me to the help desk. I'm on the road and my laptop is giving me fits.'

Secretary: 'I'd be happy to. I'm transferring you now ...'

Since the hacker has been transferred to the help desk from an internal line, it is likely that his call will appear to have originated from within the corporate campus (Mr Bigshot's office, no less), which lends an added appearance of legitimacy. Now when the attendant seems unsure about giving out the password, the hacker can assert that he must, in fact, be Mr Bigshot because how else could he be calling from Mr Bigshot's office?

Even if this fails, the hacker may simply try again on a different day with a different approach. Maybe he will try being as sweet as sugar and finesse his way into the good graces of the victim. By adding a sob story he may find a sympathetic soul on the other end that will break the rules 'just this once' for him. From the hacker's perspective, the worst they can say is 'no'. Nothing ventured, nothing gained.

In short, a hacker's boldness and your inability to fathom it provide numerous cracks in the infrastructure which he or she is willing and able to exploit. Hackers simply have more gall than most people could imagine and this helps tip the scales in their favour.

(10.2) It's a dirty job but somebody's *going* to do it

Another low-tech source of information about your company may be sitting in the place where no fine, upstanding person would be found – in the garbage bin. Of course, this is precisely what the hacker is counting on. That's why 'dumpster diving', as it is called, works. Every day literally tons of potentially valuable hacking information are tossed aside and treated as worthless junk. But, as they say, 'one man's junk is another man's treasure'.

Hackers know that even some of the things that you think are harmless can be used as weapons in their attack. For instance, even something as seemingly unrelated as payroll records could be valuable. Let's say that these records indicate that a low-level clerk has been passed over for raises and promotions for many years. One might reasonably assume that this clerk has less than the warmest of feelings for the people he or she works for. Such a person might be a prime candidate for a professional hacker to bribe in order to get what might seem like fairly innocuous information. This information, along with information culled from other sources, might be pieced together to complete the hacker's puzzle.

This scenario is bad enough in its present form but what if we were talking about a system administrator instead of a clerk? The magnitude of the threat could grow substantially based upon the unique knowledge of this employee.

The tendency of people to write down passwords on slips of paper also represents a gold mine for the hacker because one day or another these all end up going out with the garbage. Even if the passwords are obsolete, hackers may be able to discern a pattern in password choice that allows them to predict future passwords.

System access records, which show connect times for employees on corporate systems, could give hackers a list of userids from which to start. Usage patterns could help them know when is the best time to do their work and even what kind of work a particular person does. All of which helps narrow down the list of possibilities that they must attempt.

Even the trend towards making companies greener and more ecologically sound can increase the risk of attack. The fact that paper is saved in special bins for subsequent recycling may be a great way to save the rain forests but, without adequate security, it can represent an even greater boon to hackers snooping around for information. Now they don't even have to get their hands dirty when they sift through your discarded business papers. Your colleagues have dutifully sorted out all the messy stuff by putting the dirty tissues and banana peels in another container. The result is the creation of a prime target for a hacker's dumpster diving efforts – your paper recycling bin, which might as well have a bright red bull's eye painted on it (Figure 10.1).

The moral of this story is that you need to treat your garbage like a hacker's treasure. This means that papers, even the seemingly unimportant ones, should either be shredded before being disposed of or placed in locked bins (or both, depending upon your level of paranoia). Obviously you should also do what you can to ensure that the company that carries off the bin contents treats your material appropriately as well. You can't control everything, of course, but you should do the best you can with the areas that you can affect.

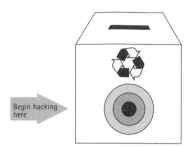

FIGURE 10.1   Recycling can make a hacker's job even easier

(10.3)   I know who you are and what you did

A famous cartoon that appeared in *The New Yorker* magazine during the time that the Internet was beginning to make its way into the public's attention has one dog sitting on a chair in front of a PC confidently explaining to another dog by his side that 'On the Internet, nobody knows you're a dog' (Figure 10.2). In a single frame this cartoon captured the essence of some of the problems that anonymity can introduce if you are depending upon someone or something you can't see because they're on the other end of a wire.

"On the Internet, nobody knows you're a dog."

FIGURE 10.2   The anonymous Internet (Reproduced with permission from *The New Yorker* © The New Yorker Collection 1993, Peter Steiner from cartoonbank.com. All rights reserved.

A lesser known variation on this cartoon (Figure 10.3) depicts a dog stepping up to a laptop PC thinking to himself 'On the Internet, nobody knows you're a dog.' Obviously, liberated by this anonymity, he proceeds to go to the 'Butcher Net' Web site where he decides to pass up the opportunity to download a lean meat recipe and, instead, selects the 'marrow bone' page. The final frame concludes with the dog staring at a Web page saying 'You're a dog, aren't you?' The point being that *where you go and what you do on the Internet says a lot about you.*

One enticing aspect of the Internet is that it allows seemingly anonymous communications. I can put up a Web site which you can visit whenever and wherever you like. You don't know me and I don't know you – and you might like to keep it that way. After all, you don't know if I'm a nice guy or a creep. You're merely interested in some information I had on my Web page. You aren't necessarily interested in starting a long-term relationship at this point.

The whole arrangement sounds harmless enough until you realize that what you do, in fact, says an awful lot about you. Some of this information may be completely

FIGURE 10.3   Not so anonymous after all (Cartoon by Nik Scott, *http://toons.net*)

benign, but others, if used in combination, could be more revealing than you might realize.

While this might be a violation of your personal privacy, what relevance does it have to corporate security? The examples of *social engineering* covered earlier involve incidents where the hacker attempts to extract information from otherwise unsuspecting victims using some sort of ruse or deception. Another form of manipulation, however, could involve something as blatant as extortion.

Imagine, for instance, that an employee visits Web sites or newsgroups involving some sort of illegal or incriminating activity. Hackers could threaten to expose this information to the employee's boss, spouse, son, daughter, law enforcement agencies, etc. unless their demands for information are met. If this information is particularly inflammatory (e.g. child pornography), the extortion target might be willing to do nearly anything to keep it quiet.

Just to show you how easy such information is to obtain, one need look no further than the Deja.com (formerly 'Deja News') Web site. Newsgroup servers are typically only able to save posts for a fairly short period of time owing to the enormous amount of storage required. Deja.com performs a valuable service by archiving posts to thousands of newsgroups and providing a search engine that allows subsequent lookup. This capability in and of itself is perfectly legitimate but, as with most things, it can be exploited for malicious purposes.

Let's say a hacker wants to target a fictitious company named Widgets-R-Us. He brings up the Deja.com search engine and enters the company's email server name (i.e. the part after the '@' in an email address), which happens to be 'widgets-r-us.com'. Then, to make things really interesting, he selects only the 'adult' oriented newsgroups and initiates his search. If he finds any postings he can then view them to see if anything really incriminating has been left lying around.

When he finds something really juicy he can use Deja.com to provide him with an 'author posting history' which shows all the postings by this person to all newsgroups. From this he can learn a lot about a person he has never even met. He might find that his victim also posts to other shady newsgroups.

He might also try reformatting his search to look for other similar email account names on other mail servers as this person might also have a personal account through an Internet Service Provider (ISP) that, while unrelated to his business account, shares a common name before the '@'. In other words, bigshot@widgets-r-us.com may also be bigshot@freespam.com. The search can be widened even further by searching for variations on the victim's name or nickname which might turn up other posts from other personal accounts.

The collection of all these posts together gives the hacker the ammunition needed to threaten the extortion target. If this information is sufficiently incriminating and the victim is sufficiently sensitive to its disclosure, the hacker's new-found knowledge can be used to further his attack.

(10.4) Plugging the leaks

A less sinister, yet just as potentially damaging vulnerability that arises from employee use of the Internet is the obvious potential for leakage of confidential information. In some cases employees may send email to business partners, colleagues or friends assuming that only the intended recipient will read it. As a result, they may be more candid than they would ordinarily be when speaking in a public forum.

In fact, there are numerous ways for hackers to get their hands on these communications. For example, your colleague may send an email to a business partner which contains information about a new project he is working on. He assumes that both his and his partner's email servers are secure. You've done your job and tightened up your defences around your server but the business partner's IT staff hasn't been so diligent. Since the email is stored on both servers (at least temporarily), an attack on either could reveal the contents of the message. Even if the servers are secure, there are weak points all along the path in between where hackers could position themselves and intercept the message.

The point is that unless you have a private network or use some form of encryption to ensure privacy, you should assume that your communications are available for all the world to read. This must be the mindset of all employees communicating with the outside world and, based on the high rate of insider attacks discussed earlier, it might be best to assume the same posture regarding internal communications as well.

Other more insidious forms of information leakage should also be considered. Recall the earlier example of the discovery of incriminating evidence culled from an employee's newsgroup postings. Let's say that instead of posting to forums of dubious character, the victim follows the corporate policy of using the Internet

```
Posting History: Techie <joetech@widgets-r-us.com>

              There are 239 unique messages by
              Techie <joetech@widgets-r-us.com>
              (numbers may be slightly skewed by cross-postings)
                              Get all 239 messages


        Number of Messages          Forum
               115                  alt.engineering.electrical
                53                  alt.cellular
                41                  sci.electronics.design
                22                  alt.cellular.gsm
                 8                  sci.electronics.components
```

FIGURE 10.4   A revealing history of newsgroup postings

only for legitimate business purposes. Through the normal course of his work he posts to various technical forums to learn the latest and greatest information.

A hacker might be able to deduce the nature of your company's secret R&D project by observing a sudden flurry of posting activity to a particular set of newsgroups. When viewed separately each post reveals nothing, but when taken together they unveil an unmistakable trend. From the simulated posting history in Figure 10.4, what are the odds that the fictitious 'Joe Tech' might be working on the design of a new cell-phone? Better than average it would seem ...

Another example of information leakage that might seem to be innocent but could later come back to haunt you are details regarding your internal systems. In asking a valid question on a technical forum, an employee may unwittingly reveal vulnerabilities to hackers lurking in the background. A question such as:

'How can I change the settings on our Brand X firewall?'

or

'How much memory will that new application use on a V3.2 Brand Y UNIX server?'

tells hackers what sort of defences they must overcome. By knowing the vendor and the release level of the systems in question, they can easily search the publicly available list of known vulnerabilities for those systems and tailor their attack accordingly. This information saves hackers time and allows them to strike with greater precision.

(10.4) The spirit of the law

So what should you do about surfing, posting, and emailing by people within your company? Can you just shut down all Internet access? This is probably not a viable option any more. Businesses of all kinds are moving quickly towards greater and greater dependence upon the Internet. Draconian measures are, therefore, likely to reduce your organization's access to critical information – driving it slowly but surely toward extinction.

The answer begins with the establishment of a solid security policy (see Chapter 5 for more information) with emphasis on what is and is not 'acceptable use'; but it doesn't end there. In order to truly affect human behaviour in such matters it is critical that the user community have an understanding of not only the *letter* of the law but also a sense of the *spirit* behind it as well. If users don't have at least a rudimentary appreciation of the potential consequences that could result from their actions, then they are likely to try to find loopholes to slip through (or simply ignore the policy entirely). In other words, *education* is the key. No amount of threats, mandates, or edicts from on high will ever be as effective as a well-informed and properly motivated user community.

chapter 11

Hackers don't want you to know that ... *passwords aren't secure*

Treat your password like a toothbrush. Don't share it with anyone else and get a new one every six months.

Cliff Stoll, 1987

Chapter summary

- Why passwords are often vulnerable
- How hackers steal passwords
  - password guessing
  - shoulder surfing
  - password sniffing
- How hackers crack encrypted passwords
  - dictionary attack
  - hybrid attack
  - brute-force attack
- Poor password choices
- Good password choices
- The importance of effective password rules

- The value of single sign-on solutions
- Alternatives to using passwords to prove user identity
  - smart cards
  - security tokens
  - biometrics

Let's say we've set up a userid just for you to use on a given system. It allows you to do all that your job requires – no more, no less. You're ready to work, so you want to access your system. But how does it know that you are really you – and not some impostor pretending to be you? In other words, how can we *authenticate* your identity?

The typical answer is that we will tell you the name of your userid and let you pick a password that only you and the system know. When you go to access the system, you present these two pieces of information as proof of your identity. The system sees if the password you have submitted matches the one it has on file for the userid you've been assigned. If they match, then it is presumed that you are the only person that could have known this password and, therefore, you must really be you and access is granted.

Since passwords are the most common form of authentication in use on today's IT systems, you might be tempted to believe that they must be reasonably effective. In fact, passwords are so common that most people never even consider using alternative forms of authentication. In this chapter we will discuss some of the inherent weaknesses of password-based authentication, some things you can do to shore up these weak areas, and some alternatives that could potentially provide even more reliable forms of authentication.

Passwords are the most common form of authentication in use on today's IT systems.

11.1 The problem with passwords

At its core, the problem with password-based authentication schemes is that they assume that if you know the password you must, therefore, be an authorized user. The implication, of course, is that we know that you are, in fact, you because you have special knowledge (i.e. the secret password) that no one else should know.

The weakness in this approach, however, is that while your identity is unique, the knowledge required to prove it to the system, may not be. For instance, it is possible for you *and* someone else to know the same thing. The mere fact that your brain has some bit of information does not necessarily preclude another's brain (which may belong to a hacker) from containing that same information. Clearly, if this information is contained in more than one brain it ceases to uniquely identify the person that goes with that brain. Said more simply – a secret is not a secret if other people know it.

Password-based authentication schemes ultimately rely on the *secrecy* of the password. The security of such a system hinges entirely on the level of secrecy that is maintained. As you will soon see, there are a number of different ways that this secrecy can be compromised. Each represents a potential threat to the health and welfare of your IT systems and, ultimately, your company.

(11.2) Insecurity administrators?

The threat is compounded by the fact that so many resources are protected by passwords alone. User accounts provide varying degrees of access to important business functions. Administrator accounts can be even more dangerous in the wrong hands as they control the very fabric of the underlying IT infrastructure. With a database admin id, hackers could copy confidential information or destroy it altogether. With a LAN (local area network) administrator's id, they could reassign access privileges at will. With a Web server admin id, they could bring down one of the company's primary sales channels. Admin access to a network router or switch could allow someone to shut down the corporate network, making all the other potential problems seem inconsequential by comparison.

Many organizations profess awareness of the importance of these critical components yet fail to do much in terms of preventing unauthorized access to them. A common practice is to set up a shared admin ids which is then used by multiple administrators. This same account may be replicated on other systems as well. This makes the administrator's job easy since all they need to remember is a single userid and password combination to get access to all the resources for which they are responsible.

The problem with this arrangement, however, is that it makes the hacker's job a whole lot easier too. Now, with a single userid/password combination, the hacker can wreak havoc in a dozen different areas without having even to break into a sweat. The fact that the passwords for these shared admin ids rarely (if ever) change means that the hacker has ample time not only to discover what the password is, but to use it for weeks and months on end. Things get worse still when administrators change assignments or leave the company and carry with them this 'secret' information.

There are better ways of approaching the problem of user authentication, as we will soon discuss. Remaining obstacles, though, are that:

(1) many products, especially in the networking hardware arena, don't support more secure authentication schemes, and

(2) even when such solutions do exist, not enough organizations take advantage of them.

Certainly cost is a factor in both cases, but when you truly consider the cost of what is ultimately at stake, the decision gets a whole lot easier. Before we get to these solutions, though, let's first get a clearer look at why passwords are often vulnerable in the first place.

(11.3) Password guessing

The most primitive way for hackers to attack a password-protected system is simply to try logging on with various passwords they have guessed until they finally get in. An obvious guess would be to assume that the userid and the password are the same. This is so obvious, in fact, that you would think that it should almost never be successful but, unfortunately, it works all too often. Also, since one of the most common trivial passwords is simply the word 'password', it is likely to be one of the hacker's first guesses as well. Other easy choices include the user's name, nickname, spouse's name, child's name, pet's name, car licence number, phone number, birthday, spouse's birthday, children's birthdays, wedding anniversary, and so on. Guessing attacks work best when hackers know something about the user they have targeted and, as we discussed earlier in Section 10.3, such information may not be all that hard to come by.

There are two main things you can do to thwart such an attack:

(1) ensure that users don't choose easily guessable passwords, and

(2) disable a userid that experiences a predetermined level of incorrect password logon attempts (e.g. 'three strikes and you're out').

The latter should be fairly easy to implement as many systems allow the administrator to set this sort of threshold. They may also send an alert to the user, the user's supervisor, or the system administrator when such an incident has occurred so that further investigation can be initiated. The former case is harder to ensure unless the system actually checks that the password meets some predetermined criteria designed to weed out easily guessable passwords. These password rules could be enforced by the utility that allows users to change their passwords and reject any suggested passwords that don't meet the standard.

These measures certainly help, but, as you will see, they are far from foolproof. In fact, according to one of Murphy's laws:

'It is impossible to make anything foolproof because fools are so ingenious.'

Perhaps nowhere is this statement more true than in the area of insecure passwords.

(11.4) Password nabbing

Of course, hackers can remove the guesswork entirely if they can devise a way to nab a password outright. **Shoulder surfing** is one classic, low-tech approach that hackers have used for years. A nonchalant glance over the shoulder of their intended victim while they enter their password may tell hackers all they need to know to gain unauthorized access. Passwords such as 'qwerty', 'asdf' or 'zxasqw', which are chosen because of the easily remembered geometric patterns they form owing to their physical location on the keyboard, are particularly vulnerable to this attack (Figure 11.1). However, when this approach fails, technology can assist by picking up where shoulder surfing leaves off.

Another way to swipe a password is to read it after it has been entered into a prompt window. Of course, most applications that rely on this sort of authentication scheme are smart enough to obscure what is displayed on the user's screen by substituting asterisks ('*') for each character that is entered. This way users can see that the system is responding without revealing their actual password to anyone attempting to steal a glance at their display screen. They assume that since the password doesn't actually appear on the screen, it can't be seen. They may also choose to make life easier for themselves by allowing the application to save their password so that it doesn't have to be re-entered time after time. Again, they figure that since they can't see the password, no harm can come of it.

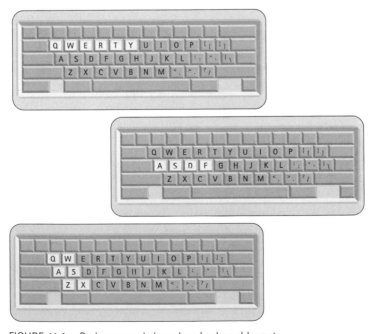

FIGURE 11.1   Bad passwords based on keyboard layout

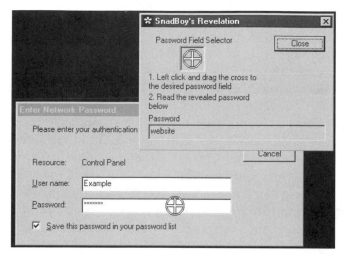

FIGURE 11.2   Revealing 'hidden' passwords with Revelation

These assumptions could come back to haunt them, though, because a freeware program called Snadboy's Revelation[1] can effectively peel back the asterisks and reveal the underlying password (Figure 11.2). This tool is something of a double-edged sword. In the right hands it can help a user recover a saved password that has been forgotten. In the wrong hands, however, hackers can use it to steal a user's password. All they need to do is slip a diskette containing Revelation into the target machine, start up the tool, drag a crosshair icon over the obscured password field, and ... voila! ... the user's password is plainly displayed in Revelation's password window.

Of course, telling users not to select the option for the application to save their password could eliminate the most common instance of this vulnerability. The problem is that an edict of this sort is unlikely to have much effect as the convenience offered by this feature is just too good for most to pass up. A more realistic approach would be to have users ensure that they never leave an unsecured workstation unattended. At minimum, a keyboard-locking screen saver should be invoked when they need to step away. However, even this protection can be circumvented if a hacker simply powers the machine off and back on again. This is why a power-on password should also be configured. This way even if the hacker turns the machine off, he or she won't be able to proceed with the boot-up process.

Hardware-based options such as IBM's SmartCard Security Kit secure a system with a smart card (discussed in more detail in Section 11.11) which, when removed by the user, will automatically lock up the keyboard until the user reinserts his or her smart card and enters a PIN (personal identification number). The keyboard even remains locked after the system has been rebooted until the user has proven his or her identity.

1. www.snadboy.com.

UNIX systems offer additional password-stealing opportunities. For example, some of them store passwords along with other account information in a publicly available file (e.g. */etc/passwd* for many systems). In fact, there are a number of ways for a hacker to obtain a password file by exploiting 'an unprotected *uucp* link, well-known holes in *sendmail*, or via *ftp* or *tftp*' (Klein, 1991). Thankfully, the passwords in these files are saved in an encrypted[2] format but, as you will see in the next section, even this is no guarantee of security. Even encrypted password files need to be protected.

Shadow password files provide one such approach. These are formed by splitting up the password file into two files. The account information is still saved in a file in the public area but the encrypted passwords are saved in a shadow file, which can only be accessed by the *root* userid. Since *root's* access is strictly limited to certain critical system processes and the system administrator (at least that's how it should be), the chances of a hacker getting a copy of even the encrypted passwords is diminished.

Windows NT systems have similar vulnerabilities (CIAC, 1997). The SAM (Security Account Manager) file saved on an NT server contains key security information, such as encrypted passwords. This file is normally available only to the system administrator and, even then, only through specific interfaces. The reason for this is that the operating system locks the file during initialization and keeps it locked until the system is shut down. However, it still might be possible for hackers to get to this file by rebooting the machine with a DOS diskette, thereby subverting the native NT security facilities. Using a utility such as NTFSDOS,[3] hackers can get access to the NT file system (which is not normally recognizable by DOS). Of course, they would need physical access to the system in order to launch this attack, but given our earlier discussion on insider attacks in Chapter 9, you can see that this is not necessarily a significant problem to overcome.

Another means of accessing the SAM file may be created when the administrator creates a backup copy. This is a good idea for disaster recovery, but creates a potential risk in that this security information is also copied. This means that hackers now have a variety of sources for the SAM file they seek. It may be on a tape backup, an Emergency Repair Disk, or on the machine itself in the *winnt**repair* directory.[4] This is not necessarily a problem as long as the backup copies are protected sufficiently. The problem arises from the fact that many system administrators are lulled into a false sense of security because they know that the stored passwords are in an encrypted format. They figure that 'if it's encrypted, it's secure'.

However, hackers know that encryption is no guarantee of security. They rely on the administrator's complacency and exploit it to their advantage. If they can get a copy of the SAM file, they can begin a password-cracking attack. In fact, they may

---

2. Technically speaking, a special one-way encryption, or hashing function, is typically used. The fundamental concept of hashing is discussed later in Section A.6.
3. Available at www.sysinternals.com.
4. L0phtCrack readme file, L0pht Heavy Industries, Inc., www.l0pht.com.

have at their disposal a tool such as SAMDUMP,[5] which can cull encrypted password information from the SAM file automatically for them. As we will soon see, they can then feed the results into a cracking tool and then sit back and wait for the passwords to start dropping out.

Still another way to obtain passwords is through network sniffing. This subject will be covered in greater detail in Chapter 12, but for now, suffice it to say that it is possible for hackers to obtain a copy of packets transmitted across the network. If they are looking just for passwords they can use something like L0phtCrack, a tool which is discussed in Section 11.7. L0phtCrack includes an SMB Packet Capture facility which saves a copy of only the relevant logon information from all the packets it sees. Hackers simply start the collection process from their workstation (or on one that they have hacked into) and then check back in a few hours or days to see how many encrypted passwords they have snagged. Their job couldn't be simpler since the tool has already filtered out all the unneeded packets. Of course, some packets may actually contain unencrypted passwords for some legacy applications, which makes the hacker's job far too easy, but even encrypted passwords may be vulnerable, as we are about to see ...

11.5 Password cracking

Since passwords are often stored and sent in an encrypted form, many people assume (incorrectly) that they are impervious to attack. Unfortunately, reality doesn't support this widely held belief. Hackers know this and benefit from the fact that most other people don't.

Even encrypted passwords may be vulnerable to cracking attacks. Once hackers have a list of encrypted passwords they can launch an offline attack. An advantage of offline attacks is that once hackers have captured some encrypted passwords, they no longer even need access to the target network to do their work. They can do their password guessing and testing on their own system, which allows them to avoid detection and get around the limits many systems have against consecutive failed logon attempts. These offline attacks usually take the form of one or all of the following approaches:

- dictionary attack,
- hybrid attack, or
- brute-force attack.

All are based upon a substantial amount of trial and error, but since hackers can let a computer do all the heavy lifting, they don't mind. In fact, they can start the

5. Available at www.l0pht.com/l0phtcrack.

process running and then go on to do other things. They then simply check back in a few minutes, hours or days to see what has turned up.

In fact, if the passwords to be cracked are for an NT server, hackers may also have something else working in their favour – weak encryption. Microsoft's LAN Manager, a predecessor to NT server, used an encryption scheme that is widely considered weak by today's standards. However, in the interest of maintaining compatibility with the large existing installed base, NT was designed to handle both the stronger NT encryption scheme as well as the weaker LAN Manager mechanism. While this approach certainly helps with migration cases, it just as certainly hinders security by carrying forward a large number of poorly protected passwords. These passwords, then, become the soft underbelly that hackers aim for when they launch a cracking attack. This makes perfect sense. Who wouldn't choose to focus on a weakly encrypted password when the alternative is to try to chip away at a more strongly encrypted form of the same data?

11.6 Throwing the book at them

As its name implies, a dictionary attack involves making password guesses based on words in a dictionary. Hackers know that their victims are humans, not machines, and that they have limited memories. As a result, humans are likely to choose passwords that are easy to remember. However, if a password is easy to remember, it's also probably easy to guess. The chosen password has a very good chance of being an actual word that could, in fact, appear in a password dictionary. Therefore, the hacker need only feed the encrypted password and a list of guesses from the dictionary into a cracking program and wait to see if a match pops up. The cracking program does all the hard work by encrypting each password guess from the dictionary with the same password encryption algorithm that the operating system in question uses. If the encrypted dictionary word is the same as the encrypted password the hacker is trying to uncover, then the crack has been successful.

> If a password is easy to remember, it's also probably easy to guess.

You might think that you don't have to worry about this because your password is the name of your dog, cat, spouse, sports car, etc. and that no dictionary would actually have entries for such unique names. You'd probably be wrong. Password dictionaries, which are widely available on the Internet, include all sorts of words, including common variations, in many different languages across many different subjects. For example, some FTP sites[6] contain not only common English words

---

6. UIUC Archive, ftp://ftp.cso.uiuc.edu/pub/security/wordlists/, University of Illinois at Urbana-Champaign.
    Central ZEDZ FTP archive, ftp://utopia.hacktic.nl/pub/crypto/wordlists
    Also http://cert.unisa.it/pub/Tools/Password/dictionary.

but also dictionaries for Afrikaans, Esperanto, Hindi, Swahili, Yiddish and even Klingon just to name a few. There are even dictionaries that contain terms from the realms of literature, religion, science, music, television and film. In other words, they've got the bases covered, from the ridiculous to the sublime.

What if you try to be a little more clever by creating a variation or hybrid of your desired password, assuming that no dictionary would anticipate your scheme? Nice try but no cigar. A common variation on the dictionary attack involves feeding password guesses through a mutation filter which tries things like converting the letter 'o' to the number '0' and the letter 'L' to the number '1'. They don't stop there either. Other mutations involve mirroring ('cat' becomes 'cattac'), mixed capitalization ('smith', 'Smith', 'sMitH', etc.), and concatenation ('john', 'john1', 'john01', etc.). In other words, any slick variation that you might come up with is likely to have already been dreamt up and included in a mutation filter to augment a dictionary attack.

If you are still feeling that you can outsmart hackers with an obscure or ingeniously disguised password, think again. Remember that hackers don't necessarily have to get *your* password in order to be successful. They simply need to get *someone's* password. The higher the privileges, the better – but anyone's password will do. If they can get access to just one account, they can establish a toehold for further investigation. When you consider the possibility that a quarter of the passwords on your system can be discovered with these sorts of attacks (Klein, 1991), you ought to be more than just a little concerned. For instance, if this vulnerability rate held up for a modest system of only 50 users, a dozen or more userids could be compromised. Since hackers only need one userid to do damage, it's easy to see that this could represent more than a small crack in the security infrastructure. Looking at it another way, would you feel secure if the front door to your home was locked but every fourth window was left ajar?

So, what can you do to guard against dictionary attacks? The solution sounds simple enough – don't allow passwords that can be easily guessed. How do you actually do this, though? The answer begins with your security policy, which should spell out a set of *password rules* that disallow trivial passwords. To be effective, these rules need to be completely unambiguous or you run the risk of each user coming up with his or her own interpretation. More on this in Section 11.9.

11.7 Doing it the hard way

Of course, the strength of any password-based authentication system lies in the assumption that:

(1) only the legitimate user of the account knows the password, and

(2) the password is virtually impossible for an impostor to guess.

We've already discussed various ways that these two assumptions can be violated, therefore resulting in a vulnerable authentication system. What happens, though, if the dictionary attack along with its common variations fails? It turns out that hackers are still far from being out of business. There's always the old brute-force method of trying every reasonable password possibility looking for a match.

The assumption of many system administrators is that there are an impossibly large number of potential passwords that hackers would have to attempt. In other words, the system is secure because there are simply too many combinations to be tried. If it takes longer than the hacker's lifetime to try them all, then theoretically, the system is safe. If a password system is implemented properly, this may be a reasonable assumption. However, there are a number of common pitfalls that make the job much easier for hackers and skew the odds back in their favour.

Let's take a simple example of a system in which passwords are comprised of a string of four numbers, similar to a bank ATM (automated teller machine) card protected by a personal identification number (PIN). If a PIN is four digits long and each digit is numeric (0–9), the total number of permutations would be:

$$10 \times 10 \times 10 \times 10 \quad \text{or } 10^4 \quad \text{or } 10{,}000$$

A 4-digit numeric password could be cracked on a modest PC in 0.02 seconds – faster than you can blink your eyes.

Unless the hacker got really lucky it would take an enormous amount of time to try each of these by hand. Consider, however, that a good cracking program such as L0phtCrack[7] can try over 450,000 guesses per second running on even a modest Intel Pentium II processor. Then imagine configuring this program to search only for four-digit password combinations. The result would be that what initially seemed an impossibly long task has suddenly been reduced to a mere 0.02 seconds[8] – faster than you can blink your eyes. If you increase the length of the password from 4 digits to 6, you find that the time to crack would be increased to only about 2 seconds – still a trivial task. If you increase the string of digits yet again from six to eight, you end up with just under 4 minutes to crack. Better, but still not secure by any reasonable definition.

You can see why numeric-only passwords aren't such a good idea. What about alphabetic characters? If you use only single-case characters (e.g. all upper or all lower) you get a cracking time of over 5 days. Clearly better than the numeric-only approach but still no match for a cracking program with spare CPU cycles and time on its hands. Allow both numbers and single-case characters to be used and the time increases to over 2 months. Throwing special characters (e.g. @, #, %, *, -, etc.) into

7. Although L0phtCrack is designed to work with NT passwords and not ATMs, the principles in this example still apply.
8. This assumes that an exhaustive search of all possibilities is tried. Calculated by dividing the total number of possible passwords (10,000) by the number of tries per second (450, 000). As will later be pointed out, one would more reasonably expect the actual number of tries to be *half* that many.

the mix yields a 32-year cracking time and if both upper- and lower-case characters (i.e. mixed case) are allowed, a cracker is facing about 430 years of cracking to do the whole job (Figure 11.3). (Hackers can be extraordinarily patient, but even they have their limits.)

Another element you can add to the password mix that will help make life even more miserable still for the hacker is to allow variable-length passwords. The previous examples all assumed passwords of a fixed length. A simple variation such as allowing passwords to be 6, 7 or 8 characters in length might help. Here's how it works …

If you insist that all passwords be 8 characters in length and comprised of only case-insensitive alphanumerics, the total number of potential passwords would be:

26 alphas + 10 numerics = 36 alphanumeric characters

therefore,

$36 \times 36 \times 36 \times 36 \times 36 \times 36 \times 36 \times 36$ or 36^8 possibilities

which comes to

2,821,109,907,456 or roughly 2.82×10^{12}

If the same assumptions hold except that you allow the length to vary from 6 to 8 characters, the total would be:

$36^6 + 36^7 + 36^8$

which comes to

2,901,650,853,888   or   roughly 2.90×10^{12}

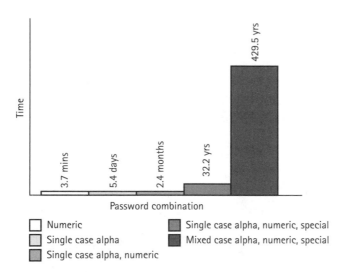

FIGURE 11.3 Maximum time required to crack various password types

This means that simple variation in password length bumps up the total number of possibilities by:

$$2.90 \times 10^{12} - 2.82 \times 10^{12} = 0.08 \times 10^{12} \qquad \text{or roughly 80 billion}$$

At a rate of 450,000 tries per second, you may have bought yourself a couple of days. Not a lot, but it helps ... or does it? If hackers suspect that users will choose the minimum password length (a reasonable suspicion since most users take the path of least resistance and do the bare minimum), they can run their attack for all six-character passwords first and then move on to the longer ones later (assuming they still need to). Again, since this can all be automated, such an approach is quite simple.

In other words, the mathematical analysis, alone, may be misleading. You also need to take into account the likely behaviour of real-world end users as well as the capabilities of available cracking tools when you start formulating password rules.

Of course, the more often you change your password, the harder it is for hackers. If it takes them six months of brute-force cracking to get your password and you change your password every two months, you have effectively made brute-force cracking a fairly unattractive option. After all, what's the point of cracking passwords that will expire before you can use them? A good rule to have, then, might involve the lifetime of a password. The length of that lifetime, also, must be considered carefully so as to get the maximum benefit.

11.8   Exceptions to the (password) rules

The lesson, clearly, is that the greater variety of characters allowed, the harder a password is to guess. There are a number of problems with the theoretical numbers stated here, though.

(1) These numbers represent the time required for an exhaustive search of the entire set of possible passwords. A cracker would have to be unbelievably unlucky if every possibility had to be tried to break a given password. On average, only half of the total permutations would have to be attempted which, of course, cuts the cracking time in half.

> A cracker would have to be unbelievably unlucky if every possibility had to be tried to break a given password.

(2) Many systems, such as Windows NT, are case insensitive. In other words, they allow the user to enter both upper-and lower-case passwords but ultimately convert them all to a single case. Other systems may not allow the use of non-alphanumeric characters. Of course, these restrictions dramatically cut down the size of the cracking job. Fortunately, UNIX systems typically don't suffer from this problem.

(3) Even if all such possibilities are allowed, users are unlikely to take advantage of them because they result in passwords that are very difficult to remember. If, for example, a user chooses a password that is all numeric (e.g. phone number, birth date, social security number, driver's licence number, etc.) and the hacker suspects this (which is not at all unlikely), the theoretical strength of the password becomes irrelevant since it is, in fact, far weaker.

(4) Password rules, created in order to prevent users from choosing easily guessable passwords, limit the number of possibilities that must be tried. For instance, if hackers know that passwords must be 8 characters long and are not allowed to be comprised of only numeric characters, they can immediately eliminate from consideration 1 billion possible passwords,[9] thereby speeding up their cracking efforts.

In some cases, however, the trade-off is worth the cost as the few minutes that they gain by eliminating these possible combinations are more than offset by the fact that a large number of trivial passwords, which a user might otherwise choose, have also been taken off the table. This is not true for all rules, though. Careful analysis is needed to ensure that as you define rules intended to eliminate trivial passwords, you don't also allow hackers, who might discover these rules, to narrow their search to a manageable set of possibilities.

While all this cracking work might sound tedious beyond belief, bear in mind that cracker programs automate the entire process very nicely. Hackers can initiate their cracking activity and go on doing other things while this process runs in the background.

LOpht Heavy Industries, a group of hackers who have turned their expertise into a security consulting business, claim that during a corporate audit they performed for a 'large high technology company', they 'cracked 90% of the passwords in under 48 hours on a Pentium II/300'. They further state that '18% of the passwords were cracked in under 10 minutes'.[10] While these figures may not be typical, they do, at the very least, put an exclamation point on the vulnerable nature of passwords. When you consider that LOpht's tools are generally available as shareware to anyone on the Internet and that only a modest computing platform is needed to run them, it becomes quite apparent just how easy password-cracking attacks really are.

You might be tempted to bemoan the fact that such tools are so easily accessible, but that, of course, wouldn't change anything. A more productive use of your energy would be to turn these tools around and use them to test your systems for vulnerabilities *before* the bad guys do. This way you can fix the problems before disaster strikes. Consider it a pre-emptive first strike against future intruders.

---

9. The number of eight-character passwords consisting only of numeric digits would be $10 \times 10 \times 10 \times 10 \times 10 \times 10 \times 10 \times 10 = 10^8 = 1$ billion.
10. LOpht Heavy Industries, Inc., www.l0pht.com/l0phtcrack/.

11.9 Following the rules

Setting up rules is one thing – enforcing them is another. If you really want to make sure that the rules are followed you need to customize the logon procedure in each system so that it disallows passwords that don't follow the rules. You might even go so far as to distribute a program to the user community which can generate cryptic passwords that meet the criteria. However, the randomness of such a program would be difficult to guarantee so if hackers ever got hold of this program, they might be able to find a predictable pattern which could be exploited.

Even if you got all this to work perfectly, there are still issues involving the human element of this arrangement which are often overlooked. The dilemma is this:

(1) The best password is one that can't be guessed.

(2) If a password can't be guessed, it's probably difficult to remember.

(3) If a password is hard to remember, the user will probably write it down somewhere.

(4) If a password is written down, it is probably no longer secure.

If users need access to multiple systems, the problem becomes particularly acute. Such a 'catch-22' scenario points out the need for a different sort of solution.

11.10 Sign me on

Let's say a user needs to logon to five different systems through the normal course of his or her work responsibilities. Let's also say that each of these five systems employs a rigid set of password rules which essentially eliminate any trivial password choices. Finally, let's assume that each system requires that passwords be changed every 60 days in order to keep the hackers guessing.

What we have just described is an environment that many IT specialists might think is reasonably secure. After all, it would seem that any cracking attempts based on guessing and brute force have been deterred substantially. Confident in this belief, they turn their attention to more pressing matters. Unfortunately, this nice, neat solution could be little more than a mirage, lacking substance upon closer inspection.

Such a false sense of security is just what hackers need. They know that this arrangement is inherently weak because people will find this environment impractical. They know that people can't remember five different hard-to guess passwords that change every couple of months. They know that one of two scenarios is likely to occur:

(1) users will reduce the complexity of their part of the problem by making all their passwords identical or

(2) users will write down all their passwords on one of those little yellow sticky pads and 'hide' it in some really clever place, such as under their keyboard (who would ever think to look there?!), in their desk, or even on their display.

The former option means that if one password is guessed, all five systems are vulnerable. Clearly not a good situation. The latter option means that anyone with physical access to a user's work area can steal his or her password when he or she gets up to take a break, attend a meeting, go to lunch, etc. As we've already discussed, 'insider attacks' are to be feared at least as much as 'outsider attacks', so the second option is not to be taken lightly. The security policy insists that we allow only hard to guess (and, therefore, hard to remember) passwords which are changed frequently and are unique across each of the systems a user logs on to. The human side cries out for an alternative that is usable and doesn't hamper productivity. What is needed is a solution that satisfies both sets of requirements.

Single Sign-On (SSO) tools are one possible answer. They represent a rare exception to the 'security vs. usability' trade-off discussed in Section 2.2. Such tools allow you to optimize both sides of the equation. SSO solutions such as Tivoli's Global Sign-On product provide client software which the end users interface with during logon. Once users have been successfully authenticated, they are presented with a list of systems that they are allowed to access. They simply select the desired system and the SSO tool takes care of the rest. No additional password prompting is necessary.

Under the covers the SSO client retrieves the appropriate sign-on information for the selected system either from its local database of encrypted passwords and userids or from a centralized logon coordination server. Sign-on dialog is carried out between the client software and the target system. The next thing users see is the application they intend to use. From their perspective, nothing could be simpler.

Since users only have to remember one password (their single sign-on password), their task is now considerably more manageable. Unlike the human user, the SSO

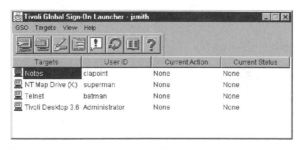

FIGURE 11.4   A single sign-on GUI

tool doesn't mind remembering lots of different, seemingly random passwords that change on a regular basis, so the security policy is also satisfied. An additional benefit is logons are quicker and more efficient. The cumulative effect of the time saved across the organization could offset the cost of the SSO infrastructure in relatively short order. An illustration of this saving appears in Table 11.1.

TABLE 11.1   SSO savings: a hypothetical example

	Average end user	Single sign-on
Number of passwords to remember	5	1
Average minutes to sign on/system	0.5	0.5
Hours/years spent signing-on (assuming 1 sign-on/system/work day)	10.42	2.08
Employee burden rate (avg.)	$35,000	$35,000
Sign-on cost/employee/year	$175	$35
Number of employees	10,000	10,000
Cost to the enterprise	$1,750,000	$350,000
Potential annual savings		$1,400,000

Another important area of savings that tends to be overlooked in the SSO discussion is the potential reduction in the number of calls to the help desk for password resets. When you consider that for many companies the 'forgotten password call' is the most common problem they see, it doesn't take long for support cost decreases in this area to add up.

SSO has the potential to produce some impressive savings while reducing the likelihood that users will need to write down their passwords. Therefore, with one solution you can make a positive dent in the company's balance sheet while improving security. Instead of requiring end users to keep up with complicated passwords, which are necessary to prevent cracking attacks, only a single, secure password needs to be remembered. By moving the storage of the various underlying passwords from the user's head to a secure server both security and usability are improved.

However, SSO doesn't really address the problem of having a single password that allows access to multiple systems. If hackers figure out a user's SSO password, they can still break into all of that user's accounts. In order to address this problem, a different technology is needed.

11.11 Are you really you?

How can we answer the question 'are you really you?' in a way that avoids many of the weaknesses of password-based authentication schemes? Let's review the basics. Authentication mechanisms are based on something you:

- know,

- have, or

- are.

Password and PIN-based systems rely on the assumption that you *know* something that no one else knows. Of course, if your password is guessed, found, or cracked, this assumption is no longer true and the authentication scheme breaks down.

Other schemes are based on the fact that you *have* something that no one else has. Just as the key to your home affords you easy entry but makes it more difficult for intruders, have-based authentication systems insist that the user possess a special device in order to gain access. For instance, you might be required to present a so-called 'smart' card in order to prove your identity.

A *smart card* looks like an ordinary credit card but actually contains a tiny, embedded microprocessor. The smart card's memory stores a unique identifier which, when recognized by a smart card reader, will prove that you are who you claim to be. The presumption is that only one person can have the smart card at any one point in time and that the possessor is, therefore, a legitimate user. Knowledge, however, can be possessed by more than one person simultaneously. If

FIGURE 11.5   SecurID token from RSA Security Inc.

hackers steal your password you may never know it. If they steal your smart card, you will definitely know it the next time you go to logon and can't find it, at which point you would contact the security administrator and have the system configured to reject any subsequent use of the device. Additional protection against theft is provided as many smart card systems require the use to enter a PIN. This *two-factor authentication* approach is based upon something you have (the smart card) and something you know (the PIN). A hacker would now have to steal both your smart card and your PIN in order to break in.

Other have-based authentication methods might require that you present another sort of unique security token. RSA Security Inc.[11] produces what is known as an RSA SecurID token. These tokens often look like a credit card or a small key fob[12] with an embedded numeric display (Figure 11.5). With this system users must enter not only their userid and password but also the number that appears on the RSA SecurID token or a small keyfob at that instant in time. Since the number on the token is changed every minute and since hackers can't predict which number will come up next, they would, as with the smart card, have to steal the token and a password in order to break in – another example of two-factor authentication.

Still other methods require that the client system present a *digital certificate* containing the public encryption key for the users. As long as users keep their *private* key secret, information can be scrambled using their *public* key in such a way that only they can unscramble it (more on this in Appendix A).

The final class of authentication systems is based on something you *are*. These systems involve biometric devices which can measure certain physical characteristics unique to you. This could take the form of a fingerprint, voiceprint, retinal scan, facial recognition, hand geometry, or even the electromagnetic field that you emit. Sound like science fiction? It's not. While some of these technologies are still in their infancy and have yet to be proven over the long haul, others have shown themselves to be acceptably reliable.

The advantage of biometric authentication is that there are no passwords to remember (or for hackers to steal) and there are no proof of identity devices that you have to carry around with you (and potentially lose). The downside is often the cost. In fact, the reason that passwords are so popular is that they cost virtually nothing to implement. Of course, there are plenty of hidden costs in terms of password administration (e.g. calls to the help desk for lost password resets) and lower security, but, on the whole, they work and they are cheap. When tokens of some sort are introduced, security increases, but so do the costs. Biometric solutions often are the most costly of all but they have the *potential* to be the most secure (depending upon the particular technology you choose, of course).

> Biometric solutions often are the most costly of all but they have the *potential* to be the most secure.

---

11. Formerly known as Security Dynamics Technologies Inc.
12. For more information see www.rsasecurity.com.

Biometric authentication systems, though, introduce other issues that must be properly accounted for. Since no biometric system is perfect, a decision must be made as to which sorts of errors are more tolerable than others. Consider a voice recognition system as an example. A **false positive** (erroneous approval) would result if an impostor were able to gain access either by imitating you or by playing back a recording of your voice. The consequence of such a scenario is a security breach. On the other hand, the system could also err by failing to recognize your voice on a day when you are suffering from a cold. In this case the resulting **false negative** (erroneous rejection) could range in significance from a mild inconvenience to a total business shutdown, if you are unable to gain access to the resources you need to perform a mission-critical task.

Biometric systems typically allow an administrator to specify how precise a match must be in order to be considered a positive identification. The organization's tolerance for false positives and false negatives will dictate this parameter. If the value of the resources being protected is extremely high, the administrator might opt for a higher likelihood of false negatives. This is because the protected resources are deemed to be worth the added inconvenience of a higher rate of improper rejections. On the other hand, if denying access to legitimate users is a more costly risk than the possibility of failing to prevent an occasional unauthorized access, then the prudent decision might be to opt for a lower level of precision.

Until biometric systems are able to perform a non-invasive analysis of your DNA with sub-second response time (don't hold your breath on that one), the issue of how to strike the right balance between false positives and false negatives is likely to persist. For this reason biometric systems may work best when used not as a replacement for other authentication schemes (password, PIN, smart card, etc.), but in conjunction with those other mechanisms.

Also, there exists the possibility that end users could face a threat to their own personal safety if the resources being protected are of substantial value. Some biometric systems include additional checks to guard against such threats. A voice recognition system might listen for audible cues that the user is overly anxious, for instance. As you might imagine, though, such detection is less than 100 per cent accurate. Other options involve allowing the user to perform a predetermined behaviour that would not be identified as unusual by the attacker, but that would alert a security guard that something was amiss.

(11.12) The burden of proof

As mentioned previously, you might choose to combine two or more of these schemes into an integrated procedure. An example of this type of two-factor authentication is an ATM which can be used to withdraw money from a bank. Typically these devices exploit the 'something you have' (the ATM card) and 'something you know' (the PIN) methods in order to establish your identity. Since this approach involves multiple levels of authentication, it is potentially more secure (assuming you don't write your PIN on the back of the card!).

It is also possible to combine strong authentication via smart cards, tokens or biometrics with a single sign-on system to maximize security, usability and productivity all at once (a rare feat in the realm of IT security!). With this arrangement you can circumvent the 'single password for multiple userids' problem by elevating the level of proof required to access the SSO logon coordinator.

Clearly, there are trade-offs that must be considered. A 'one size fits all' approach to authentication is probably not the best option. The decision should be based upon a risk analysis which considers the cost of loss or compromise along with the likelihood of such an occurrence (see Chapter 4). Obviously, you wouldn't want to protect the proverbial 'keys to the kingdom' with a weak password, nor would you want to spend inordinate sums of money to protect something of little value. The best solution is the one that fits the needs of the business and keeps hackers at bay.

Hackers know that password-based systems can be defeated. They have human nature and a host of cracking tools working for them. With dogged persistence they can go where they aren't supposed to be. However, you can use this same information to your advantage if you design defence systems that take the vulnerabilities discussed in this chapter into account. That's what hackers don't want you to know.

chapter 12

Hackers don't want you to know that ... *they can see you but you can't see them*

Remember the old 'party line' telephone systems? By sharing the same line with other people in your neighbourhood, the telephone company was able to reuse their facilities across multiple customers. This resulted in a more economical service for everyone concerned. The problem was that anyone sharing your line could also listen in to what you were saying. This required that everyone on the line exercise a considerable degree of courtesy in order for private conversations to remain private. Of course, all it took was one nosy neighbour to eavesdrop on another person's call to throw the whole system of trust into a tailspin. As soon as private lines became available at a reasonable price, everyone moved to this service and the party lines went the way of the dinosaur. Or did they?

Hackers don't want you to know that your corporate network may be a lot more like a party line than a private line. They know that LAN technologies are built on the concept of a shared medium. That means that it is, in fact, possible for them to eavesdrop on what are presumed to be private data exchanges in order to glean useful information to further their attacks. They are, in essence, like a nosy neighbour on a party line.

12.1 What's that smell?

Most LANs are based on a protocol known as **Ethernet**, which is, at its heart, a broadcast technology. The idea is that if a client station wants to get data from its server (or another client station, for that matter), it formulates a data packet, tacks on the appropriate communications header, addresses it to the server, and then sends the packet out over the line to be transmitted to the intended destination. The server, and all the other workstations on that LAN segment, sit listening for any packets that might be intended for them. Packets addressed to another station are simply ignored. An inevitable consequence of this arrangement is that every station on a given LAN segment can hear what every other station on that segment is saying. Since no one would normally want data that isn't applicable to them in the first place, the system works quite well. But all it takes is one bad apple to spoil the barrel, as we will soon see.

Token Ring is another popular LAN technology which suffers a similar fate. In a Token Ring network each station is basically responsible for:

- receiving the 'token' (a specially formatted message) and any accompanying 'frames' (the data to be sent) – it might be helpful to think of the token as a bucket carrying its contents (frames) to the intended destination,

- determining to whom the frame is addressed,

- copying the data to the machine's local memory, if the frame is addressed to this station, and

- sending the packet along to the next station on the ring.

(Of course, much more goes on than this, but this is enough detail for our discussion.)

With both Ethernet and Token Ring technologies the normal mode of operation is for stations to only look at the header of a given packet to see if it is addressed to them (Figure 12.1). If it isn't, they don't bother to examine the rest of the packet's contents. There is an exception to this typical case known as *promiscuous mode*. Promiscuous mode, as its name implies, isn't as well behaved. With this mode the LAN adaptor is not restricted to dealing only with its traffic, but it saves a copy of the packet contents for *all* the packets it sees, whether they are addressed to that particular station or not. An adaptor can be switched from 'virtuous mode' (not an official term but it is the opposite of 'promiscuous', right?) to promiscuous mode through software running on the workstation.

Why would LAN adaptor manufacturers create such a security loophole in their products in the first place? Surely, they understand that they have created an environment that is ideal for eavesdroppers, don't they? It turns out that this capability has some legitimate uses in the proper hands. Network technicians often use tools that allow them to monitor all traffic on a network in order to do problem determination and performance analysis. Such tracing tools are often called **sniffers** (after the product of the same name from Network General Corp. which rose to fame in the

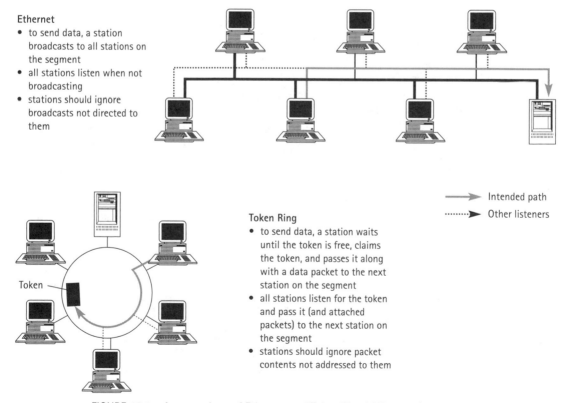

Ethernet
- to send data, a station broadcasts to all stations on the segment
- all stations listen when not broadcasting
- stations should ignore broadcasts not directed to them

Intended path
Other listeners

Token Ring
- to send data, a station waits until the token is free, claims the token, and passes it along with a data packet to the next station on the segment
- all stations listen for the token and pass it (and attached packets) to the next station on the segment
- stations should ignore packet contents not addressed to them

Token

FIGURE 12.1   A comparison of Ethernet and Token Ring LAN operation

early 1990s). A minimal sniffer might consist of a PC (possibly a laptop for the sake of portability) containing a LAN adaptor capable of promiscuous mode and software designed to analyze the traffic it sees. It might classify traffic based on network protocol, workstation, size, volume, etc. In addition it would be able to show the actual byte-by-byte composition of selected packets so that protocol errors could be diagnosed.

Such information in the right hands can be a valuable asset when trying to tune a network or simply keep it up and operational. This same information in the wrong hands could spell disaster.

12.2   Aroma or stench?

What happens if hackers gets their hands on a promiscuous mode LAN adaptor (which isn't at all hard to do) and the requisite software to exploit it? The answer is that they start snooping around your network looking for anything that might interest them. It turns out that the same commercially available sniffer tools intended to help the good guys are a double-edged sword that can be exploited by the bad guys just as well. The difference isn't in the tool but in the *reason* the tool is being used. **Sniffing** can be a legitimate technique used by authorized network technicians or a means for hackers to eavesdrop on corporate communications. Since network traffic could include passwords, confidential reports, or even incriminating email, the stakes can be extremely high.

Unfortunately, the barriers to entry into the world of malicious network sniffing are quite low. Since most Ethernet adaptors support promiscuous mode (many Token Ring adaptors do, but they are somewhat less common), all hackers need is a LAN adaptor and some readily available sniffing software and they're in business at minimal (if any) cost.

One of the more effective sniffing tools for swiping passwords is L0phtCrack's built-in **Server Message Block** (**SMB**) packet capture facility. This tool takes a look at all the packets going across the LAN, saves a copy of any server logon packets it sees, and discards the rest. This way, hackers end up with a nice, neat listing of userids' encrypted passwords which they can then feed into the tool's cracking facility (see Section 11.5 for more information). In other words, if hackers are interested in just stealing some passwords, L0phtCrack makes the job easy by filtering out all the other extraneous transmissions and saving only the desired packets. When you consider that the vast majority of LAN packets don't contain logon information, you quickly realize that this weeding out process can save hackers a considerable amount of work.

A compelling argument can be made for the legitimate use of L0phtCrack's password-cracking facilities as they can be used by system administrators to test the strength of the passwords their users have chosen. However, the case for sniffing tools such as the SMB packet filter is on shakier ground. Of course, there's the stand-ard 'if we didn't do it someone else would' argument, but the fact remains that while sniffing for the purpose of diagnosing network problems is valid, sniffing in order to swipe passwords or other corporate communications is highly unethical and most probably illegal. The reason for including such information in this book, of course, is not to tell hackers how to steal passwords, because they already know how to do this and are probably very familiar with tools such as L0phtCrack. The objective is to alert IT professionals who, for the most part, don't know that such dangers exist, in order that they may take appropriate actions.

(12.3) The 'silent attack'

What can you do to defend against a sniffing attack? You might think that you are safe since hackers would have to gain physical access to your LAN in order to do any real damage this way. It turns out that this is only partially true. In fact, even if it were completely true, it still wouldn't be reason enough to justify a sense of secu-rity. Here are just a few of the reasons why ...

Many people say 'it doesn't matter if someone hacks this particular system because it doesn't contain anything of value anyway'. Hackers don't want you to know that if they can gain access to *any* client or server workstation on your net-work, they can install a sniffer which could run unnoticed in the background. How could attackers get access? Wouldn't they have to actually put their hands on the keyboard of the target workstation in order to plant the sniffing tool?

Not necessarily. In fact, the entire attack could be executed from halfway around the world. Hackers could simply email a **Remote Access Trojan** (RAT) to their victim and let it do the rest of the work for them. The RAT might appear to be an innocuous program that produces an entertaining screen show (e.g. a holiday greeting) when, in fact, its real intent is to install a sniffer on the target system. Once installed, the RAT might send back a message to the hacker, via either email or an Internet Relay Chat (IRC) session, telling him or her where to attack. In addi-tion to broadcasting the location of the compromised machine, the RAT might also steal a telnet password on that machine and pass it along to the attacker. At this point all the hacker would need to do is logon to the compromised system from time to time to see if anything interesting had been snared by the sniffer.

This illustrates why security must be dealt with on a corporate, rather than indi-vidual, level when considering issues such as password security mechanisms, firewalls, and virus/Trojan horse protection. Even if you do a good job of repelling outsiders, you need to remember that insiders are already in an excellent position to sniff your network. They already have physical access to your LAN and probably have a clearer idea of what information is valuable and what is not.

Complicating all of this is the fact that sniffing truly is a 'silent attack'. As you will soon see, the passive nature of this sort of eavesdropping makes it very hard, if not impossible, to detect. Since most Ethernet adaptors support promiscuous mode, any station could be copying data packets and go completely unnoticed. Initially, Token Ring adaptors were somewhat better in this regard since very few had this capability. This fact offers little comfort, though, as many of the newer adaptors are capable of promiscuous processing.

Some adaptors are conscientious enough to automatically broadcast the fact that they are operating in promiscuous mode. A LAN management tool could detect these messages and warn you of a potential intruder. However, you can't depend on this capability to save you since it's ultimately left up to the adaptor (or, more likely, the software controlling it) to generate these notifications. So while legitimate sniffers used by authorized network technicians might alert you to their presence, the kinds used by hackers won't – and it is the latter that you need to be the most concerned with.

12.4 Sniffing for sniffers

Since you can't rely on the sniffers to broadcast their presence and turn themselves in, you have to find another way to locate them. There are no foolproof methods guaranteed to sniff out the bad guys, but there are some techniques that can be used to *predict* whether a sniffer is about. Many of these are based upon the idea of trying to detect some of the tell-tale signs that sniffers unintentionally leave in their wake. In other words, you can't directly test for promiscuous mode on other machines but you can borrow a page from the hacker's book and do a little snooping on the snoopers.

12.4.1 Antisniff

One such tool that can help is AntiSniff[1] from L0pht Heavy Industries (Figure 12.2). AntiSniff combines a number of different detection techniques into a single program, which can proactively test systems that are suspected of running in promiscuous mode. AntiSniff looks for specific operating system quirks that can indicate promiscuous mode processing. For example, some versions of Linux (a popular UNIX variant) can be tricked into exposing themselves when confronted with a specially modified PING[2] request. The trick is to build a PING request using the Internet Protocol (IP) address of the suspected machine but address it to a LAN

1. AntiSniff, L0pht Heavy Industries, www.l0pht.com/antisniff.
2. PING (Packet INternet Groper) is a command which generates an ICMP echo request. This packet is sent to a specified address in anticipation of a reply (which indicates that the station is reachable by the network).

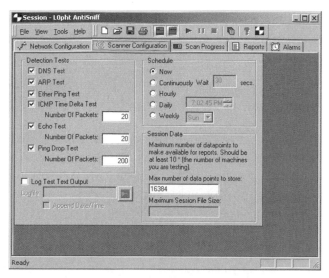

FIGURE 12.2   Sniffing for sniffers with AntiSniff (Copyright © 1994, 1995, 1996, 1997, 1998 LHI Technologies)

adaptor that doesn't actually exist. Adaptors not operating in promiscuous mode will ignore the request because it isn't addressed to them. But since a promiscuous mode adaptor copies all packets (not just those addressed directly to it), the eavesdropping station passes the request on to its own IP software which, in turn, takes the bait and responds to the PING. AntiSniff simply listens out for the PING response and, if it gets one, it concludes that a sniffer has been unearthed. This test can be circumvented, though, by hackers if they update their system with the appropriate patch or choose an operating system that doesn't make this same mistake.

Another test that AntiSniff can perform relies on the fact that most systems use the DNS to look up the numeric IP address (e.g. 10.1.2.3) for a given symbolic name (www.widgets-r-us.com). Reverse DNS lookups, which do just the opposite, are far less common. Sniffers, however, frequently make use of this function because their users often want to know the *name* (rather than just the IP address) of the workstation whose packet they just copied. AntiSniff exploits this fact by manufacturing bogus network traffic that appears to come from a station that, in fact, doesn't exist. AntiSniff then switches its adaptor to promiscuous mode and waits to see if anyone attempts to resolve the fictitious address with a reverse DNS lookup. When the hacker's sniffing tool steps out from the shadows in an attempt to figure out the name of the non-existent station, AntiSniff zeroes in on the sniffer's location.

AntiSniff can also make educated guesses as to which stations are in promiscuous mode by observing the latency or delay that occurs during a burst of bogus network traffic. The theory is that stations that aren't in promiscuous mode aren't likely to be adversely affected by 'background noise' which they quickly realize is not intended for them. However, a promiscuous mode station will be slower to respond when the network is flooded because it will be busy trying to process all the additional traffic (which is bound for the non-existent station). AntiSniff, then, takes advantage of this behaviour by PINGing stations during normal network operation to establish a baseline response time. Then it generates a flood of meaningless traffic and tests the machines again with another set of PINGs. The second set of results are then compared to the baseline and if a significant delay is found only on certain stations, they are considered to be sniffing suspects, since they were bogged down trying to process traffic they should have ignored. Of course, this technique can be error prone and, therefore, any conclusions drawn can only be considered preliminary. Nonetheless information gathered during this test can be used as the basis for a follow-up investigation.

12.4.2   Sniffer detector

A completely different approach to promiscuous mode detection involves a bit of misdirection which, when pursued by the hacker, is a dead give-away to malicious sniffing. In this case a series of client machines randomly logon to a designated server, issue a few commands, and then logoff. Since the server performs no meaningful work and, therefore, exists only for the purpose of acting as a hacker *decoy*, it is assumed that any attempt to logon to it by anyone other than the clients assigned to participate in the charade must be the result of sniffing (Figure 12.3). The server's job is simply to record all logon attempts that originate from an IP address other than those of the decoy clients and alert a system administrator of the suspicious activity.

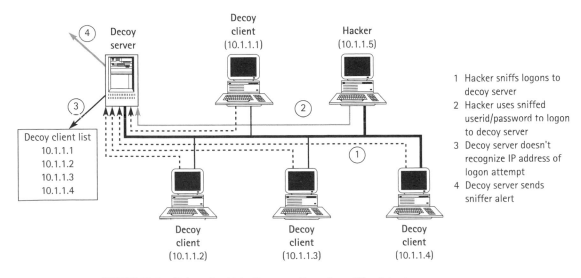

FIGURE 12.3   Bait and snitch: the operation of a sniffer detector

This indirect approach can be particularly effective because it can be easily auto-mated and run in the background. By using particularly intriguing machine names like 'topsecret' or 'payroll' and powerful-sounding userids like 'root' and 'sysadmin', the decoy server can appear especially inviting to hackers.

A more sophisticated variation on this theme came from IBM's Global Security Analysis Lab (GSAL) and was presented at RAID '99, an industry conference dedi-cated to intrusion detection (Grundschober, 1999). GSAL's 'Sniffer Detector' also includes a separate Manager system which oversees and coordinates the entire process by instructing decoy client systems when and where to logon. In addition, a 'Probe' system is used to sniff out any logon attempts to the decoy servers.

As you can see, most of the techniques for detecting sniffers involve setting a trap of one sort or another and then sitting back and waiting for hackers to take the bait. Clever hackers could, of course, 'fly below radar' if they were careful to avoid leaving traces of their presence. So while there may be no conclusive method for sniffing out the sniffers, there are any number of useful ways to narrow down the search.[3]

(12.5) Hanging up on the party line

So while sniffing is hard to detect in many cases, all is not lost. There are some things that you can do that will restore at least some degree of confidence into your corpo-rate communications. Probably the most effective of these options involves encrypting transmissions as they traverse the network. As mentioned in Section 1.2, TCP/IP was not originally designed for secure communications. As a protocol for use in military networks it was assumed that all data would flow over private lines and that the endpoints would be protected by soldiers with high-powered weapons. In such an environment, the need for secure network protocols is diminished.

However, as TCP/IP has made its way into popular use in both public networks (like the Internet) and private corporate networks alike, the need for greater secu-rity has become obvious. To address this requirement the *Internet Engineering Task Force (IETF)*, the group that controls the TCP/IP standard, launched an effort to design a next-generation version of the protocol which came to be known as IPv6.[4] Among many other improvements, an increased level of security has been added. During this process, though, it was realized that the need for security was simply too great to wait for widespread IPv6 deployment (which would take many years), so they decided to retrofit these enhancements into the existing IPv4 standard.

The name given to these security improvements was IPSec, which stands for **Internet Protocol Security**. IPSec defines a framework for setting up and operating

---

3. For more information on sniffing see Robert Graham's 'Sniffing FAQ' at
   www.robertgraham.com/pubs/sniffing-faq.html.
4. IPv4 is the predominant form at the time of this writing.

a **Virtual Private Network** (**VPN**) where transmissions can be authenticated and encrypted. Authentication features allow you to know if the message really came from the person you think it came from, while encryption helps ensure no one else can read your messages. As such, encryption gives us the 'P' (for 'private') in VPN. The 'V' (for 'virtual') comes from the fact that while the communications are, in fact, private, the network is not. In other words, if a message is scrambled in such a way that only the intended receiver can read it, then it's safe to send it across a public backbone because eavesdroppers won't be able to make sense of what they've just received. A brief tutorial of IPSec is presented in Appendix B.

Of course, it's more complicated than that as there are numerous issues regarding cryptographic strength, protection of private keys, and so forth, that ultimately determine the security of such a system (see Chapter 19 for a brief treatment of crypto issues).

The point is that VPN technologies *are* available today and can be used to keep your private communications private. However, setting up the necessary infrastructure can be time consuming and expensive. Its appeal, though, lies in the fact that a VPN over a public network can be substantially cheaper than private, leased line connections. In fact, Infonetics Research estimates that VPNs can save anywhere from 20–80 per cent when used for external network connectivity (Infonetics Research, 1997). As a result, this approach is probably best deployed sparingly within the corporate intranet for particularly sensitive applications but used extensively when communicating to remote offices, business partners, and mobile employees who dial in for remote access.

Often overlooked in the deployment of VPNs for these workers, is the fact that more and more classified data will be making its way out of the corporate campus and onto the far less controlled environment of laptops and home PCs. Some have observed that using strong crypto to encrypt credit card numbers over the Internet is like using an armoured truck to deliver a paper sack full of money to a park bench.[5] While this statement is an extreme illustration of e-commerce insecurity, its basic point is just as applicable to VPNs. It doesn't do much good to use strong crypto to obscure transmissions over the network if they will be stored 'in the clear' (i.e. unencrypted) on an unprotected platform at the other end of the VPN tunnel. The increased use of high-speed, 'always connected' services (often in conjunction with VPNs) for remote workers only compounds the problem, as you will see in Section 23.3.

This means that while VPNs represent an effective defence against sniffing, they aren't the total answer in and of themselves. Sensitive data should be encrypted when it is stored on disk and frequent backups should be taken in order to avert disasters.

---

5. Based on an example by Gene Spafford in Garfinkel and Spafford (1997).

12.6 Moving to a private line

Another option to foil sniffing attacks on the LAN involves isolating workstations in order to minimize the shared nature of the communications media. Today's switching hubs (networking hardware which provides improved manageability for LANs) could hardly be imagined by the originators of Ethernet because the price per port was prohibitively high. Now, however, in the interest of better performance, many companies are moving toward greater and greater degrees of segmentation on their LANs. By essentially putting each workstation on its own private segment, you can dramatically improve throughput (Figure 12.4). Think of it this way: if you have to share a connection with 10 or 20 other people, you know there will be some contention for the available bandwidth (i.e. capacity). On the other hand, if you don't have to share with anyone, you can effectively have full use of the connection and its capacity.

Owing to decreasing costs, switching hubs have turned this dream into a reality. The great news, from a security standpoint, is that if you're the only one on your segment, hackers can't camp out on an adjacent workstation and sniff your packets. This isolation not only improves performance but it also improves security.

Still, even this offers no guarantee. If hackers plant their sniffers in the server, they still will be able to listen in on a great deal of what is being transmitted because many transmissions will be directed there anyway. There also exists the possibility that packets will leak out from their intended segment and end up on other segments. This really shouldn't happen if the switch is doing its job, but people who have tested these devices continue to report cases where it does, indeed, occur. Therefore, anyone intending to rely on such a mechanism for security would be well advised to test their LAN for this sort of leakage from time to time.

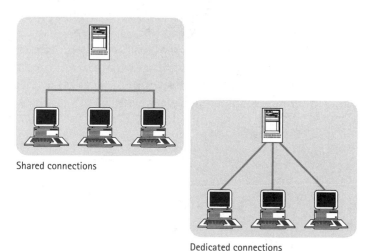

Shared connections

Dedicated connections

FIGURE 12.4   Before and after extensive LAN segmentation

(12.7) Choices, choices, choices ...

Sniffing attacks are among the most difficult to defend against but all is not lost. Here's a quick review of your options:

- *Encrypt data using VPN technology*. This is the most secure option, assuming strong cryptography is used, but it isn't cheap. Also, the overhead of encryption could degrade performance to some extent and setup/administration is far from trivial.

- *Extensive LAN segmentation*. By moving to switched hubs and putting every workstation on its own segment you can isolate LAN traffic so that it isn't broadcast to everyone within earshot. This could be expensive if you have to replace existing equipment but, once implemented, wouldn't have the maintenance problems of the VPN option. However, once packets leave the segment and hit the server or the WAN (wide area network), hackers may be able to position themselves in a sniffing position anyway.

- *Sniff out the sniffers*. If Token Ring LANs are involved it may be possible to detect some promiscuous mode adaptors via network management tools. Such an event could then trigger an alert to notify the proper personnel. However, since there are many ways for hackers to get around this, don't put too much stock in this as a line of defence. Better still are some of the sniffer detection methods mentioned in Section 12.4 which involve baiting a trap and waiting for hackers to break their silence.

- *Maintain tight physical security of the LAN*. Of course, you should do this anyway, but the potential for sniffing is just one more reason why. The deficiency with this approach is that it's very difficult to do and, even if you succeed, hackers could still plant a sniffer on a legitimate LAN workstation. This could even be done by a hacker outside the corporate intranet via a RAT (Remote Access Trojan). Also, physical security may not help much in the case of insider attacks since restrictions often must be eased to accommodate office and equipment moves and mobile employees.

chapter 13

Hackers don't want you to know that ... *downlevel software is vulnerable*

Essentially all software has bugs. I'm sure that won't come as a surprise to anyone who's operated a computer for more than about 10 minutes. Software, unlike fine wine, doesn't get better with age – it only gets increasingly more vulnerable. How can this be? Since computer programs are essentially nothing more than detailed lists of instructions to be followed in a precise order, it would seem that they would not be subject to decay. Of course, they aren't, but it may appear as if this is the case when you consider that the older a piece of software is, the longer its list of vulnerabilities seems to be. In part, this is due to the fact that the longer a program has been around, the longer hackers have had to probe it for weaknesses. The fact that some of these bugs can affect the security of your IT systems should not come as a great surprise. However, if you were to look at the vast numbers of systems that are vulnerable because they have failed to keep up with the latest level of fixes, you might be led to conclude otherwise. What should be common knowledge seems to be a well-kept secret.

Why is this problem so pervasive? Perhaps it's because IT support staff are already 'up to their ears in alligators' just trying to deal with the steady flow of problem reports generated by their end-user community. The proverbial 'stitch in time saves nine' wisdom gets drowned out by a cacophony of other, seemingly more pressing issues. Of course, in ignoring the more mundane call for regular software maintenance, these same overworked souls create for themselves the possibility of even greater headaches down the road when an intrusion occurs.

A contributing factor to the problem is the fact that many IT organizations live in a constant state of denial with respect to the hazards they face. Working so close to the fire has desensitized them to the peril that lies in wait for a singular lapse in judgement. 'I never thought it would actually happen to us' might be an appropriate epitaph for most victims of computer hacking.

Of course, hackers live for such things. They thrive on the ignorance and apathy of their victims. They count on the fact that well-known software bugs fail to get fixed within a reasonable time. Word of such vulnerabilities spreads like wildfire through the hacker community. Before you know it, any kid with a computer can bring a Fortune 500 company to its knees. Unfortunately, the word doesn't travel nearly as fast through the corporate IT community, which explains why hackers are so successful.

(13.1)   It's déjà vu all over again

What has been is what will be,

and what has been done is what will be done;

and there is nothing new under the sun.

Is there a thing of which it is said,

'See, this is new'?

It has been already,

in the ages before us.

Holy Bible, Ecclesiastes 1:9–10 (RSV)

Yogi Berra, an icon of American baseball, almost certainly didn't have buffer overflows in mind when he said 'it's déjà vu all over again', but this famous utterance would certainly apply. When it comes to software defects, especially as they apply to security, it seems the more things change, the more they stay the same. For proof one need look no further than the highly respected Computer Emergency Response Team (CERT) of Carnegie Mellon University.

CERT tracks the comings and goings of the computer security world and, when it deems appropriate, it issues advisories for problems it believes deserve special attention. In 1998 CERT issued 13 advisories. That relatively small number should tell you that they don't take such actions lightly. In other words, when CERT speaks, people listen. Of those 13 advisories, 10 involved software which had failed in one way or another to properly handle unexpected input.[1] Breaking it down even further, 7 of those 10 were caused by the same underlying defect – *buffer overflow*.

If you aren't a programmer, you may not be familiar with such a term, but you don't need a degree in Computer Science to understand the one thing that has eluded the programmers responsible for these bugs – 'those that fail to learn from history are destined to repeat it'. Validating input to a program and dealing gracefully with all possible outcomes is something that is taught in any respectable programming class. Some instructors go so far as to say that more than half the lines of code written should be dedicated to error-handling scenarios in order to prevent the sort of problems that CERT has highlighted.

Unfortunately, in the rush to crank out more and more functionality, such lessons too often get lost in the shuffle. What may sound like some new, exotic system vulnerability that hackers have exploited is quite often nothing more than a variation on this basic theme. As the philosopher wrote in Ecclesiastes, 'there is nothing new under the sun'.

13.2) Pardon me, but your buffer is overflowing

Buffer overflows are one of the oldest exploits in the book. The hacker simply sends more data than the receiver is expecting and if the receiver's system doesn't do sufficient error checking, unexpected behaviours can result. In some cases the receiver's program simply crashes. In other cases a system may be rendered completely unavailable to its legitimate users. If there is a silver lining to this dark cloud, it is that these attacks are usually easy to detect and relatively easy to fix, assuming a patch (i.e. software fix) is available.

In other cases the data that overflows the buffer may be mistakenly identified by the system as a continuation of the program it was running. When the system tries to execute the extraneous data undesirable things can happen. If hackers decide to plant malicious code in this data, they may be able to effectively do whatever they want to do to your system. This could range from destroying valuable data to stealing corporate secrets and everything in between.

1. Computer Emergency Response Team, Carnegie Mellon University, www.cert.org.

Further evidence of how common such problems are surfaced in the spring and summer of 1998 when it was discovered that three of the most popular email programs on the Internet – Microsoft Outlook, Netscape Communicator, and Qualcomm Eudora Pro – all suffered from buffer overflows bugs.[2] In some of the 'best' cases these bugs might only crash a user's system. In other more sinister cases the hacker's program might be given control of the victim's system. Once this occurred, any number of catastrophic outcomes might result. In all cases the malicious behaviour was triggered by the receipt of an email containing a filename which was unusually long. When the victim read in the email, the buffer overflow condition occurred and the fireworks began.

Prior to these incidents the conventional wisdom was that the mere act of *reading* an email did not expose a system to attack. It was well known that *detaching* and *executing* an email attachment could be dangerous, but *reading* was viewed as safe. Of course, this assertion assumed that the email program would act appropriately. In hindsight, it is easy to see how naive this assumption was.[3]

As we look to the future, we should be careful not to make similar assumptions. For example, Java applets running in a Web browser *should* be safe since they are confined to operate within a narrowly defined 'sandbox' on the user's system.[4] This sandbox is designed to contain the downloaded program by preventing it from modifying the computer's storage or interfering with other programs currently running. However, a defective browser implementation of the Java Virtual Machine (JVM) can throw all that we know about Java security out of the window. This is not to say that users should avoid Java applets at all cost, but it does mean that the IT group needs to keep a close watch on the development of software used by its users and issue fixes in a *proactive* (rather than *reactive*) manner.

(13.3) You're breaking me up

A variation on the buffer overflow problem involves other sorts of unexpected input conditions. One well-known network exploit goes by the name of *Teardrop*.[5] A Teardrop attack intentionally breaks the rules for splitting up large data packets into smaller ones that the network can handle. If networking components fail to check for malformed packets the results can be hazardous to your network's health as any vulnerable machine may crash without warning.

2. CERT Advisory, 'CA-98.10 Buffer Overflow in MIME-aware Mail and News Clients', August 1998, www.cert.org. (Note: While not mentioned in this CERT Advisory, Eudora Pro was already known to suffer from an overflow bug which could crash a user's system if it encountered an email containing a filename longer than 233 characters.)
3. In November of 1999 the 'BubbleBoy worm' (a.k.a. VBS.BubbleBoy) served to remind the IT Security community that the simple act of viewing an email could, in fact, make a system vulnerable to attack.
4. Under the newer Java 2 security model, the user would need to deny any requests that an applet might make for additional privileges in order for this assumption to hold true.
5 CERT Advisory, 'CA-97.28 IP Denial-of-Service Attacks', December 1997, www.cert.org.

A similar attack known as *Land*[6] involves IP packet spoofing. Spoofing is essentially impersonation. The spoofed packet claims to be from somewhere that it's not. In the Land attack a spoofed packet contains the same origin address, destination address and port number – a condition that should clearly never occur. Vulnerable network components simply don't know how to handle this obvious error condition and may crash or hang as a result.

Hackers know about these vulnerabilities and have access to widely available software which automates the entire attack for them. It is, therefore, quite easy for them to run these attacks again and again until they find a soft spot.

Such attacks are classified as 'Denial-of-Service' or 'DoS' attacks since they deprive access to legitimate users by making key resources unavailable. Since DoS attacks are some of the easiest attacks to launch, they are especially popular among novice hackers. The effect on the company's bottom line, however, can be just as devastating as the consequences of more sophisticated attacks.

DoS attackers aren't likely to gain anything that would be of value, but to them, the mere act of creating a disturbance is reward enough. In one sense DoS attacks are the Internet equivalent of a drive-by shooting – a quick, unpredictable and lethal strike against what may be a random target. Not only are DoS attacks easy to execute but they can offer a greater degree of anonymity for the attacker than other types of attack. Emboldened by this fact, hackers may feel that they can act with impunity – and often do just that. As with senseless violence in the real world, DoS attacks often affect innocent bystanders – people who depend upon IT systems for their livelihood.

Hackers know all about DoS attacks – how easy they are to pull off and how damaging they can be – and they hope you don't know the same things that they do. Because if you are wise to ways of DoS, you can stop many known attacks dead in their tracks.

13.4 This doesn't belong here!

DoS attacks can also result from all sorts of unexpected conditions. For instance, telnet sessions normally connect to port #23 on the target machine. However, if a hacker telnets in an unexpected way, such as to port #135, into a vulnerable NT server, enters a few random characters and promptly disconnects, the CPU utilization on the target system will jump to 100 per cent and stay there until the machine is rebooted. This, of course, renders the machine useless to anyone that might need its services.

A fix for this problem has existed for years, but a surprising number of servers still haven't received it and are, therefore, little more than disasters waiting to happen. If you think this is an overstatement, consider the impact to the business

6   CERT Advisory, 'CA-97.28 IP Denial-of-Service Attacks', December 1997, www.cert.org.

if this NT machine happens to host the corporate e-commerce Web site. The effect is the same as closing the door in the face of potential customers who were ready with cash in hand to buy your products or services. When they find the doors to your online shop closed during regular business hours (which are 24 hours a day, 7 days a week, 365 days a year when the Internet is involved), they are likely to find another place to spend their money.

(13.5) A cure that's worse than the disease?

Of course, if you build a better mousetrap, eventually someone will build a better mouse. This is precisely what happened in response to the Microsoft Outlook bug mentioned previously. A group of hackers from Bulgaria decided to capitalize on the hysteria created by the original buffer overflow bug by providing a free 'fix' to the problem. It turns out, though, that this fix amounted to nothing more than yet another attack on the systems to which it was applied (Cornetto, 1998).

The bogus fix was included as an email attachment sent along with a message which discussed the original problem and included instructions to the user indicating that he or she should apply this fix immediately and send it to all his or her friends in order to defend against the attack.

Clearly, the lesson here is that while it is essential that you apply fixes for known security exploits, it is equally important that you know *what* you're installing. Since it's not practical to try to determine from merely browsing the binary files that make up the fix what it will actually do, you ultimately have to trust the source of the fix. In other words, know where the fix comes from before you apply it and spread the word to your user community that only fixes from specific, authorized sources should be applied. You should include all of this in your corporate security policy and make sure that everyone knows about it.

This might seem obvious to a systems programmer, but as the Bulgarian hackers well knew, it is far from obvious for the vast majority of Internet users. It was this bit of information that hackers didn't want their victims to know, because if they had, the attack would never have got off the ground.

(13.6) Exterminating the bugs

The sad truth is that a significant number of attacks resulting from software vulnerabilities never needed to happen in the first place. The exploits are often very well known (at least within the hacker community) and fixes are readily available. The goal of the IT organization, of course, is to keep everything up and operational. But how they go about doing that isn't always as clear.

On the one hand some will argue that 'if it ain't broken, don't fix it'. This makes a lot of sense. Why subject yourself to the rat race of trying to keep up with all the various software vendors, their products, and their '*fixes du jour*'? Wouldn't things be a lot simpler if you just left well enough alone? How many new bugs will be introduced with new fixes? Some companies go so far as to mandate that they will not run any new software release until it has been generally available for six months to a year. Of course, all of this is intended to maintain stability.

On the other hand, if that software is three or four fix levels behind, how many security holes, which have subsequently been found and fixed, does it contain? Many vendors are slow to issue security fixes in the first place because they don't want to draw attention to the vulnerabilities that exist in their products. Unless they are publicly shamed into action, some will remain silent on the issue entirely. A less than obvious consequence of this behaviour is the fact that many fixes that are finally released for one stated reason may also address unpublicized security issues that the vendors know they must deal with. By issuing a 'stealth fix', vendors may hope to nip a problem in the bud without drawing undue attention. After all, what vendor wants to advertise the fact that their product contained a gaping security hole in it for the past six months?

The point is that while you may believe that you're maximizing stability by slowly moving forward with your software maintenance, you may be doing just the opposite. How stable is a system that is littered with well-known hacker exploits? Answer: not very.

(13.7) Spreading the word

Of course, publicly accessible systems need to be impervious to hacker exploits but you can't stop there. Back-end servers that supply data to Web-based applications could be attacked through the very ports they use to communicate with the 'outside world'. Even clients and servers that have no direct presence on the Internet could fall to insider attacks or Trojan horses (discussed in Section 16.3) downloaded from the Web. In fact, every system, both on the external Internet and internal intranet, needs to be updated regularly with the latest security fixes.

Maintaining software currency on a few Web servers is one thing, but doing it for *every* system in the organization is another matter altogether. One alternative is to employ a low-tech, 'sneaker net' approach where software is loaded onto a diskette which is carried from machine to machine where each fix is installed manually. In order to distribute fixes in a timely manner you will need lots and lots of feet on the street. Dispatching this 'Mongolian Horde' will require substantial coordination and inordinate cost.

A better scheme, however, would be to utilize automated software distribution tools to do the same job. This way the IT staff can determine which fixes should be applied and when it should take place. If done properly, the impact to end users is inconsequential. The initial installation and setup cost for the necessary infrastructure might seem prohibitively expensive at first glance, but a deeper consideration of the long-term savings (e.g. no Mongolian Horde to feed and care for!) and the resulting improvement in security (read: reduction of risk) could quickly offset this expense.

As with all things, balance is the key. You don't want your production systems living life on the 'bleeding edge' but, by the same token, you certainly don't want a hacker to compromise your company's business activities by exploiting a three-year-old bug that could easily have been prevented. Whatever decision you make, be sure to include it in your corporate security policy and make sure that all the right people know about it.

chapter 14

Hackers don't want you to know that ... *defaults are dangerous*

In his best-selling book entitled *The Cuckoo's Egg* (1990), Cliff Stoll, an astronomer working in the Lawrence Berkeley Lab computer center, tells a compelling tale of how he tracked a 75 cent billing error all the way to the very bowels of the hacking underground. Through incredible ingenuity (and even more incredible persistence), Stoll tracks the source of the error to a group of hackers in what was then communist East Germany. This group, known as the Chaos Computer Club, was breaking into research and military computers all across the US in order to find out whatever they could about the Strategic Defense Initiative (a.k.a. 'Star Wars'). They apparently planned to sell this information to the USSR. Stoll's creative retelling of the cat-and-mouse game he played in order to track down the hackers makes for a story that is both captivating and informative at the same time.

While the book reads like a novel it is, in fact, a book of non-fiction. One of the more shocking details revealed in the story is the ease with which these hackers entered various systems, some of which contain classified information. It turns out that some of the operating systems involved were shipped from the vendor with a set of preconfigured default userids and passwords which were never changed.

In one example, Stoll points out that the system manager's account, which is afforded the highest privilege level on the system, had a default userid of 'system' and a password of, you guessed it, 'manager'. It doesn't take a rocket scientist to figure that one out. In fact, rocket scientists (or at least their IT support staffs at the Jet Propulsion Labs in Pasadena, CA) didn't. They failed to realize the potential damage that could result from not removing such defaults and, therefore, unwittingly allowed their systems to be used as stepping stones by hackers. These hackers were dedicated to getting the lowdown on how the US was planning to defend against Soviet missiles. Such secrets involved technology that would allow the American military to shoot down incoming warheads with laser beams fired from earth-orbiting satellites. Clearly, a system containing sensitive information like this is not one that you would want just anyone with a PC and a phone line to be able to access.

14.1 'De'faults are *your* faults

It is in the vendor's best interest to have their product look its best when you install it. After all, if you are satisfied with the product you might buy more or even tell your friends and colleagues who might buy more still. If you install the product and find that it has some additional capabilities that you hadn't originally considered, but now find useful, this pleasant surprise will increase your level of satisfaction and could, the vendor hopes, lead to even more sales.

However, the vendor's best interests and yours may not always intersect. From a security standpoint you should never have additional userids lying around on a system because each represents a potential door through which unauthorized users might enter. By this same reasoning, additional capabilities and services that you don't plan to use should also be turned off until they are needed in order to reduce the number of attack points the hacker might exploit. Privilege levels should be set to deny access at the time of installation so that each resource you make available to a given user is done explicitly and not by accident.

This effort to limit risk by turning off all non-essential features is known as 'hardening'. In essence, it makes a system less vulnerable to attack because there are fewer entry points for a hacker to exploit.

14.2 The security afterthought

The fact that many Web sites are built and maintained by Web masters, who may have no training or interest in computer security, only adds to the problem. Web masters tend to focus on providing compelling content within the context of a dazzling display of digital technology. Their attention is more likely to be directed toward flashy visual effects and other 'eye candy' rather than on the invisible security and stability characteristics of the underlying platform.

This is understandable. In fact, it's not necessarily even a problem so long as someone else is tending to the details of ensuring that the system is bulletproof. Unfortunately, it is this critical aspect that is far too often given only superficial attention – with disastrous results. Security considerations must be dealt with during the design phase, implemented during installation, and maintained through constant vigilance. Security, manageability and scalability are frequently the first casualties in the rush to get a virtual storefront up and running against a calendar measured in three-month 'Web years'. John Wooden, former men's basketball coach of the UCLA Bruins during the 1960s and 1970s, advised his players to 'be quick but don't hurry'. That advice served his teams well as they won 10 national championships in 12 years – a record that no one else has even approached either before or since. These same words are just as applicable to today's e-business efforts. The winners know this already. The losers will learn it eventually.

(14.3) Minding the virtual store

Suffice it to say at this point that if a vendor-chosen default makes your corporate data vulnerable, it will be you, and not the vendor, who will pay the price of this poor decision. Therefore, it behoves you to take the proper steps to make sure that you know what you are, in fact, installing and what it can and cannot do.

You should also look to do *vulnerability testing* of your systems so that you can learn of any cracks in the security infrastructure and fix them before they turn into gaping holes. Scanning tools, which will be covered in more detail in Chapter 16, can help automate this process. Such tools can be a tremendous help but do not, in and of themselves, solve the problem.

Smart hackers know this. They know about the various default userids, passwords, vulnerable services, and so on. They know which level of operating systems have these weaknesses and which ones don't. If they can find out what level of software you are running, which is not hard to do in many cases, their job is just that much easier. They know all this because the information is widely available on the Internet to anyone who knows where to look for it – which is the subject of the next chapter.

chapter 15

Hackers don't want you to know that ... *it takes a thief to catch a thief*

Chapter summary

- Hackers as thieves
- How to keep up with the hackers
- Learning to think like a hacker
- Learning about vulnerabilities
- Hacker Web sites
- Other online sources for security information

Whether they want to admit it or not, hackers are essentially thieves.

- When they logon to a system that they are not authorized to use, they *steal* valuable processing power, memory, bandwidth, and other system resources that can, at that point, no longer be used by legitimate users.

- When they make a copy of classified corporate data, they *take* something of value that doesn't belong to them and, in some industries, intellectual property is far more valuable than physical property.

- When they *hijack* a server or a router with a Denial-of-Service (DoS) attack, they hold up critical resources by blocking the door to lawful business activity.

● When they deface a corporate Web site with what is essentially high-tech graf-fiti, they *rob* an enterprise of one of its most valuable assets – its reputation.

The courts have been slow to recognize this modern form of thievery, but it is thievery, nonetheless. One such example where a computer-illiterate legal system fell behind is the 1977 case of 'Lund v. Commonwealth' (Lusk et al., 1982). In this case the Commonwealth of Virginia pursued criminal charges against a graduate student at Virginia Polytechnic Institute (a.k.a. Virginia Tech). The defendant was accused of using large amounts of the university's computer time without author-ization in the development of his PhD dissertation. The Commonwealth argued that such improper use amounted to grand larceny of computing resources on the order of $5,000, based on information contained within the printouts, which they had obtained, of Lund's work.

The Virginia Supreme Court, however, reversed a lower court's decision, saying essentially that larceny only applied to 'goods and chattels' and 'cannot be inter-preted to include computer time and services in light of the often repeated mandate that criminal statutes must be strictly construed'. In the eyes of the court, nothing but a bunch of printouts was actually carried away. Since the University admitted that the printouts, themselves, were worth little more than 'scrap paper', the court ruled that there was insufficient evidence to convict.

In an era of personal computers and cheap desktop MIPS (millions of instruc-tions per second) it's easy to forget what a precious commodity mainframe computer processing time was on batch systems during the 1970s. Nevertheless, anyone with an understanding of computers realizes that more was involved here than a bunch of scrap paper. However, the law in 1977 was unable to recognize this basic fact. Of course, new laws and legal precedents have been established since that time which better deal with the issue of computer crime, but the relevance of this case remains as technology continues to outpace the law even today. Hackers know this all too well and frequently get away with their crimes because of the ineptitude of the criminal justice system.

The more recent case of the infamous 'Love Letter' virus/worm in May 2000 caused an estimated $10 million worth of damage in just a few days. Despite a global effort to apprehend those responsible for the attack, the prime suspects could not be prosecuted as the Philippines – where the attack originated – had no legislation to deal with a high-tech crime of this sort (Associated Press, 2000b).

(15.1) Levelling the playing field

Hackers are able to do what they do because they are bold, persistent, sometimes ingenious (although not always, as you will see in Chapter 16), but above all, they know things that you don't. If you know their 'tricks of the trade', you can defend against them. If you don't, you can take a place in line along with all the rest of their other victims. As the old saying goes, 'it takes a thief to catch a thief'. To catch these thieves you need to know what they know. You need to understand what makes them tick (see Chapter 3). Ultimately, you need to be able to think like they do in order to adequately protect your IT environment.

How can you get this kind of knowledge? In fact, it's easier than you might think. In the early days of hacking, information about vulnerabilities and exploits was a highly guarded secret known only to a few. Such information might be kept on, more or less, secret **Bulletin Board Systems** (**BBS**s). In order to gain access you had to know the proper telephone number to dial in to and have a userid and password for the BBS. Elite hackers would tightly control access to these systems because they knew that when it comes to hacking, information is power, and whoever controls the information is the one in power. They derived enormous pleasure from the fact that they knew something that no one else knew. It made them unique – special. A hero to some and a villain to others but, in any case, you couldn't ignore them when they wanted to be noticed.

Such secret places still exist but, like you, the vast majority of hackers don't have access to them. In fact, they don't necessarily need them. The rise of the Internet has been something of a double-edged sword in this regard, though. On the downside is the fact that hacking information is more readily available to the bad guys than it's ever been before. Anyone can put up a 'How to Hack in Three Easy Steps' Web site in a matter of minutes at no cost to them whatsoever. The upside, however, is that much of this same knowledge can be just as easily obtained by the good guys as well. While the sheer volume and transient nature of such hacker sites would prohibit a comprehensive coverage of the subject here, it is worth noting some of the more popular and more enduring (endearing, if you're a hacker) sites that have served the hacker community. If used properly, these hacker rest stops along the information superhighway can be a valuable resource to the defenders of corporate information systems.

Some might argue that a discussion of hacker Web sites only helps hackers and, therefore, represents a threat to people trying to earn an honest living on the Net. But this assertion fails to recognize the singularly undeniable fact that *the bad guys already know this stuff*. In other words, hackers aren't going to learn anything from the disclosure of this information because it's old news to them. The only people that stand to benefit from further disclosure are the good guys who, by and large, don't know about its existence. The intention here, then, is to 'level the playing field' by removing an advantage that the other side has enjoyed and exploited. The information available to one and all on the sites discussed here can, therefore, help you learn to think like a thief in order to catch a thief.

15.2 Eating from the same trough

Many hacker exploits are known by colourful names such as Teardrop, Land, Snork, Smurf, Ping of Death, Bonk, Boink, and so forth. These attacks become famous (or infamous, depending upon your perspective) as word of them spreads throughout the hacker community. Where can you go to get wind of these attacks and, hopefully, discover a way to defend against them? Certainly there are reputable places like CERT,[1] discussed in Chapter 13, which are a must. There, information concerning incidents and advisories is published for all to see.

This, however, is not the most likely place for a hacker to go (although it's not a bad place to start). Hackers hang out at places that are more on the 'bleeding edge'. Some of these places make a compelling case for their existence on the grounds that they provide a service to the computing community as a whole. By exposing weaknesses in commonly used products they maintain that they intend to shame vendors into fixing these problems. The way they have it figured, they are actually making things safer for everyone.

In order for this to really be true, however, vendors and IT support staff need to keep a close watch on the comings and goings at such places. Otherwise, these sites end up being nothing more than a central clearing house of how-to's for aspiring hackers. Of course, one might argue that publishing information on how to make a bomb is hardly the sort of thing that makes the world a safer place, but, unlike bombings, which are virtually impossible to defend against on all fronts simultaneously, effective countermeasures can usually be taken against most hacker attacks.

After CERT, perhaps the most well known of the vulnerability sites is *Bugtraq*.[2] Bugtraq allows anyone to post to the site so it is much more informal in nature than CERT, which is tightly controlled. It is also more comprehensive than CERT, as its voluminous archives on all sorts of weaknesses will attest. It originally focused only on issues relating to UNIX systems but has, more recently, expanded to cover Windows NT and other common operating systems. While the information here is not scrutinized as closely as the CERT site is, Bugtraq is a must for anyone trying to stay one step ahead of the hackers.

At the other end of the spectrum are Phrack[3] and 2600.[4] Both are well-known sites in the hacker community and have stood the test of time (if your calendar runs on Web years). They are more eclectic and devious in nature. Here you might find anything from how to pick a combination lock to ways you can get free long-distance phone calls illegally. Why would hackers want such information? Simple. Why waste your time trying endless password guesses when you can break into a

1. Computer Emergency Response Team, Carnegie Mellon University, www.cert.org.
2. Bugtraq, www.securityfocus.com.
3. Phrack, www.phrack.com.
4. 2600, www.2600.com.

safe or locker which might have them all stored on bits of paper or diskettes for safe keeping? Also, if hackers can make phone calls for free, they can hide their tracks better by dialling into distant systems and let someone else, namely legitimate telephone customers, foot the bill.

Another place to look for hacking information is in the common search engines. Yahoo!,[5] for example, has links to both traditional computer security sites as well as hacker sites. About.com[6] (formerly the Mining Co.) maintains a very thoroughly researched set of references as well. Also, meta search engines such as Metacrawler[7] allow for more extensive searching as they consolidate the results of several other well-known search engines into a single list that is weighted so that the best matches are at the top.

(15.3) Keeping up with the hackers

The point is that there's no need to remain ignorant of hackers, what they're after, and how they are likely to go about getting it. Thanks to the openness and ubiquity of the Internet, you have access to most of the same information that they do.

You can bemoan the fact that hacking techniques and tools are so easily accessible if you like, but it won't do any good. Even if you could find a law enforcement agency that is willing to shut down a hacker site, the courts would be likely to reverse this action on the grounds of free speech, press, etc. And even if you could get the legal system to agree with you, hackers would simply move their sites to another jurisdiction with a more *laissez-faire* point of view. Since the Internet is global, it doesn't matter where a Web site is physically located so, ultimately, information (including hacking exploits) cannot be shackled as long as Netizens (citizens of the Internet) persist in posting such information.

> Learn what your adversary already knows and use this knowledge to *your* advantage for a change.

Instead of cursing the darkness, light a candle. Learn what your adversary already knows and use this knowledge to *your* advantage for a change.

---

5. Yahoo!, http://dir.yahoo.com/Computers_and_Internet/Security_and_Encryption/Hacking/.
6. About.com, http://netsecurity.about.com/compute/netsecurity.
7. Metacrawler, www.metacrawler.com.

chapter **16**

Hackers don't want you to know that ... *attacks are getting easier*

A few years ago, these programs were traded among hackers like baseball cards. Now anybody who can search Yahoo can get these things.

Chapter summary

- How hacking tools have become easier to obtain
- Probing for insecurities
    - vulnerability scanners (SATAN)
- Some powerful hacking tools
    - L0phtCrack
    - Back Orifice
- Why computers are vulnerable to Denial-of-Service attacks
- Email bombs
- How to avoid being used as a spam relay
- How some infamous Denial-of-Service attacks work
    - SYN flood
    - Ping of Death
    - Smurf

● The danger of distributed Denial-of-Service attacks

- high-profile attacks on Yahoo!, Amazon.com, eBay, CNN, E*TRADE, and others

- Tribe FloodNet 2K

Like a prized collectable, hacking tools were once the exclusive possessions of small communities of elite hackers. Exchanges of these precious commodities occurred in the darkened back alleys of the Net – such as it was in those days. Exclusivity and secrecy were the watchwords of the special few. Knowledge of often obscure details of IT systems which led to potential exploits was the currency of this underground world. Since this knowledge could be packaged neatly in computer programs which could be sent over a network at the speed of light, the exchange of these tools could occur quickly and easily regardless of time and distance.

But still, you had to know *where* to go and *how* to get in if you wanted to play serious hacker games. You had to know somebody who would let you in on the secrets. In exchange, however, you needed to show that you were worthy of such treasure. You had to have something to offer the gatekeepers in order to make it worth their while. 'Something for nothing' was just not going to cut it when it came to these valuable secrets. In fact, half the fun lay in the power that the hacking 'haves' could lord over the wannabes.

That was then, this is now. Now the Internet has replaced the obscure, tightly controlled BBSs that served as almost inaccessible hacker clubhouses with far more reachable gathering places. Transactions can take place in the full light of day. Hacking tools can be posted to a Web site for all to download. The barriers to entry have essentially disappeared. Where once it was the rare individual who had a PC with a network connection, in many communities it is now the rare individual who doesn't. Secret BBS phone numbers have given way to public URLs. It's as if the genie has been let out of the bottle.

Of course, there still is an elite hacker community that guards its secrets as it did so many Web years ago. Individually, they possess the greatest potential for harm, but when compared to the far larger number of aspiring hackers and script kiddies, one might argue that their threat seems to pale in comparison. Through sheer volume, the collective, yet uncoordinated, efforts of the novice hackers could represent the greatest concern. Their desperate and often ungraceful attempts to make a name for themselves so that they can join the ranks of the elite enable them to attack more sites in more different ways than their more seasoned counterparts. Their own ineptitude and ignorance can lead to unintended consequences that outstrip the goals of the original attack. As was pointed out earlier in Chapter 3, elite hackers are to be feared for what they know and novice hackers are to be feared for what they don't know.

> Elite hackers are to be feared for what they know and novice hackers are to be feared for what they don't know.

16.1 A deal with the devil?

In 1995 a great controversy spread through the IT community like wildfire. A couple of programmers, Wietse Venema and Dan Farmer, had developed a tool which could be run on one machine and targeted at another. Once unleashed, this tool would make numerous attempts to enter the target system through any of a number of predefined mechanisms. Through sheer brute force, this program would simply try to open a connection through a given port, report its success or failure, and then move on to the next port. Also, other well-known exploits were launched against the target system, with the results of these attacks being reported back as well. An analogy would be trying to break into someone's home by turning all the doorknobs and trying to open all the windows in order to find out if the house was really locked up or not.

What would be the purpose of such a tool? That depends upon whom you ask. The creators of this program, **Security Administrator Tool for Analyzing Networks** now known as **SATAN** justified their work by asserting that it could be used by legitimate IT support staff to assess the security of their systems and, ultimately, address any weaknesses that were uncovered. Opponents argued that such a tool in the hands of hackers spelled trouble since what had previously been a tedious, manual process of trial and error had now been neatly automated. They contended that making such a tool generally available was an irresponsible act as it would surely lead to increased hacker activity, which would undermine the safety of businesses, governments, schools, militaries, and the like. The tool's sinister name served to reinforce the hysteria that resulted.

Heated debate raged for many months. Eventually, the 'IT establishment' resigned itself to the reality that, despite their bitter complaints to the contrary, the spread of SATAN was now inevitable. The best thing they could do was to try to stay one step ahead of hackers by getting a copy of the program themselves and running it against their own systems. This way they could discover any weaknesses and batten down the hatches before the hacker storm arrived.

In the intervening years, the 'SATAN controversy' has died down and **vulnerability scanners**, as such tools are also known, have grown up. Next generation tools have been developed both by the hacker community and by legitimate businesses, which market their products as an important component in a larger defence system against intruders. 'If you can't beat them, join them' is the best response to such tools.

16.2 Tools of the hacker trade

By comparison to today's hacker tools, SATAN, which has not been rigorously maintained, appears quite tame. In addition to vulnerability scanners, which check for weaknesses but, as a general rule, don't try to actually exploit them, there are tools now which can be used to both 'seek' and 'destroy'.

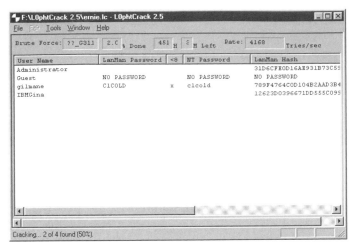

FIGURE 16.1   L0phtCrack at work (Copyright © 1994, 1995, 1996, 1997, 1998 LHI Technologies)

One such tool discussed previously is L0phtCrack which automates the time-consuming and tedious task of password cracking.[1] Its cracking process includes the ability to perform both dictionary and brute-force attacks against a list of encrypted passwords. It also includes a built-in SMB packet capture facility that, when combined with a promiscuous mode LAN adaptor, can pick off encrypted passwords as they flow over the network. L0phtCrack is controlled from an easy-to-use graphical user interface (GUI) and has even been ported to run on client operating systems such as Windows 95.

The significance of these last two details should not be overlooked. By simplifying the interface and making it available on the most widely available platforms, L0phtCrack has 'lowered the bar' on password cracking. Anyone with a PC and access to a network can be a cracker. No special knowledge of cryptography, network security, or system administration is needed.

The good news is that legitimate companies can use these same tools to ensure that their passwords are, in fact, hard to guess. The bad news is that so can the hackers. A tool like L0phtCrack clearly can be used by both the good guys and the bad guys. Some tools, however, are of a more dubious nature.

16.3   Coming in through the back door

One example is *Back Orifice*[2] (BO) from the Cult of the Dead Cow (cDc),[3] a hacker organization. Back Orifice's name is, of course, a play on words the name of Microsoft's Back Office software suite. BO can be slipped in through the back door,

1. *CRACK* is a similar tool for cracking passwords in a UNIX environment.
2. Another similar tool is NetBus available at http://netbus.org/main.html.
3. Cult of the Dead Cow, www.cultdeadcow.com.

as it were, by a hacker who wraps it up in a seemingly harmless program that might pop up an entertaining graphic sequence or even perform some useful function. It can be unintentionally installed by unsuspecting users who run what they believe to be a benign program sent to them as an email attachment (not a good idea unless you really know what you're running). Such malicious software is called a *Trojan horse* because, like its ancient namesake, its victim unwittingly facilitates the attack. (For more information on Trojan horses, see Section 17.3.)

Once installed, BO erases any obvious traces of its existence. For example, on a Windows 95 machine it will not even show up in the list of active programs displayed when the Ctrl-Alt-Del key sequence is depressed, despite the fact that the program really is running. BO can even be set up to notify hackers via either email or IRC (chat) of the IP address of the new target system so that they will know exactly where to direct their efforts. It's almost like the victim's system is sending up a flare announcing 'here I am, come and hack me'. With this information hackers can then completely take over and remotely control essentially *all* aspects of the compromised machine. Among other things they can:

● monitor and store keystrokes entered by the user (including 'hidden' fields often indicated by a string of asterisks);

● look over the user's shoulder by capturing screen images;

● execute commands of their choosing on the user's system;

● rename, copy and delete files on the user's system;

● connect to other systems via telnet or FTP;

● open and close the CD-ROM drive (just for kicks!).

And if that wasn't scary enough, they can even turn the victim's machine into their own remote surveillance system. If a microphone or video camera is attached to the user's system, hackers can turn these devices on and then sit back, listen in, and watch what their victim is doing. You might be inclined to dismiss this last threat by assuming that such peripherals are rare in corporate computing environments where they aren't often required, but you might be unpleasantly surprised when you realize that many laptops, which are increasingly being used as desktop system replacements in the office, are equipped with built-in microphones. Imagine what the consequences would be if Back Orifice were to be slipped into a system administrator's machine where critical passwords are entered as he or she telnets into various servers throughout the day. What if the compromised system was that of the CEO? Even the most private of meetings held in his or her office could be eavesdropped.

The damage that could be done with this one hacker tool alone is incalculable, but that's just the beginning ...

16.4 Burning bridges

Denial-of-Service (DoS) attacks are some of the simplest to launch. Unlike more sophisticated exploits, DoS attacks involve a minimum of penetration into the target network and are often easy to automate and initiate from any vantage point. DoS attackers don't gain unauthorized access to a critical system, don't steal classified information, and don't even get the satisfaction of airing their grievances (either real or imagined) against the faceless enemy whose Web site they might wish to deface. DoS attackers simply deny legitimate users access to services that they are authorized to use. An 'if I can't have it, no one else will' sort of attitude forms the basis of this class of attack.

The reason DoS attacks work is that despite their tremendous capabilities, computers are essentially pretty dumb. They will mindlessly perform the same task over and over and over again *ad nauseam* unless they are specifically instructed otherwise. This insensitivity to boredom is one reason we like them. Unlike the humans that operate them, computers obey without complaining, no matter how repetitive or how long it takes to get the job done.

This same endearing quality can be their downfall, though. Unless special precautions are made in advance, computer systems will fail to recognize the difference between productive, meaningful work and simply spinning their wheels. It's as if every time the phone rings they dutifully answer it.[4] A human would realize, after a few successive calls with nothing but heavy breathing on the other end of the line, that there's no point in repeating this scenario. A computer, however, never seems to tire of such nonsense and can be tricked into diverting all its available energy toward an endless stream of what are basically crank calls. In fact it will do so with such vigour that it consumes all its resources responding to unproductive requests while leaving bona fide users with the computing equivalent of a busy signal.

16.5 'You've got mail ... bombs'

Examples include email bombs which, unlike real-world mail bombs, are not explosive but whose effects can be just as devastating to an email system. In these attacks, hackers simply send an abnormally large (e.g. 10 MB) email to their intended target. If repeated enough times, they may be able to overwhelm the email system by forcing it to use up all its available storage keeping copies of the useless data it is receiving. The effect, then, is to starve out legitimate emails which can no longer get through.

4. Adapted from Fessler (1998).

Email bombing requires very little technical expertise and can be easily automated. Such attackers can also hide their tracks by using so-called anonymous remailers, which act as email relays. By spoofing their origin addresses (i.e. impersonating another machine) or by initiating their attack from any of a number of free email services they can achieve a similar effect. Services abound which allow anyone to set up an account in a matter of minutes and do little, if anything, to verify the actual identity of the account owner.

As with real-world bombings, there is also collateral damage to unintended victims as well. Sometimes attackers have chosen to bomb a spammer in order to 'teach them a lesson'. However, even Hammurabi, the ancient Babylonian king who codified the principle of 'an eye for an eye and a tooth for a tooth', would have to disapprove because such an action fails to deal with only the specific perpetrator and exaggerates the punishment with respect to the crime. Even though the email bomb may be directed toward a specific account, the failure of the email system on either the sending or receiving side may be the ultimate result. In fact, more innocent victims than guilty perpetrators will have to pay the price should such a counterattack take place.

The best way to defuse email bombs is at the source. This means that email systems being used to launch the attack should be configured to recognize such an exploit and shut down the originating account immediately. The problem is that too many system administrators are concerned only with the consequences they face when they are being attacked and not about the case where they are, in effect, assisting in an attack themselves.

Legal liability in such situations, however, should not be overlooked. If you can't prove that you did everything within reason to prevent your systems from being used by a hacker, you may be held responsible (at least in part) for the actions of such a person.

There are a number of things you can do to protect your email system from attack. These actions are, of course, limited to the capabilities of the software you use. For example, you may be able to set a threshold for the amount, either in terms of number or size, of email that a specific user is allowed to send or receive. Anything beyond that limit is discarded. You might also establish a limit as to the amount of email your server will accept from a particular sender within a given time frame.

Another precautionary measure would be to configure your mail server so that it cannot be hijacked by spammers (people who send unsolicited 'junk' emails usually trying to sell you something you couldn't possibly need). Unless you reject all traffic that either didn't originate from your network or isn't destined to someone in your domain, you could unwittingly facilitate spam activity by acting as a third-party relay. Why would spammers want to use your systems to propagate their offence? The answer is that they can hide behind your identity and spam with impunity.

Why should you care? First of all, spam is by definition unsolicited and, by implication, probably unwanted in the first place. Allowing your resources to be used by someone who hasn't paid for the privilege ought to be enough motivation to shut down this kind of abuse. But if that's not enough, consider the fact that the people that end up receiving the spam that your systems have helped deliver may see you as the perpetrator and not as an innocent bystander. They might use a service such as the *Realtime Blackhole List*[5] which keeps track of offenders and warns other system administrators who might want to block out all email (including the legitimate stuff) that comes from your organization.

Finally, consider the fact that while spammers are making themselves at home on your mail server, they are also stealing cycles from the legitimate users that the system was intended to serve. If the problem is allowed to get out of hand it could result in a potentially costly Denial-of-Service scenario. Fortunately, there are some good Web sites that can point you to more information on the nature of the problem and how to fix it. Here are just a few:

Mail Abuse Prevention System (MAPS)
   http://maps.vix.com/
Open Relay Behaviour-modification System (ORBS)
   http://www.orbs.org/

The point is that while email bombings are easy to launch, they are also fairly easy to defend against and can be essentially eradicated if all email system administrators and ISPs take the proper precautions to eliminate them at their source and penalize the offenders.

16.6 I hope you can swim

In 1996 Panix, a New York-based ISP, found that their on-ramp to the 'Information Superhighway' was completely blocked. No one could get in or out of their network. Businesses and consumers had been cut off from the Internet and no one knew why. Eventually the source of the outage was isolated and diagnosed. A hacker was to blame.

This hacker was exploiting a weakness in the TCP/IP protocol which had eluded some of the biggest vendors in the computer industry.[6] During normal TCP session setup, the originator sends a special packet which synchronizes the sequence numbers that will be used by the session partners. This packet is called a **SYN** (short for SYNchronize) packet. Upon receipt of the SYN packet, the destination system reserves certain resources that will be needed during session setup and returns a **SYN/ACK** (SYN/ACKnowledgement) packet to the originator. It then waits for a reply before proceeding with the rest of the session setup process.

5. Mail Abuse Prevention System Realtime Blackhole List, http://maps.vix.com/rbl/.
6. CERT Advisory, 'CA-96.21 TCP SYN Flooding and IP Spoofing Attacks', September 1996, www.cert.org.

FIGURE 16.2   A SYN flood attack

The Panix hacker realized that if he spoofed the IP address in the original SYN packet by inserting a bogus address (i.e. one which pointed to a non-existent machine), the target system would wait patiently for quite some time listening for a reply to its SYN/ACK before proceeding (Figure 16.2).

Since the target system had been duped into sending the SYN/ACK to an unused IP address, the packet basically fell into a black hole never to be seen again. Eventually, it would give up on waiting for the reply which would never be forthcoming anyway, and free up the session resources so that they could be reused by another session. The problem was that the time spent waiting was simply too long and the number of resources too small. The hacker realized this and launched a flood of spoofed SYN packets which tied up all available session resources for an extended period of time. The results were catastrophic to the ISP and its customers.

Eventually, fixes were developed by all the networking vendors to eliminate or, at the very least, substantially lessen the effects of the 'SYN flood attack'. Solutions involved simple things such as decreasing timeout values and increasing the number of available session resources. More complex remedies actually recognized the bombardment of SYN packets from a single address or range of addresses and discarded all subsequent traffic from these locations.

In the end, though, a lesson was learned about the fragile nature of the TCP/IP protocol – a protocol which was designed to exist in an environment where end points were well-known and, therefore, trusted. TCP/IP would be vulnerable in an open environment where individual accountability was nearly non-existent.

Clearly this would not be the last such exploit that would threaten to bring down at least some portion of the Internet. Given that corporate intranets are built upon the same technology, it is reasonable to assume that they may suffer from many of the same ills as their public counterparts. Even those not directly affected by the Panix SYN flood attack had received a warning shot across the bow.

16.7 Lowering the bar

Other types of DoS attacks exploit additional weaknesses in the networking protocol or in common vendor implementations. One example is the so-called *Ping of
Death*[7] attack in which an oversized packet is sent to the victim. Networking software breaks up the packet into smaller, more manageable pieces which the victim's
machine obediently puts back together. The problem is that a machine that is vulnerable to this attack fails to realize that the packets it is assembling are
unreasonably large and, therefore, threaten to overflow the buffer area it had allo-
cated to hold the complete transmission. When the last piece is reassembled …
bang! The machine may crash, freeze or reboot as a result. This is analogous to a
mail bomber sending a bomb in pieces along with a set of assembly instructions
which the victim dutifully carries out.[8]

Another well-known DoS attack involves the use of directed broadcasts. In the
Smurf[9] attack, as it is commonly called, hackers exploit a special feature of TCP/IP

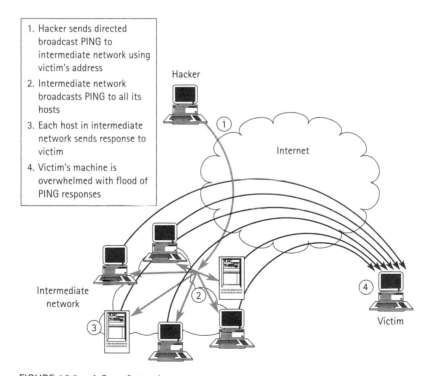

FIGURE 16.3   A Smurf attack

7. CERT Advisory, 'CA-96.26 Denial-of-Service Attack via ping', December 1996, www.cert.org.
8. Adapted from a description of the Ping of Death attack by David Gamey, IBM Corp.
9. CERT Advisory, 'CA-98.01 smurf IP Denial-of-Service Attacks', January 1998, www.cert.org.

to direct a flood of traffic to their victim's machine (Figure 16.3). Here's how it works ... a PING request, an innocuous packet used to determine if a host is operational, is sent to an intermediate network which acts as an unknowing accomplice in the attack. However, instead of being directed to a single host, as most PING requests are, this directed PING is sent to an address ending in either 255 or 0 (e.g. 10.1.2.255 or 10.1.2.0), which causes it to be forwarded to *all* of the hosts in that network. The sneaky part, though, is that the hacker modifies the PING packet he or she sends so that it appears to be coming from the *victim's* machine rather than the hacker's (i.e. spoofing). This way, when all the machines in the intermediate network respond, they do so to the victim's machine – not the hacker's.

In effect, the intermediate network is unintentionally acting as an *amplifier* for the DoS attack. If, for instance, there are a few thousand hosts in the intermediate network, hackers can easily overwhelm the victim's system with just a few malicious PINGs because each packet is quickly multiplied for them.

The good news regarding Smurf attacks is that they can be easily thwarted if network administrators simply take the time to configure their routers so that IP-directed broadcasts are disabled. The bad news is that not enough administrators have done so. The netscan.org[10] Web site proves this point vividly by maintaining a list of what it calls the 'most egregious offenders'. Based on network scans performed by netscan.org, these networks are vulnerable to this attack and, therefore, act as Smurf amplifiers. Of course, hackers love this information. From a single Web page they can find out just which networks are ready, willing and able to help them execute a DoS attack – but this isn't why netscan.org maintains this list. In fact, it is for just the opposite reason. As they put it:

We're a small group of concerned network administrators who got fed up with being smurfed day after day simply because a few admins aren't doing their jobs. This site serves to inform and educate 'the rest' in hopes of eliminating this problem ...

This attempt (and others like it) to shame network administrators into blocking well-known DoS attacks could turn out to be the best way to call attention to the problem and, ultimately, improve the situation. In this case, bringing what might otherwise be closely held hacker secrets out into the light of day for everyone to examine will, hopefully, defuse the danger. Hackers don't want you to know this because Smurf attacks rely on ignorance and apathy – both of which can be counteracted with the right information and motivation.

Other spoofing variations allow hackers to hide their identities when attacking. Unfortunately, the process of tracking down the true origin of such attacks can be very difficult. If the attack spans multiple Internet Service Provider networks, the

10. www.netscan.org.

level of cooperation necessary to bring together the disparate pieces of the puzzle may be in short supply. However, as with the Smurf attack, there are things that you can do to make sure that you don't act as an unwitting accomplice to attacks on other networks. **Egress filtering**, or preventing suspicious traffic from leaving your network in the first place, can be accomplished with only a few minor configuration changes to perimeter firewalls and routers. If these 'gatekeepers' check to make sure that all traffic leaving the internal network did, indeed, originate from that network (i.e. the traffic is not merely passing through from another source), then hackers' ability to use your systems as a jumping off point to further their attacks can be limited.[11]

Teardrop and *Land* are other similar examples which were mentioned in Chapter 13. During the final days of 1999 the *Tribe FloodNet 2K* (*TFN2K*)[12] exploit burst onto the scene as exaggerated concerns over the Y2K bug[13] and the impending doom it was purported to cause reached their peak. TFN2K combined a damaging payload like that of Teardrop and Land with a distributed amplifier similar to Smurf to make for one very nasty DoS attack sequence. The hacker would first plant TFN2K server software on unsuspecting intermediate systems (sometimes

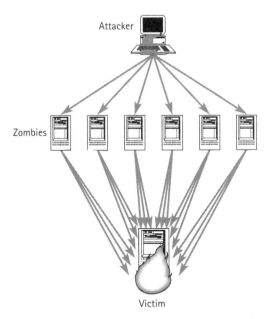

FIGURE 16.4   DDoS: multiplying the effects of a Denial-of-Service attack

11. For more information see 'Egress Filtering', Chris Brenton, SANS Institute, Global Incident Analysis Center, www.sans.org/giac.htm.
12. CERT Advisory, 'CA-99.17 Denial-of-Service Tools', December 1999, www.cert.org.
13. The 'Y2K bug' refers to the fact that many computer systems and their associated software were not originally designed to deal with years that didn't begin 19xx.

referred to as 'zombies'). Then, from a client controller the hacker could instruct the various TFN2K servers to join the attack, each from their own unique vantage points on the Net (Figure 16.4). The result was a **distributed DoS (DDoS)** attack that was damaging not only because of the payload it carried but also from the sheer volume of the packets generated by the exploited intermediate systems. What made this attack particularly difficult to defend against was the fact that it emanated from so many different places all at once.

The devastating potential of DDoS attacks was realized soon after the IT security community had been warned of these risks. During the week of 7 February 2000, some of the Internet's most visited Web sites were assaulted by overwhelming network traffic emanating from a multitude of sources. The list of victims read like a 'Who's Who' list of Web sites. Over the course of three days the Web's most popular search engine/portal (Yahoo!), largest bookseller (Amazon.com) and most popular online auction site (eBay) were hit. Victims also included a leading Internet superstore (buy.com), online brokerage (E*TRADE) and a couple of top Net-based news outlets (CNN.com and ZDnet) (Crouch and Mainelli, 2000). The cost of this three-day rampage was estimated to be in excess of $1 billion, which didn't even include the damage to the various corporate brands represented (Niccolai, 2000). Clearly, the threat was not merely theoretical.

16.8 The bottom line

Of course, there are far too many different types of DoS attacks in existence (and more being devised every day!) to be covered adequately here. The bottom line is that the unmistakable trend in hacking is that attacks are getting easier and not harder over time. The widespread availability of tools which automate various attacks means that the level of expertise required to launch them has plummeted. Now anyone can launch a debilitating attack even though they have no idea how it actually works. In fact, some DoS attacks are launched unintentionally by inept hackers or users unaware of the consequences of their actions.

The fact is that the bar is constantly being lowered for hackers. If we were involved in a limbo dance, that would be good news, but, unfortunately, defending your systems is more like a high-jump event. However, if you can build a brick wall between the uprights, it won't matter how low the bar goes.

chapter 17

Hackers don't want you to know that ... *virus defences are inadequate*

... and armed hosts, an unexpected force, Break from the bowels of the fatal horse.

The original Trojan horse as described in Virgil's *The Aeneid*, 19 BC

Chapter summary

- The malware threat
    - virus infection statistics
- Profiles of some early worms
    - the CHRISTMA worm
    - the Morris Worm
- Various forms of malware
    - viruses
    - worms
    - Trojan horses
- How malware damages systems
- Menacing malware
    - macro viruses
    - BubbleBoy

  - Remote Explorer

  - Melissa

  - CIH/Chernobyl

- Hoax viruses

  - what they are

  - how to spot them

  - what to do about them

- Malware defences

One of the things we like about computers is that, unlike people, they are willing to work day and night. They don't show up to work with a bad attitude. They are incredibly dependable. They never call in sick. Or do they? While it may seem that these tireless workers are immune to the biological frailties of their carbon-based counterparts (that's you and me), they can, in fact, exhibit some of the same weaknesses.

Of course, computer viruses don't really make a machine sick, *per se*, but this analogy is not without merit. Like a human victim of a biological virus, a computer infected by a software-borne virus:

- may not show any obvious signs of infection for days, months, or even years;

- can infect other systems that it comes in contact with;

- can be partially or completely incapacitated when the virus expresses itself;

- could cause inordinate hardship and angst to those people that depend upon it.

The good news is that some very good virus protection tools exist which, along with prudent end-user behaviour, can work together to form an effective barrier against computer virus infection. The bad news is that many people don't seem to know this as evidenced by the increasing frequency of virus outbreaks. Hackers don't want you to know that the virus protection measures (tools, policies, behaviours, etc.) in place on most machines are inadequate for any number of reasons. They don't want you to know this because if you fully understood how vulnerable you were, you would surely close the gaping holes in your defences, making their job much more difficult.

(17.1) Merry Christmas and a Happy New Worm

The time was December, 1987. With only a few days remaining in the year, thoughts turned to the upcoming holiday season. It was a time to reflect upon past accomplishments and look forward to much-anticipated reunions with family and friends. Christmas was near and with it were to come the annual traditions of office parties, Christmas cards and the like. In the technology sector this was about as close as it could get to 'peace on earth and goodwill toward men'. However, if you happened to be responsible for keeping IBM's internal worldwide network up and operational, you couldn't celebrate just yet.

Of course, in 1987 it was the mainframe – not the workstation – that served as the workhorse upon whose back most business data processing rode. But for some reason this veritable Rock of Gibraltar seemed to be crumbling. Until you figured out why the life was being sucked out of your company's technology infrastructure the notion of a 'Silent Night' was only a distant dream.

It turned out that an electronic chain letter of sorts had entered the IBM internal network and was spreading like wildfire. A file posing as a digital Christmas card would show up in end users' in-baskets encouraging them to load its associated program onto their own account and run it. This program would then present a holiday greeting along with a crude depiction (the best you could do with the text-only terminals of the day) of a Christmas tree. What the recipients didn't know was that the program would also send a copy of itself to *everyone* in that user's address book before erasing itself. The so-called 'CHRISTMA exec'[1] seemed innocent enough. By virtue of the way it spread, victims inevitably received it from someone they knew and, presumably, trusted. Filled with the holiday spirit, unsuspecting employees reasoned, 'what could be wrong with taking a minute to view a harmless Christmas greeting?'

The answer to that question came quickly enough as one user unintentionally forwarded the program to all the people in his or her address book who then forwarded it on to all the people in their address books and so on. This process continued unabated until a significant portion of IBM's worldwide network became hopelessly bogged down with network traffic, which continued to grow at an exponential rate.

It turns out that IBM's network was not the only one affected. In fact, it is believed that this attack actually originated on EARN (European Academic and Research Network) and spread to its American counterpart, BITNET ('Because It's Time Network'), and ultimately to IBM's internal VNET. However, IBM's extensive use of the VM (Virtual Machine) operating system which CHRISTMA was designed to attack caused them to experience the greatest impact.

---

1. The program name had to be shorted to 8 characters to accommodate the VM operating system running on the affected mainframes. The term 'exec' was given to programs written in the REXX programing language (successor to VM's original EXEC programming language).

Thankfully, recovery from this crisis began nearly as swiftly as it started. Once the source of the problem had been identified, various solutions were dispatched and order was restored. The people who had to clean up the mess, however, realized that they had just witnessed a bit of history in the making. The CHRISTMA 'worm' (a name given to this type of exploit) that had eaten up untold computing cycles foreshadowed the beginning of a new era of computer insecurity (Taubes, 1996).

17.2 One good worm deserves another

Almost a year after CHRISTMA had taken centre stage, users of the worldwide Internet, then in its infancy, got an unappetizing taste of a newer, more devastating species of worm. This new attack became known as the *Morris Worm* after its creator, Robert Morris, Jr, who was at the time a student at Cornell University.

It turned out that Morris either intentionally or unintentionally (depending upon which story you believe) released a program on the Internet which began bringing systems around the world to their knees. According to the Computer Emergency Response Team (CERT), which came into being as a result of this attack, the Morris Worm 'crippled approximately 10% of all computers connected to the Internet'.[2] An age of innocence with regard to Internet security had ended. The age of Internet malware (malicious software) had begun ...

17.3 Pick your parasite

Universal agreement as to the precise definition of what is and is not a computer virus has been elusive. Nevertheless, most would agree that a computer **virus** is a program that copies itself (or a portion of itself) when it is executed. It is this replicating behaviour that makes it act in many ways like a biological virus. It may attach itself to other executable files on the user's hard disk or even to the boot record, which loads the operating system when the machine is started up.

It is the virus's **payload**, though, that does the real damage. The payload consists of a set of instructions which dictate what the virus will ultimately do when it expresses itself. The results of this expression could be as inconsequential as a bizarre message that pops up unexpectedly on the user's screen or as catastrophic as the complete loss of mission-critical data.

Some biological viruses kill their human hosts with devastating speed. Oddly enough, though, these are far less damaging, from a global perspective, than

2. 'About the CERT/CC', Computer Emergency Response Team, Carnegie Mellon Software Engineering Institute, www.cert.org/nav/aboutcert.html.

slower-acting viruses. The reason is simple. If the host dies very soon after infection, the virus will not have had much of an opportunity to infect very many others. However, a virus that takes longer to kick in can infect a large population before anyone realizes what is going on. In the same way, a computer virus that wipes out a user's hard disk soon after the machine is infected will not spread very far because its host system will have essentially died before having a chance to spread the disease. This is why most computer viruses are designed to remain dormant for extended periods of time.

A **Trojan horse**, although technically not a virus, is similar in effect.[3] Trojan horses get their name from various accounts in ancient literature where the Greeks pulled a military fast one on their opponents from the great walled city of Troy. In this story the Greeks built an enormous wooden horse and offered it to Troy as proof of their peaceful intentions. The Trojans took the bait hook, line and sinker. They wheeled the huge horse in through the gates completely unaware that a small contingent of Greek soldiers was concealed inside. Later that night the Greek soldiers snuck out and opened the gates, allowing the rest of their army to pour into the city. The Trojan defeat was profound. The Greeks had conquered the city in what has come to be known as one of the greatest diversionary tactics in military history.

Computer Trojan horses operate essentially the same way. Although they do not neccessarily replicate themselves as viruses do, they do carry a malicious payload that can do enormous damage. Like their historical namesakes, they are advertised as doing one thing that is benign but conceal a malicious alternative agenda. A Trojan horse may perform a useful or even amusing function and, therefore, appear perfectly harmless – but it is really rotten to the core.

Computer **worms** are yet another type of malicious program. Like the tapeworm, from which its name is derived, a computer worm is a software parasite that can essentially eat everything in sight. Over time it replicates itself over and over again and may, therefore, consume memory, disk space, or bandwidth in the process. If unchecked, this action can continue until the worm starves its host system of the resources it needs to do meaningful work. Like viruses, worms are capable of replication – often through a network. Unlike viruses, worms usually do not infect other programs on the host machine.

If all this terminology is confusing, don't worry about it. Although not technically accurate, it has become increasingly common for all forms of so-called malware to be simply referred to as viruses. Since the same precautions are required to detect and destroy these parasites, the subtle differences are probably irrelevant to end users anyway.

---

3. Because they don't spread on their own, non-viral Trojan horses are generally not as serious as viruses which can strike on a larger scale.

17.4 Where do they come from?

Computer viruses emanate from the dark recesses of the minds of programmers who possess more skill than good judgement. In other words, hackers create them. The fact that it doesn't necessarily require a great deal of skill to create a devastating piece of malware only makes the problem worse. In a perverse way these 'bottom feeders' draw pleasure from the fact that they can release a virus on the world and then sit back and watch as it spreads, wreaking havoc along the way. In a sense it's as if their own power reaches beyond themselves into a virtual world that spans the globe. An intoxicating sense of power is their reward when they realize that strangers who wouldn't give them the time of day must now take notice of their 'skill'.

17.5 How do they spread?

A computer virus can attach itself to a legitimate program[4] or office document through a few small modifications. As this program is passed from machine to machine, its stranglehold on the enterprise increases. In the early days of PCs, diskettes were the primary means for exchanging data. With the Internet, however, it is possible to pass infected programs at the speed of light. Email attachments, downloaded shareware/freeware, or even commercial software on CD-ROMs can facilitate the spread of the infection.

17.6 I'm not feeling so well ...

In 1992 news media outlets around the world publicized the dangers of the 'Michelangelo Virus'. This virus was set to strike infected computers everywhere on 6 March – the birthday of the famous artist it was named after. Fantastic stories of impending doom caught the attention of a gullible public for whom computers seemed about as incomprehensible as quantum physics. These strangely intelligent electronic appliances which, at the time, seemed to be taken straight out of the latest sci-fi thriller, now threatened to wreak havoc over all the earth. Machines that already were viewed with enormous suspicion by many were now proving that they couldn't be trusted. Of course, viruses like Michelangelo were really nothing new to those who had been paying attention, but somehow the story of this

---

4. Hacker tools are another potential source of unintentional infection. The hackers that created Back Orifice 2000, a highly publicized Trojan horse program, were left with egg on their faces when it was later learned that the CDs they had distributed at the July 1999 DEF CON 7.0 hacker convention had been infected with the CIH (Chernobyl) virus.

particular virus caught the fancy of reporters who, like so many lemmings, rushed to drown themselves in a sea of hysteria. Panic-stricken consumers and IT professionals alike rushed out to buy the latest antivirus software in the hope of 'curing' their system before it was too late.

As it turned out, the threat was, indeed, real, but substantially exaggerated. Some systems were hit hard, but the fact that most breezed through unscathed may have served to be more damaging in the long run. When the virtual D-Day came and went without affecting most people, the fortunate majority felt that they had fallen victim to a case of 'crying wolf'. As a result, the threat of computer viruses fell off the radar screen for most users at just the time that virus outbreaks were on the verge of epidemic proportions.

(17.7) Epidemic or hysteria?

While the prevailing attitude toward computer viruses is often nonchalant, virus statistics show why such a posture is dangerous. According to Dr. Solomon's Virus Central,[5] the number of known viruses continues to increase at an astronomical rate. Figure 17.1 shows the growth of viruses since the middle of 1990.

The trend is unmistakable. The virus problem is getting exponentially worse – not better. Another way of putting the numbers in perspective is to look at the rate of introduction of new viruses discovered each day. Again, using the numbers from Dr. Solomon's, one can infer that by the middle of 1998 nearly 20 new viruses were born each day (Figure 17.2). That's almost *one new virus every hour*! Assuming you

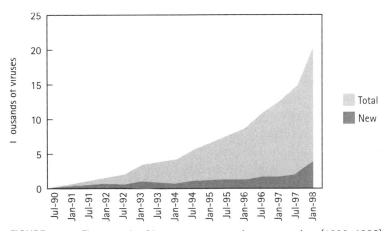

FIGURE 17.1   The growth of known computer viruses over time (1990–1998)

5. Dr. Solomon's Virus Central, www.drsolomon.com/vircen/stats.cfm. Note: Network Associates Inc. acquired Dr. Solomon's in 1998 and continues to market products in various jurisdictions as Dr. Solomon's Anti-Virus.

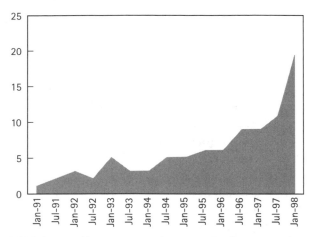

FIGURE 17.2　New computer viruses per day (1991–1998)

are like most people who installed antivirus software a year or so ago and haven't touched it since, how many of these new viruses do you think you're protected against? Answer: none.

Well, it's not quite as bad as that. Many antivirus tools also perform heuristic analysis, which allows them to spot certain abnormal behaviours which can signal a viral infection. Nevertheless, you shouldn't rely solely on this capability to catch all the latest strains.

In case you want more proof, consider the annual 'Computer Virus Prevalence Survey'[6] from the International Computer Security Association (ICSA). It found that the monthly rate of infection for corporate PCs essentially doubled each year from 1996 to 1999 reaching a level of 80 incidents per 1,000 PCs (Figure 17.3). From this you can easily see how an organization of any significant size could be impacted by the threat of malware. Even if the actual loss of data was minimal, the

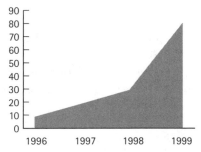

FIGURE 17.3　Monthly rate of infection per 1,000 PCs (based on first two months of 1996 through 1999)

---

6. *Fifth Annual ICSA Labs Computer Virus Prevalence Survey: 1999*, International Computer Security Association, www.icsa.net.

time spent recovering from so many incidents would detract from the company's productivity and, ultimately, the bottom line.

In fact, a 1999 study found that computer viruses and their equally malicious cousins, worms, cost businesses $7.6 million in the first half of the year alone (Reuters, 1999b). In other words, the virus threat is not just theoretical. It's quite real and its consequences can be very expensive.

Before you throw up your hands in utter defeat, resigning yourself to inevitable annihilation, it's worth noting that the vast majority of these viruses will never be seen outside a lab environment. The good news is that a far smaller, more manageable list of viruses that are 'in the wild' are the ones that you really need to concentrate on. A list of these, known appropriately as the 'WildList', was started by Joe Wells and is now maintained by the WildList Organization.[7] This group tracks virus reports submitted by experts around the world. A quick scan of the monthly WildLists from 1998 shows that the total number of viruses known to be infecting systems in the real world hovered around 250. A number of this order is one that you can reasonably hope to get your arms around. This assumes that you are diligent in applying the latest list of updates to your antivirus software.

Unfortunately, vigilance against the ongoing virus threat is not nearly keeping pace even with this more manageable number. Even if people are conscientious enough to install antivirus tools in the first place, still not enough of them actually updates this software frequently. The fact of the matter is that if you are depending upon end users to manually perform these updates on a regular basis, it simply won't get done. Antivirus vendors provide easy mechanisms for people to get updates over the Internet, but if this process relies on user intervention in any way, it will surely fail.

If, however, this process is automated, the prospects for success increase dramatically. The IT support staff could devise a means for picking up the latest list of virus signatures and automatically distributing this to all machines in the enterprise using a software distribution scheme. There are many commercially available software distribution products which can do the job quite nicely and provide a solution to a long list of other support problems that result from downlevel software. In order to really make sure that the job gets done, this approach may be the best. However, it's certainly not the easiest. The cost and effort involved in setting up the necessary infrastructure for a centrally managed software distribution system is substantial – not to mention the ensuing debate over who really should control the desktop – the end user or the IT organization.

If end-user workstations already have access to the Internet, a cheaper, easier solution might involve simply using the automatic update features that are now included in some antivirus tools. For example, Norton AntiVirus's LiveUpdate facility can pick up the latest list of viruses from an Internet-based server maintained by the vendor. LiveUpdate can be initiated manually by the user or triggered

7. The WildList Organization, www.wildlist.org.

automatically by a built-in event scheduler. The best part of it all is that updates are free to registered users. If you can just get employees to set up this process correctly when they install the antivirus tool, the rest will, for the most part, take care of itself.

17.8 Publish and perish

Initially, executable program files were the primary carriers of computer viruses. The conventional wisdom of the day held that program files – not data files – downloaded from the Internet were the most likely source of infection. However, hackers are, if nothing else, unconventional. Conventional wisdom will only carry you so far when dealing with people who possess an uncanny ability to 'think outside the box'. Most viruses are little more than a variation on a theme and, therefore, require little or no ingenuity to create. Every once in a while, a new type of virus comes along that substantially alters our understanding of the potential risks. By 1997 a new type of virus was atop the charts as the most common carrier of software-borne infection.[8] This type affected *data* files, which were previously thought to be immune to viruses.

Hackers found the macro facilities used to enhance word processing documents and spreadsheets to be fertile ground for virus growth. Microsoft Word and Excel files were the most frequent targets for these **macro viruses** because of the large installed base of these products. The fact that a well-known set of security vulnerabilities lay just below the surface didn't hurt either. Since a macro was basically a program embedded within a data file, an end user would be unaware that merely *viewing* its contents could trigger infection. Hackers relied on this ignorance to assist in the outbreak.

17.9 The virus is in the mail

As previously mentioned, in the early days of computer viruses, infection spread almost exclusively through diskettes which were passed around from PC to PC. However, with the popularization of the Internet came email and, as an unintentional consequence, a newer, more efficient way to spread viruses. As you might expect, a mass emailing could reach more people in far less time than could the more pedestrian approach of diskette distribution.

A hacker could now, for instance, write a program that displayed an amusing computer graphics animation sequence and send it to a few friends as an email attachment. In an attempt to share the delight they had just experienced from this seemingly harmless display, these people might send the same attachment to all of their friends, who would then send it to all of their friends, and so on.

8. *ICSA 1998 Computer Virus Prevalence Survey*, International Computer Security Association, www.icsa.net.

What the hacker doesn't want them to know, however, is that he has embedded a malicious payload in this attachment which will go unnoticed for many months. He has exploited the good nature of unsuspecting users and turned them, unwittingly, into a rather effective malware distribution system. Since the ill effects of the virus remain dormant for some time, the user may never suspect that this email attachment received months earlier has anything to do with his or her current hard drive failure. This, of course, allows the virus to spread even further still without being detected.

In a case such as this, defence is difficult. The conventional advice that it is not safe to run a program from an untrusted source has been subverted because the victim very likely does know and trust the user that sent the virus. Since both parties are unaware of the destructive consequences that will ultimately ensue, they feel that they are abiding by this principle and are, therefore, safe.

Another approach to this problem is to tell users never to execute a program sent to them as an email attachment, especially if they aren't expecting the file in the first place. Since email attachments are a common carrier of infected software this might sound reasonable. However, even this defence was shown to be fallible when the *BubbleBoy* worm surfaced in November 1999. BubbleBoy could, in fact, be triggered by merely *reading* an infected email. Once unleashed, it attacked Microsoft Outlook users by mailing a copy of itself to everyone in the victim's email address book. Although widely hailed as the first of its kind, such unexpected behaviour was not completely without precedent. A year earlier, vulnerabilities in popular email software had already signalled the possibility that simply reading email could be hazardous to your computer's health (see Section 13.2 for details).

The best approach, then, involves making sure that antivirus and email software are up to date as well as being particularly cautious about detaching or executing email attachments – especially if they are unexpected and likely to be unnecessary in the first place. Both aspects of this two-tiered approach to malware defence are essential.

17.10 Viruses in the pipes

Biological viruses need a host and a means of transmission in order to continue to grow beyond a very limited scope. Computer viruses are no different. A computer acts as the host and, depending upon how aggressive the virus is, it may infect a single file, many files, or the master boot record, which controls all the files on the system. Computer viruses also need a way to replicate themselves to other machines in order to avoid isolation and eradication. As previously mentioned, virus transmission has typically occurred from passing infected media (e.g. diskettes, CD-ROMs, etc.) from machine to machine or as files over a network. What is common in these cases is that end users take an explicit action which introduces the infection to their system.

In December 1998 a new means of transmission made headlines. The so-called *Remote Explorer* virus opened the world's eyes to a new threat even more insidious than its predecessors. This virus, which affected Windows NT servers, *could spread on its own* when clients logged on. The self-propagating nature of this new strain provided possibly the fastest means known at the time to create a widespread infection. An outbreak of this sort needed only a single, infected server and lots of connected client systems with shared drives. With these criteria met, it took almost no time before the entire user community was victimized.

A user of an infected machine might suddenly realize that random files had been compressed and encrypted, rendering them useless. And if that weren't enough, it was even possible that the Windows NT Registry might be affected. Given the critical nature of the Registry on Microsoft operating systems, such results could be catastrophic.

The good news is that this virus did not, in fact, spread very far because it didn't propagate across the Internet but was confined to more isolated LAN environments. This meant that the virus had to be planted on at least one server within the enterprise in order to kick off the replication process. However, the significance of this new strain of self-propagating viruses should not be overlooked, as future attacks could attempt to exploit a similar vulnerability.

In fact, only a few months later in March 1999, corporate networks around the world began bogging down with a sudden surge in email traffic. Volumes shot up so quickly that some companies were forced to take down their email systems entirely for hours or even days. Even some users who weren't directly hit by this newest malware attack were impacted as email systems were taken down as a precautionary measure. Almost instantly this critical means of communication had been crippled and the problem was spreading like wildfire.

At the bottom of this crisis lay a new virus which had been designed to propagate itself automatically. *Melissa* (or Mailissa as it was also known) was a macro virus which affected Microsoft's Word 97 and Word 2000 word processing software. When a user opened an infected document, Melissa used the victim's email program to send a copy of itself to the first 50 people listed in the address book on that system. In most cases the victim was completely unaware that he or she had assisted in the outbreak. Since the virus was sent to other users that the victim regularly corresponded with, they were likely to assume that their colleague had sent them a file that they needed to look at. Of course, when they did, they, too, became unwitting accomplices in the outbreak.

The exponential growth that resulted from one user sending copies to 50 other users who, in turn, sent copies to 50 more users who, in turn, sent copies to 50 more users, and so on, was enough to swamp email servers everywhere. The speed with which Melissa spread was breathtaking. It was like watching 'Six Degrees of Separation' principle[9] in action with terrible results. To their credit, antivirus vendors responded quickly to the outbreak by making updates available for their software. The antidote was distributed and operations eventually returned to

---

9. The 'Six Degrees of Separation' principle states that everyone on Earth is separated from everyone else by no more than six degrees of separation, or six friends of friends of friends.

normal, but the industry's understanding of the very nature of the virus threat was substantially altered in the process.

Viruses had existed for some time before Melissa came along, but their spread was typically observed over weeks and months. Even though the number of systems that were seriously impacted by Melissa ended up being fewer than was first feared, this new attack signalled a change in the urgency of the virus threat.[10] Melissa showed that an uncontrolled outbreak could result in a matter of hours – rather than days. The disturbing realization that arose from this epidemic was that for the first time on a global scale it had been demonstrated that *a virus could spread dramatically faster than its antidote*. This sobering fact served as a wake-up call for more than just a few companies to get their houses in order. Of course, this phenomenon did not go unnoticed by other virus creators. Copycat viruses such as Papa.A, Papa.B, and others quickly cropped up. Clearly, this problem was just not going to go away. In fact, the pace was only beginning to pick up.

(17.11) Killer viruses!

Despite the dire claims of some virus hoaxes (which will be covered shortly), the conventional wisdom of the day held that the worst thing that could happen to an infected system was that valuable data would be lost. Of course, that's nothing to sneeze at, but at least you could recover from most of this damage if you've been diligent in backing up your system.

However, in the perverse pursuit of a 'bigger and badder' computer virus, a new class was hatched in June 1998 and 'upgraded' in April 1999. This new type was capable of actually rendering an entire system useless. Even with a brand new hard drive a damaged system would amount to little more than a worthless heap of scrap metal unable even to boot up when powered on.

How could such a thing happen? Many newer systems are designed so that the **Basic Input/Output System (BIOS)**, which controls the fundamental I/O operations that are required for any system to function, can be upgraded (or 'flashed') after it leaves the factory. This capability allowed users to apply fixes to what used to be an essentially unchangeable component of the system. Sometimes these flashes involved upgrades to allow a system to recognize new I/O devices (e.g. a larger hard drive) that didn't exist at the time the BIOS was designed. This flexibility was a tremendous development for both users and vendors alike until ... some hackers decided to exploit this previously ignored vulnerability.

CIH (a.k.a. Chernobyl) was the name given to a virus that could actually flash the BIOS on a user's system and wipe out the 'smarts' needed to read and write to

---

10. Of course, the possibility of rapid replication was not really new as the 'Morris Worm' had shown, but it was, nevertheless, a revelation to many who were unfamiliar with the potential of malware.

hard drives, floppies, displays, and keyboards. The net effect was to render a previously functional system essentially 'brain dead'. No amount of trying on the part of the user could bring it back to life. You couldn't even install a new BIOS since the system no longer knew how to boot up.

Of course, a victim could always pack up the damaged system unit, send it back to the manufacturer and wait for them to bring it back from the dead, but it's easy to see how the expense and inconvenience of this remedy would present its own set of problems. If the system happened to be the laptop used by a travelling sales representative, you can imagine how the impact could affect the bottom line. If the system happened to be a server that many users depended upon, the adverse affects could be even more significant. If the system belonged to the CEO (never mind whether there was anything of any real significance on it or not), you know that heads are going to roll ...

Fortunately, flashing a BIOS is not a trivial task. The sequence of events that a virus must simulate is substantially different not only among systems from various manufacturers, but may even differ from one model to the next within a given product line. This means that a 'one size fits all' flash routine isn't likely. Also, as with other malware, this new strain of 'killer viruses' can be detected by antivirus software.

The point, though, is that it's not just data that's at risk any more. Adequate virus protection can mean the difference between a fully functional system and an overpriced paperweight.

17.12 The sky is falling!!!

While not as bad as a real virus a **hoax virus** is nevertheless damaging. A hoax virus is, of course, not a virus at all, but a warning of impending doom that will result from a virus that doesn't even exist. Hoax viruses typically appear as simple emails (no attachments) and carry an impassioned plea for the reader to be on the lookout for some virus that is allegedly making the rounds and leaving a path of destruction in its wake.

Join the Crew is one of the more infamous hoaxes. No one knows exactly who started it or even exactly when it first came on the scene. What is known is that no matter how many different wordings may appear, 'Join the Crew' is just as false now as the day it was first written. Here's one common form of this hoax:

```
               VIRUS WARNING !!!!!!!

If you receive an email titled 'JOIN THE CREW' DO NOT open it. It will erase
everything on your hard drive. Forward this letter out to as many people as
you can. This is a new, very malicious virus and not many people know about
it. This information was announced yesterday morning from IBM; please share
```

it with everyone that might access the internet. Once again, pass this along to EVERYONE in your address book so that this may be stopped. Also, do not open or even look at any mail that says 'RETURNED OR UNABLE TO DELIVER.' This virus will attach itself to your computer components and render them useless. Immediately delete any mail items that say this. AOL has said that this is a very dangerous virus and that there is NO remedy for it at this time. Please practice cautionary measures and forward this to all your online friends ASAP.

Who wouldn't sit up and take notice if they had just received a serious-sounding email such as this from someone they know and, presumably, trust? If both IBM and AOL are warning people about it, it must be true, right? Wrong. Of course, neither IBM nor AOL nor any other reliable source ever issued warnings about this alleged threat other than to say that it is, in fact, a hoax. In other words, there's just enough seemingly legitimate information mixed in with a generous helping of FUD (fear, uncertainty and doubt) to make most people fall for it.

Hoax viruses play on the fears and ignorance of the vast majority of users. They exploit the good nature of the user community. They rely on our most noble instinct to protect our friends, family and colleagues from what appears on the surface to be a significant threat. They are the high-tech equivalent of the ignoble chain letter scheme – with a few notable exceptions working in their favour:

- The sender is known.

- The threat, though utterly fanciful, sounds realistic enough even to some seasoned end users.

- The urgent nature is dramatic enough to prompt immediate action.

- It's cheap and easy to propagate.

- 'The computer says so, so it must be true.'

17.12.1   The sender is known

Unlike a chain letter which is typically anonymous, a hoax virus appears in the form of a normal email from a trusted person. This is usually a person who cares enough about you to send the hoax (which they think is real, of course) in the first place. In other words, the source is known to be someone who has your best interests at heart so you are more inclined to take it seriously than an anonymous, impersonal chain letter that appears to be a copy of a copy of a copy ...

17.12.2 The threat, though utterly fanciful, sounds realistic enough even to some seasoned end users

By mixing in lots of technical terms a good hoax virus can convince even people that ought to know better to take the bait hook, line and sinker. The sincerity of the plea may be enough to cause the reader to accept on faith what he or she, deep down, knows is not technically plausible. The *BadTimes* virus alert is a classic parody which pokes fun at a well-known hoax virus called *Good Times*:

Virus Alert !!!!!!!!!!!!!!!

If you receive an e-mail with a subject of Badtimes, delete it immediately WITHOUT READING IT. This is the most DANGEROUS e-mail virus ever.

It will rewrite your hard drive and scramble any disks that are even close to your computer. It will recalibrate your freezer's coolness setting so all your ice cream melts. It will demagnetize the strips on all your credit cards, screw up the tracking on your VCR, and use subspace field harmonics to render any CDs you try to play unreadable.

It will give your ex-boy/girlfriend/ex-husband/wife your new phone number. It will mix antifreeze into your fishtank. It will drink all your beer and leave its socks out on the coffee table when company comes over. It will put a kitten in the back pocket of your good suit and hide your car keys when you are late for work.

Badtimes will make you fall in love with a penguin. It will give you nightmares about circus midgets. It will pour sugar in your gas tank and shave off both your eyebrows while dating your current boy/girlfriend behind your back and billing the dinner and hotel room to your Visa card.

It moves your car randomly around parking lots so you can't find it. It will tease your dog. It will leave strange messages on your boss's voicemail in your voice. It is insidious and subtle. It is dangerous and terrifying to behold. It is also a rather interesting shade of mauve.

Badtimes will give you Dutch Elm disease. It will leave the toilet seat up. It will make a batch of methamphetamine in your bathtub and leave bacon cooking on the stove while it goes out to chase high school kids with your snowblower.

These are just a few of the signs. Be very, very afraid!

17.12.3 The urgent nature is dramatic enough to prompt immediate action

'Dire consequences!' 'Tell all your friends!' 'Act now before it's too late!' Such phrases pump up the volume on the hoax and tap into an almost primal 'fight or flight' reflex action.

17.12.4   It's cheap and easy to propagate

A hard-copy chain letter sent through the postal service (snail mail) requires that the sender make many copies, stuff them in envelopes, address the envelopes, apply the necessary postage stamps, and put the whole stack in the mailbox. Not only can this be a lot of work, but it can also get somewhat expensive if a large number of copies are to be sent. Hoax viruses spread through email where the effort involved is trivial and the cost to the end user is virtually non-existent.

17.12.5   'The computer says so, so it must be true'

Computers are smart, right? Otherwise, how can you explain the fact that, in 1997, IBM's 'Deep Blue' computer beat Gary Kasparov, the best chess player in the world? The 'magic' of computers can be hypnotic at times. We come to rely on them for so many things and their capabilities are incomprehensible to most. The fact that even people familiar with computers are willing to suspend rational thinking when presented with bogus information from a computer is the subject of the *Gullibility Virus* – a spoof on hoax viruses:

```
*********************************************************************
*WARNING, CAUTION, DANGER, AND BEWARE!
*Gullibility Virus Spreading over the Internet!

*********************************************************************
```

WASHINGTON, D.C.–The Institute for the Investigation of Irregular Internet Phenomena announced today that many Internet users are becoming infected by a new virus that causes them to believe without question every groundless story, legend, and dire warning that shows up in their inbox or on their browser. The Gullibility Virus, as it is called, apparently makes people believe and forward copies of silly hoaxes relating to cookie recipes, email viruses, taxes on modems, and get-rich-quick schemes.

"These are not just readers of tabloids or people who buy lottery tickets based on fortune cookie numbers," a spokesman said. "Most are otherwise normal people, who would laugh at the same stories if told to them by a stranger on a street corner" However, once these same people become infected with the Gullibility Virus, they believe anything they read on the Internet.

"My immunity to tall tales and bizarre claims is all gone," reported one weeping victim. "I believe every warning message and sick child story my friends forward to me, even though most of the messages are anonymous."

Another victim, now in remission, added, "When I first heard about Good Times, I just accepted it without question. After all, there were dozens of other recipients on the mail header, so I thought the virus must be true." It was a long time, the victim said, before she could stand up at a Hoaxes Anonymous meeting and state, "My name is Jane, and I've been hoaxed." Now, however, she is spreading the word. "Challenge and check whatever you read," she says.

Internet users are urged to examine themselves for symptoms of the virus, which include the following:

The willingness to believe improbable stories without thinking.
The urge to forward multiple copies of such stories to others.
A lack of desire to take three minutes to check to see if a story is true.

T.C. is an example of someone recently infected. He told one reporter, "I read on the Net that the major ingredient in almost all shampoos makes your hair fall out, so I've stopped using shampoo." When told about the Gullibility Virus, T.C. said he would stop reading email, so that he would not become infected.

Anyone with symptoms like these is urged to seek help immediately. Experts recommend that at the first feelings of gullibility, Internet users rush to their favorite search engine and look up the item tempting them to thoughtless credence. Most hoaxes, legends, and tall tales have been widely discussed and exposed by the Internet community.

Courses in critical thinking are also widely available, and there is online help from many sources, including

IBM Anti-Virus at
http://www.av.ibm.com/BreakingNews/HypeAlert/

Department of Energy Computer Incident Advisory Capability at
http://ciac.llnl.gov/ciac/CIACHoaxes.html

Symantec Anti Virus Research Center at
http://www.symantec.com/avcenter/index.html

McAfee Associates Virus Hoax List at
http://www.mcafee.com/support/hoax.html

Dr. Solomons Hoax Page at
http://www.drsolomons.com/vircen/hoax.html

The Urban Legends Web Site at
http://www.urbanlegends.com

Urban Legends Reference Pages at
http://www.snopes.com

Datafellows Hoax Warnings at
http://www.Europe.Datafellows.com/news/hoax.htm

Those people who are still symptom free can help inoculate themselves against the Gullibility Virus by reading some good material on evaluating sources, such as

Evaluating Internet Research Sources at
http://www.sccu.edu/faculty/R_Harris/evalu8it.htm

```
    Evaluation of Information Sources at
    http://www.vuw.ac.nz/nagsmith/evaln/evaln.htm

    Bibliography on Evaluating Internet Resources at
    http://refserver.lib.vt.edu/libinst/critTHINK.HTM
```

Lastly, as a public service, Internet users can help stamp out the Gullibility Virus by sending copies of this message to anyone who forwards them a hoax.

```
*****************************************************************
```

This message is so important, we're sending it anonymously! Forward it to all your friends right away! Don't think about it! This is not a chain letter! This story is true! Don't check it out! This story is so timely, there is no date on it! This story is so important, we're using lots of exclamation points! Lots!! For every message you forward to some unsuspecting person, the Home for the Hopelessly Gullible will donate ten cents to itself. (If you wonder how the Home will know you are forwarding these messages all over creation, you're obviously thinking too much.)

```
*****************************************************************
```

ACT NOW! DON'T DELAY! LIMITED TIME ONLY! NOT SOLD IN ANY STORE!

```
*****************************************************************
```

(Note that IBM Anti-Virus is now at http://www.av.ibm.com and McAfee Associates Virus Hoax List is now at http://vil.mcafee.com/hoax.asp.) While designed to be humorous, the Gullibility Virus alert contains a number of very good URLs that can tell you more about the nature of hoax viruses and how to spot them. It should be required reading for anyone with access to an email account.

17.13 Crying 'wolf'

Some might argue that hoax viruses aren't viruses at all, but when you step back and see how rapidly they can spread and the exponential growth in email traffic that can result, you quickly realize that hoax viruses do, in fact, exhibit many of the same behaviours of their real virus counterparts. The loss of productivity due to the endless forwarding of hoaxes may seem insignificant at first, but when you multiply it across the entire user community of a large corporation, the costs can add up.

The greatest threat to security from hoaxes, though, comes from the desensitization that occurs when users finally realize that they've been duped (an inevitable consequence if you are to break the cycle of hoax forwarding). The tendency, then, is for them to discount entirely the threat of real viruses and expose themselves and their organizations to real damage. Aesop's fable of the boy who cried wolf comes to mind. Of course, this all plays perfectly well into the hands of the authors of real malware.

To combat this problem it is important that users understand that under no circumstances should they take it upon themselves to try to warn others of impending viruses. Real virus incidents should be reported immediately to the proper support personnel so that the virus can be identified, isolated, and the resulting damage limited. Virus warnings from an established, well-known source within the IT organization, however, may be appropriate in extreme circumstances. In any case, warnings of viruses, whether real or imagined, that are circulated within the user community do no good and may even do harm.

(17.14) In search of a cure

So what can you do to deal with the virus threat? Here are some suggestions:

● *Minimize risky end-user behaviour.* Users should be taught that shareware, email attachments, and even shrink-wrapped software can be a virus carrier. If the source is well known and trusted, the risk of infection is *reduced* but not *eliminated*. Users also need to know that both executable programs and data files can contain viruses. In the case of macro viruses, the simple act of displaying a word processing document or spreadsheet can result in infection. All such data should be carefully screened before being detached, viewed or executed.

● *Antivirus software should be run on* all *systems.* These tools can't guarantee your safety, but they can go a long way toward minimizing the risks. Virus detection tools should be installed everywhere so that virus transmission can be arrested before infection reaches epidemic levels. Some companies go so far as to make antivirus software available to employees for use on their personal systems at home since diskettes from these sources have a way of ending up in the workplace.

● *Update antivirus tools frequently.* Since end users cannot reasonably be expected to remember to update their virus detection tools on a frequent basis, and since failure to do otherwise can result in substantial exposure, it is in the best interests of the enterprise to automate the update process in order to make sure that it actually gets done.

● *Disable automatic macro execution.* Many products that support macros also provide a means for users to control their behaviour. By either permanently or selectively disabling automatic macro execution, one of the most common forms of computer virus can be stopped dead in its tracks. The CERT Advisory for the Melissa macro virus points out that this can be done as follows:

In Word97 you can disable automatic macro execution (click Tools/Options/General then turn on the 'Macro virus protection' checkbox). In Word2000 macro execution is controlled by a security level variable similar to Internet Explorer (click on Tools/

Macro/Security and choose High, Medium, or Low). In that case, 'High' silently ignores the VBA [Visual Basic for Applications] code, Medium prompts in the way Word97 does to let you enable or disable the VBA code, and 'Low' just runs it.[11]

A further precaution that you can take to guard against spreading Microsoft Word macro viruses is to save all word processing documents you create as .RTF (Rich Text Format) files rather than in the traditional .DOC (Document) format. The advantage to this approach is that .RTF files do not contain macros whereas .DOC files can. However, even this defence can be circumvented by a *CAP* virus (named for the macro that implemented the malicious behaviour). By intercepting common user actions such as FileOpen, FileClose, FileSaveAs, etc., CAP can override even the best of intentions with its own replacement functions (Chess, 1997).

● *Have a reliable data backup and recovery system in place.* Unfortunate as it may be, there is simply no practical way to guarantee that a system will not be infected by a virus. You can limit the damage an outbreak might cause, though. A reliable system that backs up critical data on all machines (not just a few servers) may sound expensive, but the cost of doing without one could cost more in the long run. The backup system should probably be to at least some degree centralized in order to ensure that it is implemented consistently across the enterprise. It will be most effective if its backup process is automated and run frequently.

● *Establish a means of centralized reporting.* When a virus is detected, end users should automatically know whom to contact. Without this, a company runs the risk of letting untrained amateurs try to fix a problem that is beyond their capabilities. A single phone number (e.g. the IT help desk) that is known by everyone is the best way to ensure that bush fires don't turn into full-blown forest fires.

● *Put it all in the policy.* The critical importance of a well-defined and well-known security policy has already been discussed in Chapter 5. The area of virus protection serves as a classic case where a good policy can make a world of difference. This policy should spell out the points previously mentioned and should include the proper handling of both real and hoax viruses.

Unless you plan to disconnect all your systems permanently from the network, write all your own software from scratch and throw away your floppy drive, you will always run the risk of virus infection. Clearly, such a radical remedy is both impractical and unrealistic. All is not lost, though. There is much you can do to mitigate the risks that you will inevitably face. Hackers know this but they hope that you don't.

11. CERT Advisory, 'CA-99-04 Melissa-Macro-Virus', March 1999, www.cert.org.

chapter 18

Hackers don't want you to know that ... *active content is more active than you think*

Chapter summary

- Various forms of active content

  — Java

  — JavaScript

  — ActiveX

- The pros and cons of active content

- The threat of active content

- Active content defences

Active content can really spice up a Web site. It can transform a static page that looks and acts the same way each time you access it into a dynamic, interactive experience. It can animate the dullest site with snazzy visual tricks or make it more responsive to the needs of the user.

Active content, also called *mobile code* by some, can come in a variety of flavours. In its most common form it is a program written in a special scripting language that can be automatically downloaded by a Web browser and executed on the user's system. This action can be triggered either by an intentional selection made with the click of a mouse or unintentionally by merely visiting a page. It may be coded in ActiveX, Java or JavaScript. The effects may be similar but the underlying processes at work are quite different. In particular, the security considerations of each are also worth noting.

Java, invented by Sun Microsystems, kicked off the active content craze. Java was designed to be a platform-independent programming language complete with its own unique run-time environment called a Java Virtual Machine or JVM, for short. Java took aim at the heart of one of the computing industry's long-standing problems – programs written to run on one operating system had to be either recompiled or rewritten in order to run on other operating systems. Java's 'write once, run anywhere' promise appealed to many programmers. For this reason it was quickly identified as being particularly well suited for the Internet. After all, Web site builders wanted to concentrate on providing content rather than having to deal with the vagaries of the multitudes of operating systems that Web surfers might choose.

Java **applets** could be downloaded and executed in a single step. This appealed to end users. Since applets ran in a tightly controlled JVM within the browser, the threat to security seemed minuscule. This 'sandbox' security model ensured that the applet could not tamper with the user's disk storage or memory and would, therefore, not interfere with other programs that were currently running.

Java **applications**, on the other hand, were not constrained in the same way. Applications were given free reign of the system just as other programs were. While applets were downloaded by the browser and executed within the browser's JVM, Java applications were explicitly stored on the system's hard drive by the user and ran outside the browser's sandbox. This distinction allowed the Java programmers, the flexibility to choose whether they wanted more function (applications) or more security (applets).

However, in December 1998 the walls of the sandbox were knocked down to make way for the new Java 2 standard. In Java 2 the 'all or nothing' approach was replaced with a more granular discernment that allowed developers more leeway over what they could and could not do from an applet. A necessary consequence of this new flexibility, however, was that users had to take more responsibility over what they would and would not allow to run on their machines. Unfortunately, end users are rarely the right ones to be making such decisions as they usually lack the expertise to understand what they are really being asked to accept.

JavaScript, from Netscape, came along a little later and capitalized on the name recognition of Java. Though it was claimed to be based on Java, some argue that this relationship is somewhat weak. Unlike Java, the JavaScript run-time environment was only available within the context of a Web browser. This meant that a certain degree of platform independence was achieved as long as everyone used a browser that supported JavaScript. Since both Netscape's Navigator and Microsoft's Internet Explorer, the two biggest rivals in the browser wars at the time, supported JavaScript, this worked out fairly well in most cases. However, JavaScript lacked the independence of Java applications. This meant that JavaScript programs would always be constrained in much the same way as Java applets.

ActiveX, Microsoft's successor to its own OLE (Object Linking and Embedding) technology, was positioned by many as a competitor to Java. Even though ActiveX was more of a component technology than a true programming language, its effect from a user's standpoint was similar. Like other active content, ActiveX controls could be automatically downloaded by a browser and executed with or without the user's permission. Unlike Java applets and JavaScript programs, however, ActiveX did not run in its own 'sandbox' and could, therefore, read and write to the user's disk like any other program. This gave ActiveX the same flexibility as Java applications, but also made it risky from a security standpoint because it could potentially cause damage without the user knowing about it.

This vulnerability was addressed through ActiveX's 'trust model' for security. Basically, users could designate which sites they would accept ActiveX controls from and what they would be allowed to do. ActiveX controls could even be digitally signed (see Appendix A) to prove that they did, indeed, come from the place that the user believed they were coming from. The advantage of this approach was that it offered greater flexibility than either JavaScript or the original version of Java (as previously mentioned, the Java 2 Security Model put Java and ActiveX in a similar situation). The problem, though, was that the burden of security decisions was left completely in the hands of end users – most of whom hadn't the vaguest notion as to which controls they should allow or prohibit.

(18.1) Active hacking

In theory, Java applets and JavaScript programs represent no significant security threat whatsoever. But programs don't run 'in theory', they run 'in computers' and the latter have demonstrated a less than perfect track record. Errors by JVM programmers have led to flawed implementations that let things 'leak' out of the Java sandbox. Similar flaws have showed up in JavaScript-capable products. Add to all of this the inherent risks of the human element in ActiveX's 'trust model', and you can see why the whole area of active content might be fertile ground for hackers.

> Programs don't run 'in theory', they run 'in computers' and the latter have demonstrated a less than perfect track record.

In fact, in a paper entitled 'Web spoofing: An Internet con game' (Felten et al., 1997) from the Computer Science Department at Princeton University the authors describe a particularly dangerous attack that could be facilitated, in large part, by malicious JavaScript routines. In this attack the victim is tricked into believing that the Web sites he or she is viewing are authentic when, in fact, they are modified copies that are being served up by the hacker's machine. By cleverly positioning his 'Web spoofer' between the victim and the victim's intended destination, the hacker performs a variation on the classic 'man in the middle' attack and is granted complete access to all the victim's Web traffic. Since this traffic could involve the transmission of secret passwords, confidential corporate data, or even credit card numbers, this attack could be devastating. Active content is used to obscure evidence of the attack so the victim is left completely oblivious to the danger.

Imagine getting hacked by merely *viewing* a Web site. Think it can't happen? Think the Web spoofing attack is an isolated incident? Think again. The potential for attacks of this sort reached such a level that CERT felt it necessary to issue an official advisory in order to get the proper focus on the problem. They found that through the use of 'malicious scripts', an attacker could do things like:

- alter the appearance of a Web page,
- read fields in a form which have been presented to users by Web servers they know and trust,
- change the way a page behaves (even interfere with its normal operation),
- gain unauthorized access to an internal intranet Web server, and
- make the attack persistent so that every time users revisit the affected site, the attack resumes.[1]

Making matters worse is the fact that users don't know in advance that any of this will happen because there may be no obvious indication that anything is amiss. To them, one URL looks like another. The fact that even trusted sites can be exploited in the attack makes the whole situation that much more dangerous. Thankfully, solutions to known deficiencies do exist. Keeping browsers up to date with the latest security fixes, as discussed in Chapter 13, can reduce your risk of attack substantially.

But that's not all you can do. A good practice to adopt might be to turn off active content in your browser's configuration settings.[2] Of course, this will rob you of the sizzle that active content offers but it will pay you back in faster Web access (because active content won't have to be downloaded) and better security. If, however, you need to utilize the active content that's available on a Web site that you trust, enable this capability before going to the site and disable it when you're done.

Unfortunately, this can be a tedious task if you need to change these settings a lot. Another option would be to install a 'personal firewall' on your client station that is able to selectively allow or prohibit active content based on a list of sites of your own choosing. WRQ's AtGuard product, mentioned earlier in Section 8.9, is one such example. Figures 18.1 and 18.2 show how this tool can be configured to

1. CERT Advisory, 'CA-2000-02 Malicious HTML Tags Embedded in Client Web Requests', February 2000, www.cert.org.
2. See 'Remedies' section of Felten et al. (1997) and 'Solution' section of CERT Advisory, 'CA-2000-02 Malicious HTML Tags Embedded in Client Web Requests', February 2000, www.cert.org.

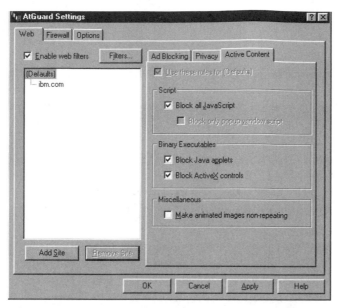

FIGURE 18.1   Blocking active content by default with a personal firewall

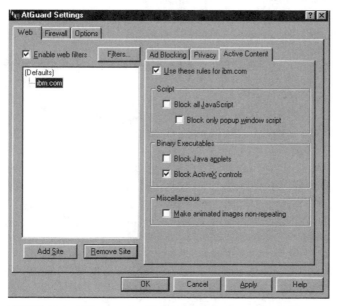

FIGURE 18.2   Allowing JavaScript and Java for a trusted site

allow certain active content from a trusted site, such as www.ibm.com, while blocking it from all other sites.

A firewall alone, though, isn't enough. The traditional role of a packet filtering firewall is to selectively allow or deny traffic based on information contained in the packet headers being transmitted. For instance, you might choose to discard all traffic except Web surfing. This would improve security by limiting the number of doors a hacker might use to slip in through. In order to do this, a filter rule would be generated which opens up port 80 (a TCP designation used for most Web traffic) but disallows everything else. This approach is fine as far as it goes but when it comes to malicious active content, that isn't far enough. The problem is that this sort of traffic can just as easily flow right through with the Web pages. The firewall typically can't discern whether this 'port 80 traffic' is good or bad.[3] This is why additional countermeasures might be useful.

One such weapon in your arsenal might be a tool that scans active content as it enters your network and blocks potentially malicious programs. Finjan Software's SurfinGate[4] product can do just that. Positioned just inside a perimeter firewall, SurfinGate can inspect and exclude active content that looks suspicious. Finjan also produces a SurfinShield tool which can do similar screening on individual desktop systems. When used in combination with the other techniques mentioned previously, these can serve as yet another barrier in a multilayered, defence-in-depth system.

The point of this discussion is that active content, which can range in usefulness anywhere from substantial business function to meaningless 'eye candy', is not without its risks. Active content has been used in the past as a means of initiating an attack. There is no reason to believe that this threat is not only still very real but may be growing. As more and more people move to the Web and more and more flawed active content platforms are made available and more and more hackers decide that this is an interesting vulnerability to exploit, the situation could get worse before it gets better.

That doesn't mean, though, that you should avoid active content like the plague. When it is used properly, active content can provide considerable e-business value. It does mean, however, that *you* should take control of what runs and does not run on *your* machines. If you don't, hackers will – and you probably won't like the decisions they make for you.

---

3. This is not to say that a particular vendor's firewall might not include some additional active content monitoring features but this additional work could cause a firewall to bog down and, therefore, become vulnerable to DoS attacks. This sort of processing is often done by specially designed software running in a separate machine behind the firewall.
4. Finjan Software Ltd, www.finjan.com.

chapter 19

Hackers don't want you to know that ... *yesterday's strong crypto is today's weak crypto*

Chapter summary

- The 'PAIN' of security

  - Privacy

  - Authentication

  - Integrity

  - Non-repudiation

- The importance of cryptography in the Internet Age

- Factors that contribute to or detract from the security of cryptography

- Cracking the code

  - cracking Enigma during WWII

  - cracking DES

- What constitutes 'strong cryptography'?

- The effect of governmental regulation on cryptography

How can you send a private message over a public network and expect it to remain private? How can you keep corporate secrets stored on your hard drive from showing up on the front page of the newspaper? How can you make sure that the person reading your confidential message is, in fact, who they claim to be? How can they prove that you are who you say you are? How can you tell if the contents of an important message or file have been tampered with? How can you make an agreement reached in cyberspace hold up under the scrutiny of a legal challenge?

An easy way to remember these requirements is through the acronym *PAIN*:

● *Privacy* A secret message must remain secret.

● *Authentication* You are who you claim to be.

● *Integrity* The message has not been tampered with.

● *Non-repudiation* The terms of the agreement are binding.

All of these requirements can be met through the use of a single technology – cryptography.

Cryptography is a method of secret writing. It involves taking an original, *plain text* message and scrambling it in such a way that its contents are obscured to unauthorized readers while still providing a means for restoration by authorized recipients. **Encryption** (scrambling) and **decryption** (unscrambling) functions are rooted in complex mathematical theories, but that doesn't mean that you need a PhD in Mathematics in order to understand the fundamental elements.

In fact, it's quite possible to get a firm grasp of the essential issues without having to know even one bit of maths, if you're willing to accept a few things on faith. Does every person that drives a car need to understand the inner workings of an internal combustion engine in order to get from point A to point B? Does a car mechanic need degrees in Chemistry and Physics in order to diagnose and repair vehicle malfunctions? Absolutely not. Of course, having an understanding of the laws of motion and chemical reactions would provide greater insight and a fuller appreciation of all that's going on under the hood, but it's certainly not a prerequisite for obtaining a driver's licence.

The rise of the Internet and its related technologies has opened up a multitude of possibilities. The world is more connected than it has ever been. The open nature of this common infrastructure is the reason for its success and is also at the heart of some of its greatest failures. Some aspects of business simply can't be conducted out in the open. When you send your credit card number to an online merchant, you would like to know that only that merchant can see the details of your order. You would not want to later see such information plastered on a Web site for all to read. In many cases, when businesses negotiate contracts or collaborate on projects privacy is a must.

When confidentiality is a requirement you can either pay the high price of private, dedicated network connections or encrypt your data so that anyone who does intercept it can't read it anyway. Since the latter provides greater flexibility and lower cost, it is increasingly becoming the predominant solution.

> When confidentiality is a requirement you can either pay the high price of private, dedicated network connections or encrypt your data so that anyone who does intercept it can't read it anyway.

In a very real sense, cryptography is becoming as important to the Internet as Web servers and routers. Without the security that cryptography can provide, many businesses will simply be unwilling to exploit the Internet to any significant degree, beyond using it as a means for presenting electronic brochures. Businesses will have little need for 'fat networking pipes' if they can't rely on the fact that what they put through them won't be compromised. This is why cryptography, an ancient technology compared to most other aspects of the Internet, has seen such a tremendous resurgence of interest over the past few years and will continue to do so for many more to come.

Cryptography has become one of the most critical and pervasive security technologies in use today. It's embedded in everything from firewalls to routers to single sign-on tools to antivirus software. Some have gone so far as to call it the 'killer enabler' for the Net. Therefore, an understanding of the issues surrounding cryptography has become essential in today's world of open networks. Hackers are well acquainted with this information and they use it to break into the systems of those who don't.

A brief tutorial about how cryptography works is presented in Appendix A.

19.1 Cracking 101

Of course, the reason that a message is encrypted in the first place is in order to ensure privacy. But how private are encrypted messages in reality? The answer depends upon factors too numerous to mention, but a few of the more common ones are the:

- strength of the chosen algorithm;
- randomness of the keys that are used;
- lifetime of these keys;
- security of private keys;
- length of the keys.

19.1.1   Algorithm strength

Inherent weaknesses in the crypto algorithm may make certain key choices inse-cure or may expose a pattern in encrypted messages which might be recognized by a hacker. For instance, a simple cryptosystem based on a fixed substitution scheme (e.g. 'A'='D', 'B'='Z', 'C'='G', ...) is easy to crack. One simply needs to know that 'E' is the most commonly used letter in the English language and apply this knowl-edge to the encrypted message. Just assume that the most common letter in the encrypted message is 'E' and repeat the substitution for the next most common let-ters and see what falls out. After enough tries, a pattern will emerge and you will have broken the code. Using a computer to do the hard work of trying these com-binations and then seeing if any words from an English language dictionary can be identified speeds up the cracking effort enormously.

Clearly, a more sophisticated encryption scheme is needed for truly important, private communication.

19.1.2   Randomness of keys

A lack of randomness in the choice of keys may also lead to weakness. If keys aren't random, then a pattern may emerge which allows a hacker to predict which keys are more likely to be chosen from among the list of all possible keys. This could dramatically shorten a brute-force attack by allowing the hacker to first try the keys that are more likely. Even though random acts seem to occur all around us con-stantly, this behaviour is, in fact, hard to simulate on a deterministic machine like a computer.

One reason we value computers is that if given precisely the same input they will produce the same output time after time after time. If this weren't the case, they wouldn't be much good for record keeping and calculations. (Who wants a calculator where 1+1 could equal 2 in one case and 153 in another?) However, there are tasks, such as key generation, when predictability is not a virtue. This is why a pseudo-random number generator is a nice feature to have. The results aren't truly random but, in many cases, they're good enough.

19.1.3   Lifetime of keys

Like freshly baked bread, crypto keys have a limited shelf life. If keys are rarely changed then a hacker who determines the key, either through skill or sheer dumb luck, will have complete access to all transmissions. On the other hand, if keys are changed frequently, the loss of privacy is limited to only those transmissions that were encrypted with the compromised key. In general, the 'fresher' your keys, the better your security.

19.1.4   Security of private keys

Asymmetric cryptosystems (discussed in Appendix A) pin all their hopes on the notion that private keys do, in fact, remain private. In the same way, symmetric key alternatives depend upon keeping the secret key a secret. However, if these keys are stored on a PC's hard drive and that system is attacked, this information could become compromised. If the keys are encrypted with a password that the user must enter, security is improved. If the keys are stored on a smart card which the user must present along with a PIN in order to use the key, security is better still. Of crucial importance with a Public Key Infrastructure (PKI) based on these technologies is the security of the certificate authority's (CA) private key. If the CA's private key becomes compromised, the underpinnings of the entire PKI are threatened because you can no longer trust that the certificates it has issued are authentic.

19.1.5   Key length

The longer the key, the larger the number of possible encrypted outcomes there are for a given message. A key that is 1 bit long will yield only two possibilities. A key of 2 bits could yield four different outcomes. Three bits yield eight alternatives and so on. The formula is simply 2^n where n is the length of the key in bits. If you want to keep your message as secure as possible, you want to choose the longest key length you can get away with. It's the 'getting away with' part that is the subject of much controversy, as you will soon see. A 1996 paper from some of the world's pre-eminent cryptographers on the subject of symmetric key lengths concluded that:

To protect information adequately for the next 20 years in the face of expected advances in computing power, keys in newly-deployed systems should be at least 90 bits long.

(Blaze et al., 1996)

One should not overlook the significance of the word '*expected*' in this excerpt. The history of technology is littered with cases where people have made the fatal mistake of assuming that the current rate of change would continue indefinitely, only to realize later that an unexpected breakthrough had shattered all their previous assumptions. Of course, computers will continue to get faster and cracking techniques more sophisticated, making it necessary to revise projections such as this. It also would not be wise to ignore the possibility that a new, revolutionary technology could come along and invalidate all that we now know. For instance, if quantum computers, which at the time of this writing are largely relegated to the realm of research papers, ever become practical, crypto-cracking capabilities could be increased dramatically. However, in light of the information available now, it would seem that

112-bit triple DES, which is widely available within the US (and to an increasing degree throughout the world), or its stronger 128-bit relatives *should* be sufficient.

From this brief list of potential crypto vulnerabilities it can be seen that the strength and, therefore, the security of encrypted messages can be affected not only by the underlying mathematical properties of the algorithms chosen, but also by the way these algorithms have actually been implemented. For instance, using an algorithm and key lengths that are generally recognized by crypto experts as being secure is no guarantee that private messages will, in fact, remain private. If the programmers and/or engineers that actually implement these functions make errors in their work (e.g. poor random number generation), it may still be possible for a hacker to access confidential information. This means that special care should also be taken to ensure that the cryptographic tools that will be used have been analyzed by a qualified cryptanalyst and/or certified by a respected industry certification organization.

(19.2) The mathematician's war

During World War II, Germany developed a machine called 'Enigma', which could be used to secure their transmissions regarding things such as troop movements, attack plans, ship positioning and bombing raids. Enigma was theoretically capable of encrypting a message in any of about 150 quintillion (150,000,000,000,000,000,000) different ways (Smith, 1998) – seemingly more than 2,000 times stronger than the Data Encryption Standard (DES), which became the crypto 'gold standard' 30 years later! A simple brute-force attack on an Enigma-encrypted message might have taken centuries to crack and by that time the information would have been meaningful only to ancient-history buffs. This marvel of German engineering was so far ahead of the cryptographic devices of its day that it was widely believed to be uncrackable. Emboldened by their confidence in Enigma, the Germans felt that they could communicate with impunity over the open airwaves – and did so on a regular basis. Fortunately for the Allies, the Germans became overconfident and made a series of procedural errors which substantially weakened Enigma's actual strength to a more manageable cracking problem.

The British exploited these mistakes by setting up a dedicated code-breaking facility just north of London in a place known as Bletchley Park. Here the finest mathematical minds from Oxford and Cambridge were assembled, along with thousands of linguists, intelligence experts, Morse code specialists, and manual labourers; all with the sole purpose of cracking the German codes and keeping the Allies one step ahead. Since their work remained classified until the 1970s, the contributions of these dedicated people, who toiled in obscurity day and night throughout the war, are only now being realized. Many now believe that the intelligence advantage gained through the work at Bletchley Park cut as much as two years off the length of the war and saved tens or even hundreds of thousands of lives (Smith, 1998).

Similar efforts by the Americans against Japanese crypto devices led to the shooting down of Admiral Yamamoto's plane and ultimately an Allied victory in the Pacific theatre as well. In a very real sense, this war was not only waged on the battlefield, in the air, and on the seas, but also in the minds of mathematicians turned code breakers who provided a decisive advantage.

19.3 Strong crypto?

Based on this short history lesson alone, you can see why governments around the world quickly saw cryptography as a critical military tool. In the US until 1996, restrictions against the export of strong crypto fell under the jurisdiction of the State Department, who treated cryptographic technology substantially the same as it did munitions. To their way of thinking, a strong crypto algorithm was potentially just as dangerous as a bomb. Their reasoning was that if the US could control the spread of strong crypto, it would possess a crucial advantage in future conflicts. The law enforcement community weighed in, saying that strong crypto in the hands of terrorists or drug smugglers would severely hamper their ability to police this sort of illegal activity and, therefore, threaten the lives of law-abiding citizens.

After prolonged protests by civil rights groups and American crypto vendors wishing to peddle their wares overseas, the responsibility for crypto import/export control was transferred to the more business-minded Department of Commerce. This might sound like a small step but, in fact, it signified the start of an important trend – crypto technology would be treated less like a live grenade (as it had been) and more like the commercial product that it was embedded in.

However, law enforcement groups such as the Federal Bureau of Investigation (FBI) weren't ready to concede just yet. Again, they argued that they needed the ability to obtain court-ordered wire taps, in certain cases. The FBI's position was they would be unable to protect the nation if criminal communications were encrypted. Since they couldn't control the use of strong crypto by American citizens within US borders (the First Amendment's 'free speech' provisions got in the way of that), they had to settle for strict limitations on the export of cryptographic technology that went beyond certain predefined limits.

Of course, one person's strong crypto is another person's weak crypto, so the debate rages on as to what key lengths are acceptably strong for legitimate business but acceptably weak for law enforcement. Stated another way, how strong is strong? As recently as 1999 the US's National Security Agency (NSA) and the FBI maintained that 56-bit key lengths (like those used in DES) were too strong for them to crack quickly and should, therefore, be limited in their use. Crypto experts in the private sector vehemently disagreed. RSA Security Inc., set out to prove that DES, the most commonly used crypto algorithm for many years, was now, in fact, weak. They, along with many others, argued that exponential growth in computing power since the invention of DES had essentially invalidated the claims of strength asserted by the US government.

To make their point, RSA sponsored a series of code-cracking contests popularly known as the 'DES Challenge' (Figure 19.1). RSA encrypted a message using DES and then offered a $10,000 reward to the first person (or team of people) to crack the secret message. In the first contest in January 1997, over 70,000 machines across the world were enlisted by one team to help. Each of the machines was automatically assigned a small portion of the 72 quadrillion possible keys to try (DES uses a 56-bit key which yields 2^{56} permutations). By using spare CPU cycles on these machines along with the Internet as a means to coordinate the effort, the winning team had essentially unleashed a massively parallel processor on the problem space. After nearly five months a winner was declared.

This first contest had proven that DES was vulnerable but that it required substantial computing power and unprecedented cooperation in order to do it. The fact that so much computational muscle, which would have been prohibitively expensive for most hackers to amass, could be assembled at virtually no cost to the winning team, however, was significant. *In a sense the Internet had helped crack DES.* Without it the enrolment and coordination of volunteer machines would have been nearly impossible. Even if you could conquer the logistical problems, the time required to do so would probably have taken years rather than months.

The next major milestone toward the downfall of DES took place just 18 months later in a subsequent DES Challenge in July 1998. In this contest a special-purpose DES-cracking machine named *Deep Crack* did the job in just *56 hours*! The Electronic Frontier Foundation[1] (EFF), a civil rights organization, built the machine for less than $250,000 (a lot of money for an individual to come up with but not a lot for a corporation, government, or organized crime syndicate). Deep Crack was capable of attempting 80 billion different keys each second. With that sort of power, it was able to beat out even the best organized teams of distributed cracking efforts.

If that weren't enough, RSA sponsored yet another contest in January 1999 during its annual conference in San Jose, California. This time EFF's Deep Crack teamed up with Distributed Computing Technologies[2] to attack DES with over 100,000 machines around the world. The combined effort exploited the power of a massively parallel 'divide and conquer' scheme based upon downloaded client code running on volunteered systems along with the enormous power of a single, special-purpose code cracker (Deep Crack). The results were spectacular. The contest was over in just over *22 hours*! For the first time publicly, DES had been cracked in under a day.[3]

1. Electronic Frontier Foundation, www.eff.org.
2. Distributed Computing Technologies, www.distributed.net.
3. Some believe that the NSA has been doing it for years in secret but that's another story. Suffice it to say that since anyone who *really* knows isn't talking, we are left to hear from those who can only speculate.

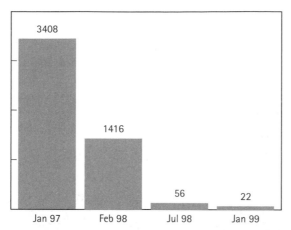

FIGURE 19.1   RSA's DES challenge: demonstrating the increasing vulnerability of DES

Of course, this work still required substantial coordination and resources to execute, but the writing was on the wall ... DES was vulnerable. This was no longer a matter of theoretical debate but a demonstrable fact. Clearly, a DES replacement would be needed before this sort of code-cracking power became widely available.

19.4   How strong is strong?

In fact, there are cryptosystems that are stronger than DES already deployed around the world. Triple DES and RC5 are a couple of examples. In order to get a sense of how the strength of a cryptosystem is affected by its key size, it is important to realize that with each additional bit the total number of permutations that a brute-force attacker must try is doubled. This means that adding just a few more bits to the key will substantially improve security. Doubling the key size increases the number of possible keys exponentially – not linearly.

One way to appreciate what this means is to consider an analogy where you imagine that all the possible keys in a 40-bit cryptosystem could fit into a teaspoon. (I know it sounds a bit farfetched but stay with me on this ...) If this were true then it would take a child-sized inflatable swimming pool to hold all the keys that 56 bits (e.g. DES) could generate. Since 40 bits used to be the limit on most US exports until 1998, it is easy to see how the shift to a 56-bit limit offered substantial relief in terms of greater crypto strength. If you take the analogy one step further to the level of 128-bit schemes, you would find that it takes a container the size of the entire earth to hold all the possible keys (Bidzos, 1999)!

From this you can see why people who want secrecy love the idea of a 128-bit cryptosystem and why, for the same reason, people who want to crack messages absolutely hate it. Since legitimate businesses typically fall into the former category and hackers fall into the latter, it should be easy to pick sides in this debate, right? Again, it's not that simple since law enforcement, oddly enough, finds itself paired up with the bad guys when you look at the issue this way.

(19.5) The politics of cryptography

In the days when the US was the prime supplier of the world's strong crypto, State Department export regulations had a substantial effect on the availability of this technology on a global level. However, those days have long since passed. Now strong crypto is available from many countries.

This fact was underscored in 1997 when NIST (National Institute of Standards and Technology) put out a request for algorithms to replace the ageing DES standard. Nominations for the **Advanced Encryption Standard** (**AES**), this next-generation algorithm, came from all over the world. In fact, 10 of the 15 candidates were submitted from outside the US. If there remained any lingering doubts over whether the US was still the world's sole source of strong cryptographic technology, they had now disappeared.

American businesses took note of this trend and argued that their competitiveness was being hampered by export restrictions. Companies around the world with legitimate requirements for strong crypto were being forced to choose suppliers from other countries. Civil rights groups pointed to events such as RSA's DES Challenge and argued that the current definition of strong crypto no longer applied. Borrowing from a well-known slogan used by the US gun-rights lobby, they said that 'if you outlaw strong crypto, only outlaws will have strong crypto'. Their argument was that criminals are, after all, lawbreakers in the first place. They will simply steal what they want. They can obtain black market commercial software or just download similar tools off the Internet. The only group that was ultimately hampered by crypto restrictions were the *legitimate* users.

The US, however, is far from being the only country that has been slow to realize this. While the American government has been focused on controlling crypto through export regulations, other countries, such as France, have focused on the import side of the equation. While it is perfectly legal to use strong crypto within the US, this is forbidden in some countries which control crypto not only at the borders but within their territories as well.

It seems inevitable, at least in the US, that such regulations are destined to find themselves in the history books rather than the law books. In fact, various proposals to relax US export regulations have slowly but surely been working their way to the forefront. At the time of this writing, no one really knows how long crypto restrictions of one sort or another will remain in effect around the world, but efforts such as the DES Challenge have helped bring focus to the matter by effectively demonstrating what hackers already knew … yesterday's strong crypto is today's weak crypto.

19.6 Securing the information highway for e-business

How can you defend against the constant deterioration of crypto strength? Efforts to repeal Moore's Law, which holds that processing power doubles about every 18–24 months (depending upon which version you are referring to), will surely fail. The key is constantly to re-evaluate the security of encrypted transmissions and data files. Information that was stored a few years ago might have been safe at the time, but may need to be re-encrypted using newer algorithms or longer keys in order to remain safe from wandering eyes.

The Roman Empire achieved previously unimagined heights in commerce. Facilitating that success was the most extensive system of roads that western civilization had ever seen. The pace of business quickened as far-flung merchants could now transport their goods to places they had only dreamt about.

The Internet has done, and is still doing, the same thing for e-commerce. However, in order for these modern dreams to be realized, the 'e-roads' must be safe enough to convince merchants that it's worth taking the risk. Strong crypto, digital signatures, digital certificates, and the like, are the critical components of this electronic infrastructure because they can help make the environment safe for business. What may have sounded exotic when first introduced can now become commonplace as companies move more and more toward the Internet as a forum to meet and greet customers, interface with suppliers, and collaborate with partners.

chapter **20**

Hackers don't want you to know that ... *the back door is open*

'If you entrench yourself behind strong fortifications, you compel the enemy to seek a solution elsewhere.'

Carl von Clausewitz, Prussian military theorist (1780–1831)

Chapter summary

- The dangers of a false sense of security
  - the Maginot Line example
- How network access points can become hacker entry points
- War diallers
  - what they are
  - how they work
  - how hackers use them to break in
  - how you can use them to detect vulnerabilities

20.1 Lessons from the battlefront

Years before the start of World War II, France knew that it lacked sufficient protection on its eastern border. In an attempt to address this deficiency, the French built an unparalleled system of defences consisting of a series of fortified, interconnected tunnels where soldiers lived, trained and fought. Prevailing wisdom reckoned that the worst-case scenario would be that invaders could at the very least be held back long enough to provide enough time to launch effective countermeasures. This 'Great Wall of France' became known as the *Maginot Line* named after André Maginot, French Minister of Veteran Affairs. This seemingly impenetrable line of defence served as a source of great national pride until ...

... until the Germans decided to outflank the stationary fortress by invading through the Benelux region to the north. In other words, they simply walked around it. Suddenly it didn't matter how strong the front line was if it was easy enough to sidestep the whole thing.

In one sense the Maginot Line didn't fail its creators at all. It did, after all, successfully fend off multiple attacks. For all intents and purposes, the Maginot Line did precisely what it was designed to do and did it well. On the other hand, however, the 'Maginot mentality' and the false sense of security it fostered contributed significantly to the fall of France to hostile invaders.

20.2 High-tech defences

Smart companies that connect their networks to other networks use firewalls to limit who can get in, who can get out, and what each is able to do. It's like putting a security guard at the main entrance. If you have anything in your company that you think others might want to steal, it's a prudent measure to take.

While many networks have the technological equivalent to a battalion of armed guards controlling access to the front door, the back door is often left unattended. Upper management might be impressed by the troops at the main entrance but will quickly come looking for explanations when they realize that 13-year-olds are able to come and go as they please. Examples of modern day Maginot Lines are all too prevalent in the world of IT security.

20.3 The door swings both ways

Chances are, if you can get out, they can get in. That's the unfortunate reality for too many networks. Your people need to connect to the Internet for a multitude of valid reasons. It may be to do research on a new technology, communicate with business partners, or even to find out what your competitors are up to. As we've discussed in Chapter 8, firewalls alone are not enough. In fact, hackers can side-step even the strongest firewall by simply using a back door.

One such back door involves exploiting undefended modems. These devices may exist for any number of reasons, such as:

- Users that can't get to the Internet through the corporate network may get what they need by dialling out through a modem installed on their PC.

- LAN administrators may resolve outages on remote servers by dialling into a modem connected to the machine. This technique is especially helpful during off-shift hours as it minimizes down time by eliminating the need to travel to the office in order to fix the problem.

- Employees who want to avoid lining up at the fax machine and having to sort through a pile of paper to find the one page they care about may choose to receive their faxes right at their desks. An auto-answer modem connected to a desktop PC running widely available fax software can do the job quite nicely.

Such uses may or may not be authorized. Some companies have made the mistake of believing that since they outlawed desktop modems, they have effectively closed this back door. This is the sort of 'Maginot mentality' that makes the hacker's job easy. They know that making rules and actually enforcing them are two completely different matters. It may make perfectly good sense to forbid alternative network access points, but simply putting it in the corporate security policy doesn't necessarily make it so.

(20.4) Dialling for dollars

The problem arises from the fact that hackers know that such modems exist. They also know that these devices, if not configured properly, can be used by insiders as a means to get out, but also by outsiders as a way to get in. But how do they find your modems in the first place? It's actually quite easy. So-called '**war diallers**', which take their name from the popular 1983 hacker movie *War Games* which introduced the technology to the general public, can automate the entire process. These programs can be instructed to dial up a long list of phone numbers one at a time and make a list of all the ones that are answered by a modem. After a few hours of repetitive dialling, hackers will often have a significant list of numbers to use as a starting point for subsequent attacks. Since large companies are frequently assigned an entire block of contiguous numbers, hackers can simply test all the lines within a predefined range in order to narrow their search to a list of likely candidates. All that's needed to get the first few numbers of the target range is a telephone book or an employee's business card.

If each phone in the office were to ring, one after another, and no one was on the other end of the line, someone might figure out that something is up. Therefore, an attack like this is typically run at night in order to avoid suspicion. The process can be kicked off in the evening and the hacker awakes the next morning with a list of potential attack points.

20.5 Switching off

Crude war diallers run through the list of candidates sequentially and can, therefore, be detected by a smart phone switch within the company. The 'signature' of such an attack is unmistakable. What other legitimate reason could there be for having all the numbers within a given range called one after the other within such a short period of time?

Smarter war diallers elude detection by calling target numbers in random order. Even these attacks can be detected by certain phone switches as they may be able to recognize the fact that a large number of incoming calls are emanating from the same phone number or group of numbers.

However, if hackers are patient enough, they can space out their war dialling attacks so that only a few calls are made each night. It might take longer, but the information they get back is just as valuable. Since hackers rarely have to work to a deadline, time is on their side. This means that their patience is often rewarded.

20.6 Locking the back door

So, how can you defend against this sort of flanking manoeuvre? There are no sure-fire solutions, but a combination of approaches can help mitigate the risks of this sort of back-door attack.

20.6.1 Policy

As with all things related to security, the solution begins with a well-understood policy. It might sound good to simply outlaw all desktop modems in the company, but such a draconian approach may simply be ignored. Educating end users as to the potential risks to which they expose the company (and themselves) with modems inside the firewall is the key.

They need to understand that if their workstation is connected to both the internal network and an external network at the same time, they could unintentionally open a gaping hole in the defence system. Their machine could be effectively transformed into a router at the hacker's disposal. They need to know that fax software may, by default, put a modem into auto-answer mode during installation instead of letting the user turn this on and off as needed.

20.6.2   War dialler detection

As previously mentioned, some telephone switches have the ability to recognize incoming call patterns and alert you to possible intrusion. Also, analysis of call records could expose abnormal patterns of late-night calls and hang-ups. This would need to be automated and run frequently in order to be effective.

20.6.3   Find the modems

Finding all the modems inside your network can be like looking for a needle in a thousand haystacks. Physical auditing used to be fairly effective when all modems were external devices. Now, however, internal modems have become commonplace and are difficult to spot with a cursory glance.

A better technique involves auditing phone lines. Many companies have switched to digital phone systems for voice communications. However, most PC modems and fax machines are designed for analog lines. This means that anywhere you have analog lines, you have potential entry points. Of course, many of these will be necessary, but some may not. It should be noted, though, that with the help of converters, even analog modems can be used over digital lines so this method is not foolproof, but it is generally effective.

20.6.4   Playing hacker

As has been pointed out previously in Chapter 15, you can use the same tools that hackers use to launch a benign attack on your own network. By running a war dialler against your own lines you may discover unauthorized modems before the hacker does.

If you do this, though, *exercise great caution*. Make sure that you have permission from all the right people within the company (and the phone company, if external lines will be used) so that you aren't mistaken for a real hacker intent on doing damage. Also, be very careful in configuring the war dialler. Mistakes could result in an unintentional attack on innocent bystanders who have no association with your company and, therefore, don't share your interest in IT security. They aren't likely to appreciate a series of accidental late-night wake-up calls due to *your* software malfunction. If you make a mistake on the list of phone numbers to be tried, you may have to explain your blunder to the police.

Securing the back doors may, in fact, be harder than locking the front door. You know where the front doors are. Someone planned where they would go and who should be allowed to go through them. On the other hand, back doors can be opened up in an instant and their ill effects may last for years. If you don't know where they all are, you can't possibly defend against attacks on them.

Hackers know this. They figure that most IT organizations are far too busy fighting fires elsewhere to be worried about a solitary modem hidden away in an empty office deep within the recesses of the corporate campus. This knowledge allows them to break in. Now that you know it, they may no longer be able to do so. (Of course, this assumes that you act on that knowledge as well.)

chapter 21

Hackers don't want you to know that ... *there's no such thing as a harmless attack*

Chapter summary

- The real cost of hacking
- The threat of electronic vandalism
  - the scope of the threat
  - past examples of hacked Web sites
- Why almost any system can be valuable to a hacker
- How vulnerable systems can be used as stepping stones to further an attack
- The advantage of intrusion detection systems
- The importance of a community effort to thwart Internet-based attacks

OK, so maybe some attacks really don't do any damage and the title of this chapter is an exaggeration. The point, though, is that it is far more accurate than most people realize. The hacker's greatest advantage is your ignorance. If you think that just because no classified data was compromised and you didn't hear from angry end users or customers complaining that the system was down then nothing of consequence happened, you could be in for a rude awakening

21.1   E-graffiti

Corporate Web sites have become a favourite target for hackers. Electronically defacing the public image of a large company by marking up their home page is the high-tech equivalent to graffiti. This new form of vandalism, 'e-graffiti', may require more expertise than its spray can counterpart, but its result is no less ignoble.

The opportunity for one delinquent soul to effectively plant his or her flag of conquest on top of a large and powerful enterprise is worth almost any cost to a hacker. In outsmarting a bastion of industry, hackers figure that they have shown themselves to be even more powerful than their victim. For someone lacking in self-esteem, the instant gratification from this reversal of fortunes is like crack cocaine for the ego – there's an immediate rush often followed just as swiftly by addiction. To have the world stand up and take notice of the actions of an otherwise unremarkable individual is sweet revenge for a lifelong underachiever. 'Who says I'm not important? I'm smarter than the corporate geniuses at a Fortune 500 company,' reasons the hacker.

Another reason this sort of attack is so popular is that it is far too easy to execute. Too many companies have assumed that since the machine hosting their Web site contained no classified business information and was not needed for any mission-critical processing, then even if a hacker did get in no real damage could occur.

This reasoning, however, is fatally flawed because it fails to take into account that the corporate home page represents something far more valuable – the company's reputation. In industries where trust is critical, such as banking and finance, anything that erodes customer confidence spells disaster. when they visit your Web page for the first time, You're asking them to trust you with their hard-earned cash because you can keep it safe ... but you can't even protect your own systems? As the saying goes, 'you never get a second chance to make a first impression'. The e-business corollary might be 'you're not going to drum up new business with a vandalized Web page'.

How likely is it that potential customers would choose to open an account with your bank if ... they are visually accosted by a parade of profanity and pornography?

Once you realize that your company's good name is a critical business asset too, you'll be less likely to leave it hanging out to dry on an unprotected (or under-protected) Web site. The US's Department of Justice learned this lesson too late. Hackers broke into their Web page and changed its title to the 'United States Department of Injustice'. And they didn't stop there. Among other things, they added a picture of George Washington saying 'Move my grave to a free country! This rolling is making me an insomniac!' and added a Nazi swastika for extra effect (Figure 21.1). They, along with countless other government agencies and private businesses, now know all too well what it's like to be a victim of a hacked Web page.

FIGURE 21.1   The Department of Injustice? Another in a long line of hacked Web sites

If you're tempted to conclude that such vandalism is (1) unlikely or (2) unimportant, think again. The 'Department of Injustice' example was selected here because it was one of the *least* offensive examples of Web site hacking. If you'd like to see just how bad it can get, try some of the following Web sites, which archive the results of past attacks, but check your moral sensitivities at the door as some contain blatantly offensive material:

● www.2600.com/hacked_pages/

● www.onething.com/archive/

● www.flashback.se/hack/

● www.freespeech.org/resistance/index.htm

The sheer volume of hacked Web pages on just these few selected archives should be enough to give you a sense of the massive scale of this problem. To make matters worse, anyone can become a target. Even UNICEF, whose mission is to care for the basic needs of children around the world, was hit in January 1998. Why attack UNICEF? The hackers knew that they couldn't steal anything of value. Surely, they didn't harbour some sort of grudge against an organization working to help needy children. Why did they do it? Because they could. Why should you be concerned about protecting your corporate Web site? Because hackers don't need any additional motivation to attack you as well.

21.2   But it's only ...

What about more obscure systems on the Net? Let's say that you have a system that serves as an FTP site for business partners that need access to schematic diagrams for the products you produce. This site contains no classified data (schematics are shipped with every product anyway), runs no mission-critical business processes (no late-night wake-up calls if it happens to crash), and doesn't host the corporate Web site. Surely, a system such as this would be of no interest to hackers, right? And even if they did break in, no real damage is done anyway. Wrong on both counts.

If you want to catch a hacker (or merely protect yourself from them), you have to think like one. Again, the vast majority of hackers aren't driven by monetary motivations. There doesn't have to be any cash on the line to make the exercise worthwhile. Their pay-off may simply come from making your life miserable. Or they may be moved by sheer curiosity – 'I wonder if I can get into that place and if I do, what else is in there?' The part about making your life miserable may just be an added bonus.

Whatever the reason, penetration into your systems puts the entire enterprise at risk. Too few people realize this and pay the price for their negligence.

(21.3) We've only just begun ... to hack

Whatever hackers learn from breaking into one system may prove useful in subsequent attacks. One example might be that if they can crack a password on a 'dispensable' (or non-critical) system, they may also have found the key that unlocks far more valuable systems. As we discussed in Chapter 11, good passwords are hard to remember and bad ones are easily guessed. This means that even if your users pick good passwords, they will probably try to reuse them on other systems because it is too hard to remember other equally good passwords.

If the cracked password happens to belong to a system administrator, the hacker may have just uncovered the 'keys to the kingdom'. He or she may now be able to logon to privileged accounts on essential systems and execute a truly damaging attack. Since administration patterns used throughout the enterprise may be deduced from a single system, the hacker may learn other aspects of how your systems are vulnerable by noting the way the 'dispensable system' is configured.

In addition to knowledge gained, such an attack provides the hacker with a 'base camp' from which to launch further exploration. This base camp might be confined to the outer perimeter of your network, but it may provide additional entry points into the inner portions as well. For instance, if this system is outside the firewall it may, nevertheless, have a port (or ports) that are allowed to pass through the firewall in order to allow for system administration and file updates. The hacker may, then, be able to squeeze through this crack and subvert the first (and for some, the only) line of defence. To internal systems the attack will appear to originate from a well-known (and, presumably, trusted) system. Secondary defence mechanisms may let down their guard, making subsequent attacks even easier.

Elite hackers know how to use a series of 'stepping stones' in order to penetrate deeper and deeper into a network. They may also use these intermediate systems as a means to obscure the true origins of their attack. If enough steps are used along the way and tracks sufficiently covered, any attempt to trace the attack will be futile. In essence, the hacker can use your own systems against you.

Worse still is the possibility that hackers may use your systems as a base camp for attacking another organization's network. Your systems may serve as accomplices in further attacks and you might be held liable for the damages. If hackers are good enough, they won't be found. However, the remaining evidence could form a trail that leads right to your doorstep. Even if you know it wasn't one of your employees who initiated the attack, your company's resources will be diverted as you further the investigation in an attempt to prove your innocence. You may also be charged with negligence for allowing your systems to be used improperly. Defending against such a charge will be costly. Even in the best-case scenario you waste a lot of money getting to the bottom of things and in the worst case, you lose even more money in legal judgements against the company for failure to perform due diligence.

Law enforcement officials may even confiscate your equipment as evidence to add to the misery. No matter how you look at it, you lose and the hacker gets off scot-free.

21.4 Winning by losing

If, as the saying goes, we can actually learn more from our failures than our successes, hackers' apparent failures should probably be viewed from a longer-term perspective. With each failed attack they can potentially learn things that will prove valuable later down the road. Thomas Edison, the great inventor who brought us the light bulb, viewed his numerous 'failures' in this way. He said, 'Why, I have not failed. I've just found 10,000 ways that won't work.'

The same is true for ingenious and persistent hackers. With each failure they learn what will not work and, therefore, move one step closer to what will. Much like the offline attacks discussed earlier in Section 11.5, when an elegant break-in tactic won't work, brute force will often suffice. Vulnerability scanning tools discussed in Section 16.1, for example, can be used to 'case the joint' before actually entering. Once inside, sophisticated hackers will size up the situation by gathering as much relevant information as they can. Finally, by covering their tracks on the way out, they are careful not to burn any bridges that might prevent them from getting back in again in the future when the real damage is to be done.

This is why it is important to be aware not only of successful break-ins, but unsuccessful ones as well. Analysis of failed attempts may reveal a pattern which can be used to:

- build a better defence against future attacks;

- determine the source of the attacks and, presumably, put an end to them (at least for the moment);

- build up enough forensic evidence for subsequent prosecution (remember, hacked systems are, in fact, 'crime scenes').

This is why intrusion detection systems (IDSs) can be so important. These tools listen out for any suspicious activity and can alert you to an attack in progress, which can be far more useful than finding out only after all the damage has been done. It is even possible to apply some of the more sophisticated data-mining techniques to the voluminous logs generated by multiple intrusion detection monitors across the enterprise. By establishing a baseline of normal activities, unusual trends could be identified through offline analysis.

IDSs are limited, however. Most are designed to look only for certain attack 'signatures' or patterns. Smart hackers know this and can vary their approach in order to avoid tripping the alarm sensors. Intrusion detectors should be viewed, along with other security tools, as just a part of an overall system of defence. Too much reliance on them (or any other single technology, for that matter) can lead to regrets further down the road.

21.5 'Unimportant' systems

After receiving a rash of Denial-of-Service attacks during the time of the much anticipated Y2K rollover, CERT issued an advisory[1] which summarized the issue of Internet security this way:

Security on the Internet is a *community effort*. Your security depends on the overall security of the Internet in general. Likewise, your security (or lack thereof) can cause serious harm to others, even if intruders do no direct harm to your organization. Similarly, machines that are not part of centralized computing facilities and that may be managed by novice or part-time system administrators or may be unmanaged, can be used by intruders to inflict harm on others, even if those systems have no strategic value to your organization. [emphasis mine]

CERT Advisory, 2000

1. CERT Advisory, 'CA-2000-01 Denial-of-Service Developments', January 2000, www.cert.org.

The point is that even seemingly innocuous attacks can be lethal. What is learned in a seemingly benign attack can be leveraged later to produce disastrous results. A system that may not seem particularly valuable to you may be priceless to hackers, who can use it to establish a foothold within your network. Once inside, they can launch further attacks against your systems and hide their tracks more effectively. If you aren't careful you may even become the unwitting accomplice to attacks on other organizations. Hackers know this already. The critical importance of 'unimportant' systems is a secret they'd rather you not know.

chapter 22

Hackers don't want you to know that ... *information is your best defence*

Information is the most valuable commodity on earth. It's more valuable than time, money, or even power because with it you can get the other three. Knowing how to best use your time – what is productive and what isn't – effectively creates more time because less is wasted. Knowing what the market will do and when it will do it creates money for investors. Knowing how to 'win friends and influence people' (or even how to make enemies that fear you) generates political power. The key to it all is information. It is this precious resource that separates the haves from the have-nots.

Social scientists have referred to the times that we live in as 'the Information Age', the reason being that at no time in history has information been such a critical element to society. Storage technologies allow us to store vastly more information in a smaller space than could have ever been dreamt of by our ancestors. Networking

Information is the raw
material that fuels the engines
of modern commerce.

technologies transport information from even the remotest areas of the planet at the speed of light, making them accessible to anyone at the touch of a button. Computing technologies can reduce overwhelming quantities of data into a manageable form that can guide our decisions. Information is the raw material that fuels the engines of modern commerce just as coal once did during the Industrial Age.

Given this, it's not at all hard to understand why information is so valuable. In the Information Age the one who controls the information is the one with the power. Edward Bulwer-Lytton wrote that 'the pen is mightier than the sword'. A modern restatement of this famous quotation might be that 'the keyboard is mightier than the gun'. Of course, guns can shoot through keyboards just as swords can slice through pens, but the point of each of these sayings is that the one who harnesses information is the *real* power broker.

22.1 The hacker's prize

Hackers know all this intuitively, whether they realize it or not. They may be on a quest for power, but they know that information is the source. That's one reason why attacks on information technology are so appealing. It's not that the hacker necessarily wants access to the proverbial red switch that controls the nuclear arsenal or is dedicated to getting rich quick (although there certainly are some who are motivated by these goals). It's that with information comes power. With power comes respect (or fear), and nothing feeds an emaciated ego like being held in high regard by people whose opinions you value.

Within the hacker community respect is gained through knowledge. The one that figures out the latest and greatest hack is revered for his or her ingenuity. If this information is used to attack a highly visible target then the entire world must take notice.

For hackers, information is what they crave. With more of it they can dream up yet more ways to attack. The snowball effect of information is, to hackers, what a high soaring stock is to a Wall Street trader. In both cases it is the pursuit of this elusive prize that gets the blood pumping.

22.2 Your best defence

Information in the proper hands can make the world a better place to live. Information gained through scientific research has freed the world of one of its most heinous killers – smallpox. However, information in the wrong hands has wrought excruciating pain upon society. That's how its dualistic nature works. It's a double-edged sword.

The problem is that the hacker's edge is usually a lot sharper than yours. That's why information, put to proper use, is also your best defence against attacks. Knowing what hackers know takes away their most valuable advantage. With the necessary information you can 'batten down the hatches' of the corporate IT infrastructure.

Of course, this all begins with an informed IT support staff. Too often the defenders of IT systems are so busy with the day-to-day operation of the infrastructure that they fail to realize that they are at war. Information warfare is being waged all around them but, through stealth, the enemy remains elusive. In many cases the damage goes unnoticed because either no one is looking for it or the people who are looking don't know how to recognize it.

> Information security should not only be the concern of the person installing the firewall. It must also be a fundamental consideration of *every* aspect of application, system, and network design.

Information security should not only be the concern of the person installing the firewall. It must also be a fundamental consideration of *every* aspect of application, system, and network design. The IT help desk must be sufficiently armed with the information they will need to recognize what should be passed along to the technical support experts for further examination. Corporate management needs an appreciation for the risks and benefits that result from doing business in an increasingly connected world.

Information security needs to be seen not as a *cost centre* but as a key *enabler* for commercial expansion. Everyone needs to understand that companies that are able to exploit a secure infrastructure effectively will be the ones that succeed in the Information Age. Information security should, in fact, be leveraged as an *asset* that provides a competitive advantage in the dog-eat-dog world of modern business. When it is done properly IT security *enables* e-business rather than *inhibits* it.

22.3 Information for the masses

IT security is not just the job of the support staff, either. As discussed earlier in Chapter 10, even the greatest state-of-the-art security technology can be rendered worthless by risky end-user behaviour. Trained support personnel comprise only a tiny fraction of the total number of people that can make a system safe or vulnerable. An informed and properly motivated end-user community is ultimately your greatest weapon in the battle to protect the enterprise.

Information such as what should and should not be done must be spelled out clearly and concisely in the corporate security policy. Too many policies are filled to overflowing with rules, but do little to actually *inform*. A collection of edicts from the security gurus at headquarters is of little value if end users don't understand the underlying principles that should be guiding their behaviour.

Another piece of critical information for users is whom they should contact when they suspect a breach has occurred. Incident reporting and resolution procedures need to run like a well-oiled machine. Attacks must be identified, isolated and repelled as fast as possible because the alternative is potentially devastating.

(22.4) Calling in reinforcements

Unless your company is willing to dedicate a significant portion of its IT staff to the job of studying all the latest hacking techniques and how to defend against them, it is wise to look outside the enterprise for help. IT security consultants can help with everything from front-end tasks such as infrastructure design and policy definition to follow-up jobs like firewall implementation and ongoing monitoring.

One popular service is the so-called **ethical hacking** engagement where you hire a consultant to try to break into your network. If they are able to penetrate (and they usually are), they then tell you how they got in so that you can plug the holes. Be careful whom you choose to do this work, though. Some of these consultants are 'reformed hackers' who have decided to make a living at what they used to do for the kicks. If someone was willing to break the law and risk the livelihood of thousands of corporate workers in the past, how do you know they won't do it again? There are plenty of honest people with enough technical savvy to pull off an ethical hack. There's no need to make a deal with the devil in order to ensure security.

An ethical hacking exercise can be enormously informative, but the results should be understood for what they are. Any conclusions drawn are likely only to be valid at that particular point in time. A few weeks, months, or years later, your environment will have changed and new vulnerabilities will probably have been introduced.

This means that ongoing vigilance must follow up any ethical hacking activities. One nice resource to have at your disposal is an *emergency response team* which is ready, willing and able to provide assistance when a security breach occurs. This can either be staffed by people from your own organization or by an outside service provider or a combination of the two. The advantage of using a service provider to do this job is that has by specialists who respond to attacks every day of the week – unlike your staff who, hopefully, only run into serious incidents on an infrequent basis. The likelihood is that any attack that you experience is one that they have already seen on multiple occasions. They have already gone through the learning curve and can direct your efforts with the precision that is needed for quick resolution.

(22.5) Winning the war

You might think it's an exaggeration to suggest that IT staffers work in a battle zone. Hackers certainly want you to think this way. It's far easier to sneak up on an unsuspecting victim than it is to launch a full frontal attack against the well-deployed resources of a multimillion dollar enterprise.

Marshalling the forces of the IT staff, end-user community and outside consultants can help bring the odds back in favour of legitimate businesses. Knowing why, how and when hackers do what they do puts the power back in the hands of the good guys. Hackers hope you don't realize this because it makes their job harder ... which is precisely the reason for this book!

chapter 23

Hackers don't want you to know that ... *the future of hacking is bright*

When in doubt, predict that the present trend will continue.

Merkin's Maxim

What about the future? Wouldn't it be great if you had a crystal ball that allowed you to peer into the future and know what would happen next? Sure, the element of surprise would be removed, but when you're concerned with IT security, the best surprise is no surprise.

Unfortunately, no one can tell for sure what will happen next (although there never seems to be a shortage of people who claim that they can). The prognosticator's proposition would seem to be that one should make as many predictions as possible. After all, no one will remember the millions of incorrect ones that don't come true and if you do get lucky a few times you'll look like a genius. Given this, and in the spirit of Merkin's Maxim, the following predictions on the future of hacking are submitted for your consideration and/or amusement ...

(23.1) I see more IT in your future ...

Our dependence upon information technology will continue to increase dramatically. The reason this is significant within the context of a discussion on IT security is that it points to the undeniable conclusion that the stakes are only going to get higher.

One might be tempted to believe that as the technology gets better and better, the risks associated with it would diminish. After all, the first bridge ever built was surely not as safe as subsequent ones that benefited from advances in civil engineering, better construction techniques, stronger and more reliable building materials, and years of learning from past mistakes. Why shouldn't IT security continue to improve as we learn more, test more, and invent more ways to thwart attacks?

The fact is that we're shooting at a moving target. Unlike the bridge whose basic function has not changed dramatically over time, IT infrastructures are constantly in a state of flux. They are always attempting to cope with new demands that could never have been envisioned when they were first designed. We won't one day expect the bridge that was designed to enable us to cross a small stream to transport us into outer space. However, we do expect analogous improvements from our IT infrastructures.

In its earlier days, the Internet was used largely as a means to exchange information among academics and researchers. Research findings could be published and disseminated quickly and cheaply to a fairly limited, albeit geographically dispersed, audience.

Then along came graphical Web browsers. As the general public began to get wind of what they were missing out on, the Internet was changed. Almost overnight it went from being a tool for the educational elite (and a few hobbyists) to a venue that quite literally offered something for everyone. Affordable, ubiquitous Net access followed and the flood gates were officially opened.

Businesses woke up to the fact that tens of millions of Web surfers could, with the proper coaxing, turn into tens of millions of customers and, thus, the era of e-commerce was born. Businesses also realized that more and more of their partners were installing Internet connections. They reasoned that if business could be transacted with consumers, it could also be performed with other businesses. As security technologies emerged to address the requirements of doing private business over a public medium, *extranets* were born.

At the time of this writing, there is nothing to suggest that these trends won't continue. Businesses will continue to rely more and more on the Internet as a means to communicate with customers and partners alike. They will become even more dependent on IT security to ensure that the environment is safe for e-business. What once was a new, experimental sales channel is becoming a primary means of doing business for some companies. What used to be an alternative means of collaborating with partners is becoming a critical link for day-to-day operations.

> Businesses will continue to rely more and more on the Internet as a means to communicate with customers and partners alike.

What once was a small capillary in an outer extremity is becoming a major artery through which the very life blood of business flows. Any interruption in the flow of information is not unlike the medical emergency that results from a heart attack. Hackers are not unlike the artery-clogging plaque which precipitates the emergency.

23.2 Upping the ante

Not only will businesses depend more upon Internet technologies, both within their own internal networks as well as outside, but individuals will be more vulnerable. It may seem bad now, but people will one day long for the good old days when the worst thing you might lose to a hacker on the Internet was your credit card number.

More and more information will be converted from hard-copy form to computerized databases that allow for sophisticated analysis and data mining. In an effort to increase efficiency and stay ahead of competitors by spotting new trends in customer buying behaviours, information about you will become more accessible to both legitimate users and hackers alike. A security breach on one of these systems could be devastating.

We were granted a sneak preview in April 1997 when the US's Social Security Administration attempted to improve customer service by offering benefits information via the Internet to the citizens it serves. By simply providing your Social Security number, date of birth, where you were born, and your mother's maiden name, the agency would send back to you via email your own Personal Earnings and Benefits Estimate Statement. It was a great idea ... in principle. Who could argue with the goal of making government more responsive to its taxpayers?

In this case, lots of people could. The reason was that not only could you access this valuable personal information quickly and easily, but so could potentially a few thousand other people ... get access to *your* personal information, that is. None of the information required for identity verification was any great secret. Social Security numbers are often used as ID numbers for all sorts of unrelated purposes such as health care and student records. Any of these records could be vulnerable in either hard-copy or soft-copy form depending upon how lax the security procedures were for handling storage and disposal of this information at each organization entrusted with its care. Your mother's maiden name and birth information is becoming increasingly more available through all sorts of genealogy resources on the Web as well. In addition, Web-based background-checking services are becoming commonplace. In other words, knowing this information doesn't constitute proof that you are the person to whom this information refers.

The Social Security Administration learned the hard way just how concerned the public was over such easy access to personal information when the public uproar reached deafening proportions. Had they been a for-profit business, they might never have recovered from the public relations damage of this *single* ill-fated decision. However, since they are a government agency with no competitors, they were able to ride out the PR storm once they admitted (sort of) their error and took down the service.

The problem, of course, with making personal information public is more than just the visceral reaction of individuals to being violated in some unquantifiable way. The fact (as was discussed in Chapter 22) is that in the Information Age we live in, information is the most valuable commodity there is. With the right information you can steal more than someone's money – you can steal their identity.

Identity theft is a threat that isn't going to go away. In fact, it's becoming easier and easier to get away with. Increased dependence upon technology such as digital certificates, passwords, and the like, mean that an imposter can essentially become you in cyberspace, if they steal the right stuff.

More and more information about you is appearing on the Web whether you know it or not. For example, your purchasing habits are being tracked by the merchants you do business with. What legitimate companies do with this information is cause enough for concern, but an additional, often overlooked threat exists in the fact that hackers might also gain access to this information by breaking into the systems that host the databases.

Also at issue are the efforts by government agencies to modernize and be more responsive to the citizens they serve by moving more and more of their public records to the Web. Since these records are, by law, public information, the thought is that there really is nothing new in this. Privacy advocates, however, argue that the increased ease of access makes misuse of this information more likely. They point to the disparity in the effort that an identity thief would have to put forth by physically going to the various agency offices during normal working hours, poring over the mounds of records, and making copies of the pieces they want versus the minimal effort required to do a Web search from the comfort of their own homes.

The ramifications of identity theft are serious because you could be held liable for illegal actions that are committed by an imposter using your identity. Your credit rating could be trashed in a matter of days, making it impossible for you to apply for a mortgage, a car loan, or even a job. It could take years to sort it all out and, by then, the personal cost to you in dollars and cents could be trivial compared to the emotional anguish you've suffered and the damage to your reputation.

> Identity theft is serious because you could be held liable for illegal actions that are committed by an imposter using your identity.

There's a moral in all of this for both consumers and businesses alike, since both can be damaged significantly. Either could stand to lose something that is priceless – their own good name. In addition, if a business is found to be involved, even unwittingly, in such a crime, the legal consequences of their negligence could be staggering.

23.3   Naked on the Net

Accessing the Internet with its wealth of graphical images, active content, and streaming multimedia through a traditional analog modem, running at something less than 56,000 bits per second, can feel like trying to drink a wonderfully thick milkshake by sucking on the end of a 50-foot soda straw. If the anticipation alone isn't enough to kill you, the red face and lack of oxygen will. This is, of course, why cable television providers and phone companies have responded with high-speed broadband access solutions. By effectively widening the diameter of the straw to something on the order of half a foot and lopping off about 48 feet in length, that shake that seemed so elusive before can now flow like a veritable Niagara Falls.

At the time of writing, high-speed cable modem and DSL (Digital Subscriber Line) services are just beginning to make their way into the mainstream. The future of fast, affordable bandwidth (i.e. network speed, capacity) looks very bright indeed. However, the future of hacking appears equally luminous. Part of the reason is that along with the greater throughput that these options offer comes the prospect of an 'always connected' link.

Not having to endure the tedium of squawks and whistles while waiting for a modem to dial up an ISP represents a tremendous improvement in accessibility and convenience for 'Netizens'. But this same feature brings along with it the baggage of a static (or reasonably static) IP address for connected systems. Instead of being assigned a different address, selected from a pool of currently available numbers, each time you dial in, you can set up a more permanent residence on the Net. 'What's so bad about that?' one might reasonably ask. 'With a fixed, unchanging address I could even run a Web server on my own machine, instead of having to pay a hosting service or endure the endless stream of ads that accompany "free" web pages – something I could never do when new addresses were doled out with each connection.'

In fact, the advantages of static addressing for the end user are substantial. Hackers know, however, that the move from dynamically assigned addresses to fixed ones transforms end-user workstations from moving targets into sitting ducks. Instead of popping up for a few minutes and then diving for cover, as is the case with dial-up services, 'always connected' users stand motionless like a row of bulls' eyes in a firing range. The fact that these machines don't often change addresses and stay online even into the early hours of the morning (prime hacking time) makes them excellent targets.

The eventual ubiquity of high-speed service only compounds the problem. As availability and affordability increase, so will the number of homes taking advantage of this capability. Anyone from telecommuters to SOHO (Small Office, Home Office) workers to typical home users will want to get on board. The problem is that many of these systems will be sorely under-protected. Most of these users have never even heard of firewalls, much less know that they need one. The fact that their neighbours sharing the same 'last mile' of the cable modem wiring infrastructure will be able to sniff their traffic (as described in Chapter 12), will be completely lost on them. They may not appreciate the risks that they are exposed to by not having updated antivirus software running on their systems.

Some may even argue that no hacker would even *want* to break into their systems because they have nothing of value stored on them – and they would be dead wrong. They don't realize that hackers don't have to profit monetarily from their attacks to be sufficiently motivated to launch them (as discussed in Section 3.3). They can't appreciate the fact that just being able to break in and cause a disturbance is reward enough. The old childhood prank of ringing someone's doorbell and then running away certainly doesn't make the vandal richer but that doesn't keep him from doing it again and again and again if he's in the mood for mischief. While such shenanigans amount to little more than a nuisance, the stakes can be significantly higher.

A budding hacker needs a place to experiment and learn the tricks of the trade. An ample supply of unprotected hosts is just what the doctor ordered. In addition, experienced hackers know that one of the best ways to cover their tracks so that they can attack with impunity is first to establish a toehold on one system and then launch their attacks from that vantage point. This way, if their activities are detected, all the evidence will point to the intermediate system rather than theirs. A vast number of vulnerable systems that are always 'open for business' fits the bill perfectly. Finally, some DoS attacks involve using other systems as unwitting accomplices to amplify the effect. Unguarded hosts sitting 'naked on the Net' make the job especially easy for hackers. In particular, the distributed DoS scenario described in Section 16.7 are tailormade to exploit these systems.

As you can see, there is a downside to all this ubiquitous high-speed capability, but the advantages are simply too great to prevent it from being rolled out on a wide scale. The challenge will be for these service providers, PC equipment manufacturers, and IT security vendors to come up with a way to build the necessary protections into a simple, unobtrusive package. At the time of writing, personal firewalls (see Section 8.9) and Internet security appliances, which combine multiple networking functions such as firewalling, address management, and LAN connectivity into a single, small-footprint box, are just beginning to take the stage. The problem with these, though, is that while they may be simpler to use than their enterprise-level counterparts, they nevertheless still bring with them a level of complexity that most unsophisticated Internet users would consider baffling. If the default settings for these tools are optimized for security, they are likely to be seen as a hindrance by users who fail to appreciate the risks and, instead, only see that the Web-content they are trying to access is out of reach. If personal IT security components are configured to be more permissive, they won't get in the way very often, but they also won't provide a lot of protection either.

In fact, the only thing that is clear about this problem is that not nearly enough people are paying attention to it. Since no easy solutions exist, and since service providers are far more concerned with selling bandwidth than in dealing with the ramifications of how this capability might be used to victimize an unsuspecting public, the problem is bound to get worse before it gets better.

(23.4) Networks out of thin air

In the 1970s large mainframe computers dominated the scene. The 1980s belonged to the PC as a new 'smaller is better' mantra came to the fore. The 1990s ushered in the era of the Internet and information technology became an even more indispensable part of doing business in a 'wired world'.

In addition to greater bandwidth, the next decade is poised to offer connectivity in a distinctly 'unwired world'. The initial capabilities of the Internet and its related technologies have only whetted appetites for more connectedness. A Net-savvy marketplace will simply not be satisfied with the limited freedom that the leash of copper (or even fibre optic) cable permits. The demand for wireless connectivity will increase as prices for such services decrease. Cellphones and pagers have already hinted at the possibilities of a ubiquitous communications infrastructure, but more is on the way.

From the standpoint of security, though, this 'wireless revolution' won't necessarily represent an improvement. The fact that confidential communications are zipping around in the sky rather than confined to physical wiring means that the possibility of interception could increase if appropriate steps aren't taken. Cryptographic technology will surely play a role, but even these solutions have their limitations, as we have previously discussed. Also, these new mobile networking devices will be going places where traditional computing devices weren't able to go, including environments that present a plethora of new security risks. Add to the mix the compact size of these devices and it isn't hard to imagine how they might more easily be lost or stolen than their larger formed factor cousins, ranging in size from mainframes to laptop PCs. Without appropriate authentication mechanisms in place, these handy gizmos could become yet another entry point for hackers intent on doing harm.

(23.5) Cryptic solutions

Increased dependence upon information technology in all aspects of our lives and our business, along with the increased threat that accompanies it, makes a strong case for keeping secret things secret. This is where cryptography can help. What might have once been viewed as an obscure field, interesting only to a small group of mathematicians, will become an even more essential underlying component of e-business than it already is. In some respects crypto will become the 'killer enabler' of e-business.

New crypto algorithms will be developed. Print and broadcast media eager to scoop the competition with the latest invention will proclaim these discoveries as the next great technology to solve all our security problems. Most of these new approaches will eventually be discarded because with each will come a brand new set of potential weaknesses and ways to exploit them, but a few will stick around.

Seasoned cryptographers view new developments in their field with a critical eye. They know that the security of a cryptosystem takes a good deal of time to establish. They also know that even if an algorithm is ultimately accepted as being strong, implementation errors can cause its use in actual products to be tragically weak.

There is, however, reason for optimism in this area. More and more people are beginning to understand how vitally important this fundamental technology is to so many different aspects of e-business. As a result, improvements are coming to the forefront faster than ever before. While at the time of this writing the problem is far from solved, governments around the world are slowly but surely relaxing import/export regulations on strong crypto products. The effect of this liberalization can only fuel the flames of e-business growth and empower individuals in ways not yet imagined.

(23.6) Computers everywhere

Consider the following scenario involving **pervasive computing** ...

Imagine that you're driving in a 'smart' car a few years from now, and it develops an engine problem. Instead of flashing you a warning light, it sends a message directly to the manufacturer over a wireless connection. Their systems diagnose the problem and transmit a fix back to the electronics complex in your car. In fact, that fix is transmitted to all models everywhere in the world. All of this is good for drivers everywhere, but imagine the power of this for the car maker.

One Voice, © IBM Corp., 1999

Indeed, such a situation would be fantastic for both car makers and consumers – and, potentially, hackers as well. Why settle for creating traffic jams in cyberspace when you can do the real thing on roadways around the world? Hackers desperately seeking to explore and to prove their technical prowess would trip all over each other in a mad dash to become the first to successfully exploit such a system of 'smart' cars.

Personal Digital Assistants (PDAs) which began showing up en masse in the late 1990s are sure to increase in popularity. The ability to fit your address book, calendar, clock, email, notepad, pager, mobile phone, Web browser, etc., all in a single device that fits neatly in the palm of your hand is an incredible improvement over lugging around a massive briefcase filled to overflowing.

Through the eyes of a hacker this impressive little gadget looks like a new playground ripe for experimentation. At the time of this writing, security features in PDAs are extremely limited. No one seems much concerned with the possibility of picking up viruses from downloaded PDA applications. This situation is likely to change in the not too distant future as news of PDA hacking starts making headlines.

Things could really get interesting when you throw **wearable computers** into the mix.[1] The ongoing move toward miniaturization has opened the door to a new class of pervasive computers which could either be worn or even implanted inside a person. The form these devices take will surely vary, but the possibility, for instance, of providing better medical care through smarter pacemakers for people suffering from heart disease, embedded blood glucose monitors for diabetics, and so forth, could substantially improve the quantity as well as the quality of many lives.

Some even believe that **implantable computers** could be used for less pressing needs as well. In 1998 Professor Kevin Warwick of the University of Reading in England went so far as to have a commercially available silicon chip surgically implanted in his arm for a few days to prove that it could be done. According to a CNN report, Warwick 'envisions a world in which humans communicate directly with computers without extraneous input devices such as mice and keyboards, and a world in which humans network continually with computers'. During the experiment, he was 'effectively wired up to the computers in his building at the university. When he [walked] throughout the building, computers automatically [pulled] up preprogrammed Web pages such as his favourite sites, doors [opened], and computers [said] "Hello, Professor Warwick", or [told] him how many email messages he [had], (Sanchez-Klein, 1998). Sounds great ... until something goes wrong.

Imagine the case where you're in a meeting and suddenly the wrist of the guy sitting across the table from you begins to twitch. A nervous tic? No, the embedded computer in his watch has been infected by a virus. Since his wearable computer has a wireless network connection it has now instantaneously transmitted the virus to all the other people in the meeting, whose wrists now begin to shake as well. Is

---

1. An IBM pilot program for wearable computers is discussed in Franklin (1999).

this a scene from a TV sitcom or could it really happen? It seems unlikely at this point, but who really knows what it could mean when wearable or implantable computers get sick?

Microsoft CEO Bill Gates, when commenting on a demo of his company's Concept Home, which was designed to simplify domestic life through automation, said 'the home will be like a computer' (Crouch, 2000). After reading this book you should be quite familiar with one of the rather unfortunate aspects of computers – they are vulnerable to attack. A home that is like a computer may also be a home that is vulnerable to some of the same inherent weaknesses that computer systems and communication networks suffer from. A computer which, as Microsoft described it, will allow people to 'send information to their car from inside the house, as well as find out what's going on at home when they're out' and can control 'PCs, printers, entertainment centers, game consoles, telephones, televisions, kitchen appliances, alarm systems and sprinklers' represents a particularly enticing hacker target (Microsoft, 2000). The possibility of being able to remotely turn on and off a neighbour's sprinkler system, lights, stereo, etc. at will, while watching from a safe distance across the street, will just be too good for some to pass up. 'Bridging the gap between the home and the rest of the world' (Microsoft, 2000), as Microsoft put it, may, for some, amount to bridging the gap between the home and the hacker community.

Of course, none of this should be used as an excuse not to proceed with exciting innovations such as these. The increase in the standard of living that could result from pervasive computers is incalculable. The point is that as such developments come onto the scene, make sure that security issues have been fully considered and dealt with appropriately. Security must be built in right from the start. Retrofits and afterthoughts never work as well and usually cost much more. Putting off security issues till the end is analogous to adding a foundation *after* you've already built the house. Consider bringing in experienced security consultants at the beginning of the project to avoid this scenario. The simple fact is that if you don't address the vulnerabilities in your systems, you can be sure that hackers will – and you're not likely to appreciate the way they choose to address these deficiencies.

> Security must be built in right from the start.

(23.7) The NC's niche

The personal computing revolution of the mid to late 1980s effectively stormed the glass house data centre and released tightly controlled computing power to the masses. It took the elements of larger systems such as CPUs, disk storage, memory, etc., and made them available in desktop form.

One of the problems, from a security standpoint, of this advancement was that it failed to bring with it many of the same protections that had guarded the 'big iron'. Things such as strong user authentication procedures, controlled access, and physical security were often left behind in the 'personal computing revolution'.

The PC that initially promised cheap MIPS turned out to be riddled with hidden costs. Software distribution, installation and administration suddenly got much tougher. Effective problem determination and performance management seemed to be constantly out of reach. Security, in some cases, went completely out of the window. Sometimes it seemed as if the systems that weren't inexplicably disappearing due to loss and theft were being threatened by computer viruses. In both cases the risk of losing important business data was substantial.

After a decade of struggling to manage a client/server environment, the industry's pendulum began to swing back in the other direction. A completely centralized computing environment was relatively easy to secure and manage but lacked the flexibility required to respond to an ever-changing workplace. On the other hand a completely distributed computing environment bordered on chaos. Enter the network computer and its cousin, the so-called 'thin' client ...

A **network computer (NC)** relies on a centrally located server for its disk storage, which makes systems management a breeze as compared to dealing with disparate PCs. It still has its own local keyboard, display, CPU and memory. This makes it possible for computing power to be distributed to the places where it is needed most while still allowing the trained IT staff to maintain control from a central location. For some environments, this is the best of both worlds – centralized management *and* distributed processing.

What all this means from a security standpoint, though, is that since an NC doesn't have any local storage (including floppy disk drives), it represents a sealed environment that is immune to many of the most common hacker exploits. Since all the data is ultimately stored on the server, it can be easily backed up on a regular basis and kept in a tightly controlled area. This way, even if hackers do break in, the damage they do is decreased. It also means that if a PC is stolen, the data on its hard drive could be lost or compromised as well. On the other hand, if an NC is stolen only the machine, and not its data, is lost since the data is usually far more valuable than the machine itself, this could be an important consideration. Also, since an NC must be connected to its server in order to operate, it is of little or no value to most would-be thieves as this dependency makes it unattractive for personal use.

Thin clients fall somewhere between the extremes of a fully configured PC and the reduced format of an NC. As such, this hybrid alternative brings with it some of the advantages and disadvantages of both approaches. Other variations on this theme beginning to break through at the time of this writing take the form of an **Internet appliance**. While these devices are initially being targeted for casual home users, it is not completely unreasonable to project a potentially larger market. As high speed bandwidth to the home becomes cheaper and more widely available, telecommuters may find that options involving reduced format computers might offer the blend of functionality they require while still allowing the enterprise to maintain better control over systems management and security issues.

NCs and their counterparts aren't for everyone, though. 'Power users' who need high performance for graphics and I/O-intensive operations are better served by a traditional PC. Mobile users, even if connected through a wireless network, clearly need some form of local storage or they risk running out of range of their important data.

Nevertheless, there are many environments where NCs are a perfect fit. Workers accustomed to using fixed-function terminals (e.g. 3270s, 5250s, VT-100s etc.) would have far more power and flexibility with an NC. Bank tellers, store clerks and clerical staff could also benefit.

NCs might also be the right answer when security is a key requirement. Some companies have gone so far as to buy full-function PCs and remove the floppy drives in order to reduce a potential vulnerability point. NCs cost less because they typically don't have a floppy drive in the first place and since they are actually designed to work this way, they may be less likely to fail than their stripped-down counterparts.

It would be foolish to predict that NCs would take the world by storm and replace all the PCs that exist today. That doesn't mean, though, that NCs couldn't have a unique role to fill when manageability and security are high priorities. For these potentially sizable niche areas, NCs and various forms of thin clients could be an effective solution.

(23.8) Conclusion

Now for some good news and some bad news. First, the bad news – hackers are justified in believing that, as the rock group Timbuk3 once put it, 'The future's so bright I gotta wear shades'. New exploits are being churned out at a dizzying pace and there is, unfortunately, no reason to expect this trend to change dramatically. If you're holding your breath waiting for a silver bullet that puts an end to the hacker threat, it would be best for you to go ahead and exhale now. There's simply not going to be a single solution for the 'hacker problem'. Like the cockroaches of the Internet, they've been around almost since the beginning and have evolved over time, as necessary, to ensure their survival. They aren't going away, but you can make sure that they don't eat you out of house and home.

The good news is that there is something you can do to defend yourself and your organization. You now know how hackers do what they do. You also know why they are able to do it time and time again. For this reason, the future of legitimate IT is even brighter.

In the process of discussing hacker tools and techniques it is hoped that you have also found in this book some of the strategies and solutions that you will need to move ahead – sidestepping the security potholes in the Information Superhighway. Through constant vigilance, ongoing education, and continuous monitoring of the health of your IT infrastructure, you really can successfully mitigate the risks facing you. In fact, this is really nothing new. Businesses have been managing risk in one form or another since the earliest days of commerce. While the threats may have changed over the years, the fundamental business philosophies for dealing with them are essentially the same.

There are no guarantees that your e-business won't be attacked. Opting out of electronic business, however, does offer you one guarantee – obsolescence. Smart businesses will choose risk and the payback it offers over extinction any day.

With a well-conceived policy, properly deployed technology, and an informed and motivated support staff and user community, you can beat the bad guys at their own game.

Now you know *what hackers don't want you to know* ...

appendix A

Crypto tutorial

The 'key' to understanding crypto

Cryptographic algorithms which do the 'heavy lifting' of encryption and decryption need two pieces of input in order to work:

(1) a message, and

(2) a key.

The message fed into an *encryption* algorithm is typically a readable, **plain text** message, while a scrambled message (a.k.a. **cipher text**) is given to a *decryption* algorithm for subsequent conversion back into the original plain text form (Figure A.1). The *key* is a string of bits which controls the output of the crypto algorithm. In the case of encryption, one key would yield one particular scrambled form of the original message while a different key would yield a substantially different scrambled output. In other words, if you choose a different key, you get a different message out the other end. The length of the key along with the mathematical properties of the specific algorithm determine how hard (or easy) it is for someone to crack the scheme and read your secrets. A discussion of the inner workings of crypto algorithms is beyond the scope of this book but is covered extensively in other works such as Bruce Schneier's *Applied Cryptography* (1996). However, a brief treatment of the impact of key lengths on crypto strength is covered in Section 19.1.

Worth noting is the fact that the security of the message should *not* be dependent upon keeping the algorithm itself secret. In fact, the very best crypto algorithms are also some of the best known. The reason for this is that well-known algorithms have been exposed to analysis by the best cryptographic minds in the world and have proven their value under the bright lights of intense public scrutiny. 'Secret' algorithms, on the other hand, are likely to contain vulnerabilities that their creators had not envisioned. Since secret algorithms have not been

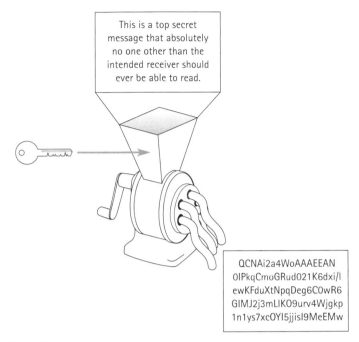

FIGURE A.1   Encryption: running plain text through a virtual meat grinder

exposed to extensive review by the crypto community, these weaknesses lie just below the surface, waiting for a hacker to exploit them.[1] As will be shown in this tutorial, it is the cryptographic keys, not the algorithms, that need to remain secret.

A.2   Symmetric cryptography

The most straightforward form of crypto is called **symmetric** (or **secret key**) **cryptography**. This scheme is called symmetric because the same key both encrypts and decrypts the message. Since you use the same key on both sides of the operation, there is symmetry of the keys. Both sender and receiver have a 'shared secret' – the symmetric key – that they both must know in order for this approach to work (Figure A.2).

For many years the most popular form of symmetric crypto has been the **Data Encryption Standard** (**DES**). Invented by IBM, it ultimately became a US government standard in the late 1970s. Relatively speaking, DES is fast, safe and reliable.

---

1. Bruce Schneier makes a compelling argument for this in 'Cryptography: The importance of not being different', *CRYPTO-GRAM*, 15 April 1998, www.counterpane.com.

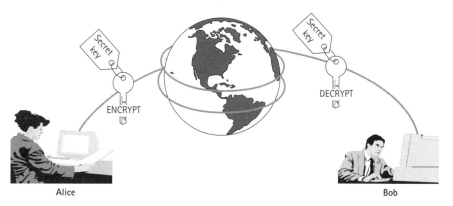

- Alice wants to send a confidential message to Bob
- Alice encrypts the message using a secret key
- Bob decrypts the message using the same secret key

FIGURE A.2   Symmetric cryptography example

It has withstood the test of time – an important criterion in choosing a security technology. More recently, however, the strength of DES's 56-bit key length has come under question (see Section 19.3).

Perhaps a more significant problem with DES (or with any other symmetric key scheme) is the requirement that both the sender and receiver know the shared secret. If Alice wants to send Bob a message, she would select a symmetric key, encrypt the message with that key and then send the encrypted message to Bob. To decrypt the message, Bob would have to know what the key is.

How can Alice give him this information? She could write down the key on a piece of paper and pass it to Bob in a clandestine meeting at a prearranged place. Just like the old spy movies, once he had read the key Bob could tear it up into lots of little pieces and swallow them in order to maintain secrecy. However, in order to keep the hackers off balance they would need to change this key every month, day or hour so that the compromise of a single key wouldn't result in a compromise of all their communications. This would require still more cloak-and-dagger exchanges and unless Bob is a goat, he isn't going to enjoy eating all that paper.

Other offline methods such as telephone, fax or 'snail' mail are too slow, cumbersome, and subject to their own set of attacks. But if Alice sends Bob the key online, then what's to prevent a hacker from intercepting it? She could encrypt the secret key and then send it to him, but how will she send Bob the key to unlock the key? You can see how the recursive nature of this problem gets out of control quickly ... unless Alice uses a different encryption scheme – one that doesn't require her to send Bob the key. No, it's not impossible and it doesn't even involve ESP. Read on ...

A.3 Asymmetric cryptography

Given that we just discussed something called *symmetric* cryptography, you can almost guess that the next section will deal with something called **asymmetric cryptography** – and you'd be right! Asymmetric crypto, as its name suggests, is just the opposite of symmetric crypto. Instead of using the same key to both encrypt and decrypt, two keys are required (Figure A.3). Either can be used to encrypt or decrypt so long as you bear in mind that *whatever you do with one key can only be undone with the other*. For example, if Alice wants to send Bob a message that only he can read using this technique, Bob (actually his computer) would need to compute two keys in advance. These keys would be mathematically related in such a way that anything encrypted with one can be decrypted *only* with the other and vice versa.

Next Bob would arbitrarily designate one key to be his **private key** and the other to be his **public key**. Bob's private key, as you would expect, *must* remain private. He would tell it to no one under any circumstance. It has been generated on his computer and should never leave his computer in order for it to truly remain private.[2]

Bob's public key, on the other hand, would be published to anyone who wanted to communicate with him. In no way is he compromising his security by telling someone what his public key is because there is no practical way for a person to derive his private key from his public key. The proof of this apparent

- Alice wants to ensure only Bob can read a secret message
- Bob publishes his public key
- Alice encrypts the message using Bob's public key
- Bob decrypts the message using his private key

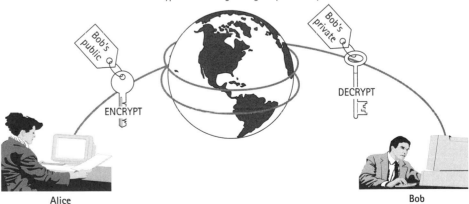

FIGURE A.3   Asymmetric cryptography example

2. One notable exception to this involves the use of smart cards which can store private keys securely and still provide the flexibility of moving from one machine to another.

mathematical paradox is beyond the scope of this book; however, the next section contains a simplified example of how such a thing could be accomplished.

A.3.1 How do they do that?[3]

Let's say that the 'secret' message that Alice wants to send is her unlisted phone number which is, for the sake of this example, 867-5309. Bob calculates a pair of asymmetric keys which have a special complementary mathematical relationship. For example, Bob arbitrarily selects one key to be 1234567 (trivial, but it will work for this illustration). The encrypt/decrypt function is based on modulo 10 arithmetic (which sounds a lot harder than it really is). This simply means that when you add two digits together, you then divide the result by 10 and only the remainder is kept. Here's an example:

   5+7=12   and   12÷10=1 with a remainder of 2

   therefore, in mod 10 arithmetic: 5+7=2

Alice could *encrypt* the secret message using a trivial algorithm involving a digit-by-digit addition in mod 10 arithmetic as follows:[4]

    8675309   the secret message Alice wants to send to Bob
   +1234567   Bob's public key
   ─────────
    9809866   the encrypted message (a digit-by-digit sum in mod 10 arithmetic)

Bob would then *decrypt* the secret message using the same algorithm with its complementary key:

    9809866   the encrypted message
   +9876543   Bob's private key
   ─────────
    8675309   the original secret message (a digit-by-digit sum in mod 10 arithmetic)

Why does this work? You know that adding 0 to anything simply yields that same thing, right? Well, in this example, it turns out that adding Bob's public and private keys together using mod 10 arithmetic is essentially the same thing as adding 0 to the original message. This is because these keys were carefully chosen to be what are called *10's complements* of each other. You might not recognize this terminology but you can easily see how it works:

    1234567   Bob's public key
   +9876543   Bob's private key
   ─────────
    0000000   the digit-by-digit sum in mod 10 arithmetic

---

3. Adapted from Stephenson (1998).
4. For example, add the digits in the one's column, divide by 10 and record the remainder. Then do the same for the ten's column, the hundred's column, etc.

At first it may not seem possible that a mathematical algorithm could not be easily reversed using the same numbers with an opposite operation. We're accustomed to the fact that if you start with 5 and add 3 to it you will get 8. We also fully expect that we can turn it all back around by taking the result (8) and subtracting (the opposite of adding, right?) the 3 we just added in order to end up where we started with 5. As you can see from the previous mod 10 example, though, asymmetric relationships do, in fact, exist as well. Of course, the actual algorithms used in real-world cryptosystems are much more complicated than those shown here, but this demonstrates how such operations are possible.

Back to the asymmetric crypto example with Alice and Bob ... if Bob has been careful to make sure that he is the only person in the world who knows his *private* key, then a message encrypted with his *public* key can only be read by him. So if Alice wants to send a private message for Bob's eyes only, she can use asymmetric encryption along with Bob's *public* key to encrypt the message and freely send it over a public network. Then Bob, and only Bob, can decrypt the message because he is the only one who knows his *private* key (which is the only key that can decrypt the message).

Conversely, Bob can turn the whole process around. This way Alice can determine if a message did, indeed, come from him. If Alice can decrypt the message with Bob's *public* key then he must have been the one to encrypt it with his *private* key, therefore, the message did indeed come from him.

In fact, Bob could take a single message and encrypt it with both *his private* and *Alice's public* keys (i.e. two separate encryptions of the same message). Alice would decrypt it with her *private* and Bob's *public* keys, and they could **authenticate** both the sender *and* the receiver of the message. It may take a few minutes for that to sink in but if you can convince yourself that this works, you will be a long way down the road toward understanding the value of asymmetric algorithms.

A.4 The best of both worlds

So now you might ask, 'Why not simply use asymmetric cryptography all the time, since it doesn't have the problem that symmetric schemes do in needing secret keys?' The reason is simple. Asymmetric crypto is about 10 to 100 times more computationally intensive than symmetric crypto. In fact, some have suggested that **RSA**, a popular form of asymmetric crypto, which was named for its inventors (Rivest, Shamir and Adleman), might just as easily stand for 'Really Slow Algorithm'.

If your message is of any substantial size, you would need to limit the amount of asymmetric crypto that must take place (unless you have loads of patience and free CPU cycles). Most commercial crypto applications strike a balance between the pros and cons of symmetric and asymmetric schemes by using something like DES or

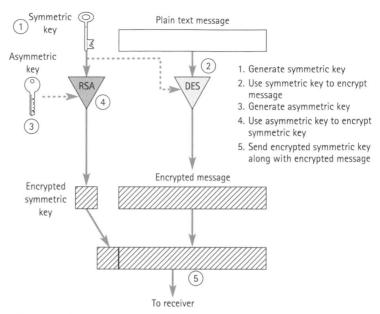

FIGURE A.4   The best of both worlds: using symmetric and asymmetric cryptography together

triple DES to encrypt the bulk of the message payload and RSA encryption to distribute the symmetric keys as show in Figure A.4. Since symmetric key lengths are relatively small (typically 56–128 bits) as compared to message payloads (which could be thousands of bytes long) the overhead from the asymmetric encryption is minimized.

A.5   Getting 'carded' in cyberspace

For RSA (or any other asymmetric crypto scheme for that matter) to work, however, we need to have a means for telling the world what our *public* keys are. This is where digital certificates come in. A **digital certificate** is a message that contains important information about you, such as your name, your public key, and when the certificate expires. You would not include any private information here as this is going to be freely exchanged with anyone that wants to communicate with you. This digital certificate, then, serves as a means of identifying you in a virtual world of electrical impulses. Since you can't very well show the other party your driver's licence, passport, or employee ID card in cyberspace, digital certificates are used instead.

But how can Bob, for example, know if the digital certificate that he has just received from Alice is really hers? How does he know that a hacker isn't simply claiming to be Alice while sending him his own digital certificate instead? The answer is that Bob deals with this in much the same way that ID cards in the physical world are handled – he relies on a **trusted third party**.

Bob might not know Alice, but if he knows that the credentials she presented were issued by the government's Passport Office or Department of Motor Vehicles, for instance, he doesn't have to take her word for it. He knows that Alice had first to prove her identity to a government agency before a physical credential (e.g. passport, driver's licence, etc.) was issued. If Alice has the valid credentials then Bob has a decent indication that she met the government's criteria and this is probably good enough for him.[5] Physical credentials often bear a handwritten signature or seal which signifies authenticity. Digital certificates, quite appropriately, contain **digital signatures** from the **certificate authority** (i.e. the trusted third party that issued the certificate) to prove where they came from.

A.6   Digital ink?

How does one 'sign' a digital certificate? Clearly, an ink pen won't work when we're dealing with the strings of 1's and 0's that digital computers operate with. The answer, again, lies in cryptography. Let's review …

When Alice wants to send a message to Bob that only he can read, she encrypts the bulk of the message using a randomly selected symmetric key. That helps ensure confidentiality. She also wants to ensure that the message Bob receives is the same one she sent (i.e. **message integrity**) so Alice runs a **hashing function** (similar to a **checksum**), which calculates a unique (or close enough to it for our purposes) **message digest** value.

This digest is, as its name implies, a summary of the full message. It doesn't actually contain the message itself, though, but rather a fixed-length numeric value that is unique to that message. One well-known hashing function, SHA-1, reduces a message of less than 2^{64} (over 18 quintillion!) bits to a 160-bit digest. A good hashing function yields a significantly different digest value even if the original message has been changed only slightly. Also, it does not allow a hacker to determine the original message based solely on the digest value. In other words, it's an irreversible, one-way function.

After calculating the message's digest value, Alice would then encrypt this digest using her *private* key. The result is known as a digital signature. She then sends this digitally signed message (i.e. the encrypted message along with the encrypted digest) and her certificate to Bob. When he receives the message, he runs the very same hashing function that Alice ran so that he can determine the message digest on his own. Then Bob decrypts Alice's signature using her *public* key (which Bob obtained from Alice's certificate) and sees if the digest value that she calculated on the sending side matches the one that he calculated on the receiving side. If they match, then

---

5. Of course, it is possible to produce counterfeit credentials but, then again, there are mechanisms for detecting this also. The same holds true for digital certificates. A brief discussion of one such mechanism follows in Section A.6.

Bob can believe, to a reasonable degree of certainty, that the message has not been modified along the way. Figure A.5 shows an example of just such a transaction.

But how can Bob know that the public key in Alice's certificate is really her public key and not that of an impostor? The answer is that her certificate has been digitally signed by a recognized certificate authority – a third party that both of them trust and whose public key is well known. Since Bob knows the public key of the CA (certificate authority) that issued the certificate (in fact, it may be hard-coded into software to prevent impersonation), he can simply run the same integrity check on the certificate that he just ran on the message. In other words, Bob can calculate a digest value for the certificate and compare it to the one contained in CA's digital signature (which is included in the certificate). Of course, Bob would need to decrypt the CA's digital signature using the CA's well-known public key before comparing the two digest values (i.e. the one Bob calculated and the one he received in the certificate), but once this is done, he can determine the validity of Alice's certificate and, therefore, the trustworthiness of her public key (Figure A.6).

Another benefit of this scheme is that Bob has also established that this message did, indeed, come from Alice because it was signed using her *private* key – something only she knows. This, then, could be the basis for **non-repudiation**, allowing him to hold Alice to the terms and conditions of any agreements they make using this technology. In fact, non-repudiation is ultimately a legal condition – not a technical one; therefore, it is the courts that must decide whether a binding agree-

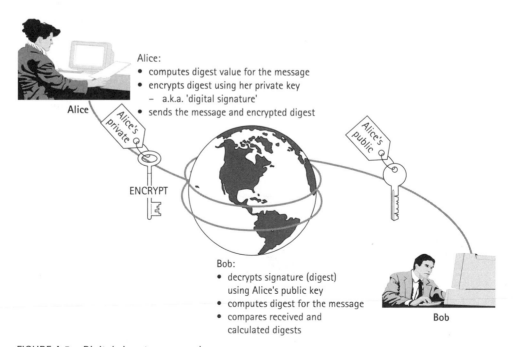

Alice:
- computes digest value for the message
- encrypts digest using her private key
  - a.k.a. 'digital signature'
- sends the message and encrypted digest

Alice

Alice's private

ENCRYPT

Alice's public

Bob:
- decrypts signature (digest) using Alice's public key
- computes digest for the message
- compares received and calculated digests

Bob

FIGURE A.5　Digital signature example

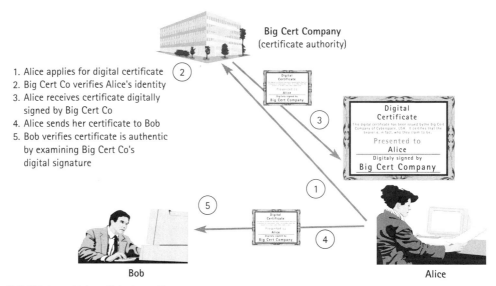

1. Alice applies for digital certificate
2. Big Cert Co verifies Alice's identity
3. Alice receives certificate digitally signed by Big Cert Co
4. Alice sends her certificate to Bob
5. Bob verifies certificate is authentic by examining Big Cert Co's digital signature

FIGURE A.6   Using digital certificates

ment exists or not depending upon their trust in not only the technology employed but also the procedures involved in its use. The point here is that digital signatures can provide a *technological basis* for non-repudiation, assuming that private keys remain private and that certificate authorities are up to the task of conclusively verifying entities before issuing digital certificates to them (which is no small feat).

VPN tutorial

B.1 Inside the VPN tunnel

Is that the proverbial light at the end of the tunnel ... or a train? If you're talking about VPN (Virtual Private Networks) tunnels, then it all depends upon your perspective. VPN technology carries with it the promise of cheap, secure, ubiquitous bandwidth. In other words, you could go anywhere in the world and still have access to your corporate network without destroying your IT budget in the process. Or you could connect to remote branch offices or even business partners over a public network, such as the Internet, and still keep your communications out of the reach of snooping competitors (Figure B.1).

Sounds interesting, right? So what's the catch? It turns out that along with the exciting upside of VPNs come some additional considerations, such as manageability and interoperability issues, that must be dealt with. Nevertheless, the potential savings over the cost of private network connections and added security have convinced some people that the increased complexity is well worth the hassle. So, let's take a look at what a VPN is and what makes it tick ...

B.2 VPN defined

What is a Virtual Private Network? Let's take the terms in reverse order. We know that a network is a series of connections that make it possible for us to send data from point A to point B. In this context, 'private' means that those communications can be read only by their intended recipients. Private networks are nothing new, however. The trouble with them is that they are expensive. The network service provider has to dedicate the bandwidth to you, so they also have to pass along all of the costs to you.

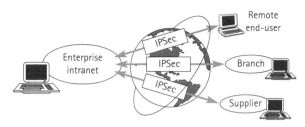

FIGURE B.1   Extending the intranet securely with IPSec tunnelling

That's where the 'virtual' part comes in. If you could use public, shared band-width but maintain the security of a private, dedicated network, then your network service provider could spread the costs out among multiple customers and you wouldn't be stuck footing the entire bill. So, instead of a 'real' private network, you set up a 'virtual' private network over a shared infrastructure. It seems to you just like the real thing – only at a fraction of the cost. In a sense it's like carving out a secure tunnel for your private communications through the public Internet.

B.3 Virtual privacy or virtually private?

But how can you send a *private* message to a business partner over a *public* net-work? Public networks are only for public information, right? Not necessarily.

If you send a postcard through the mail, you can't expect a great deal of privacy because anyone that sees your postcard can easily read what you've written on it. It's likely that only a few people, such as postal workers, would actually have access to the card while it's being delivered but, needless to say, this would not be the pre-ferred method for sending corporate secrets.

Putting that postcard in an envelope, however, would certainly help. This way a snooper would have to actually open the envelope in order to steal your secrets. Of course, opening an envelope isn't a difficult thing to do, but if that envelope was made out of reinforced steel and secured with a combination lock whose code was known only by you and the recipient, then you could reasonably expect that your secret would be safe.

Unfortunately, you can't put your IP packets in a locked, steel-reinforced envel-ope before sending them over the Internet, but you can do the next best thing – encrypt them. You could scramble the message before sending it to make sure that only the intended receiver knows how to unscramble it. This way, even if snoopers do intercept the message, they can't make head nor tail out of what they nabbed.

B.4 Standards, standards everywhere ...

The key to making all of this work, of course, is that the sender and receiver must know how to read these modified packets. Otherwise, the whole scheme falls apart.

In order to do this, both sides must agree on an encryption algorithm to use, know the appropriate encryption/decryption keys, and know the exact format of the modified packets. That's where standards help.

Standards are a wonderful thing -- which is why it seems everyone has one of their very own. VPN standards are no different. A number of competing and complementary tunnelling options are available to choose from. It's very important to understand what each is capable of (and not capable of) so that you can choose the right one for your particular needs.

One popular alternative is Microsoft's **Point-to-Point Tunneling Protocol (PPTP)**. This option is popular by virtue of the fact that it is included in Microsoft operating systems and is, therefore, easily within reach of millions of users. However, the most popular answer is not always the best. As crypto expert Bruce Schneier of Counterpane Systems points out:

They [Microsoft] invented their own authentication protocol, their own hash functions, and their own key-generation algorithm. Every one of these items was badly flawed. They used a known encryption algorithm, but they used it in such a way as to negate its security. They made implementation mistakes that weakened the system even further. But since they did all this work internally, no one knew that their PPTP was weak.

(Schneier, 1998)

This example points out one of the problems with proprietary solutions. Without an open standards-based development process, the opportunity for sufficient peer review by the best minds in the industry is minimized. Developing network security solutions in this sort of security vacuum is particularly dangerous because the stakes are so high. Ultimately, Microsoft did come up with fixes, but the initial results weren't always satisfactory in either the completeness of the solution or the timeliness of the patch.

This is why open, industry-developed standards are often a better choice. In many cases it may appear that their creators threw in everything plus the kitchen sink in order to appease all the various constituencies involved. While these added features are frequently intended to offer greater security, they can also have the opposite effect. Nevertheless a standards-based solution such as IPSec (Internet Protocol Security) is usually better. As Schneier puts it:

Although it's possible for any [VPN solution] to be flawed, you want to minimize your risk. If you go with IPSec, you have a much greater assurance that the algorithms and protocols are strong.

(Schneier, 1998)

There are other standards-based VPN technologies such as the **Layer 2 Tunneling Protocol (L2TP)** which, like IPSec, also comes from the IETF (Internet Engineering

---

1. Confidentiality can be achieved by using IPSec in conjunction with L2TP, though.

Task Force). However, since L2TP does not directly provide confidentiality for its transmissions[1] and since this capability is needed to provide protection against network sniffing, our discussion will centre around IPSec.

B.5 Opening the IPSec envelope

IPSec is most appropriately thought of as a *framework*[2] offering many choices rather than a single, monolithic standard that results in a set of look-alike VPN components. In fact, it is this characteristic that gives rise to some of IPSec's greatest strengths (e.g. flexibility) and its greatest weaknesses (e.g. complexity).

IPSec essentially deals with three important VPN issues which will be covered in the following sections:

- Authentication (Are you really you?)

- Privacy (Just between you and me)

- Key management (Who has the key?)

B.6 Are you really you?

Authentication refers to the ability to know for certain that an entity is, in fact, who it claims to be. We do this in the physical world through informal means such as recognizing a person's appearance, voice, mannerisms, etc. These work well if you already know the person you're trying to identify, but in cases where you don't, then you can use more formal criteria involving credentials such as a driver's licence, passport or ID card. In the virtual world of cyberspace, such methods are impractical. However, digital counterparts derived from special applications of cryptography can do the job.

IPSec specifies an **Authentication Header**[3] (AH), which can be added to the original IP data packet to provide the following features:

- *Authentication.* Authentication is required when we need to know that the person (or thing) that we are communicating with is really who (or what) we think it is. For example, you may want to have your firewall authenticate packets coming into your network to ensure that they really came from your business partner and not a hacker intent on penetrating your defences.

- *Message integrity.* You might also like to know that the message that you sent is the same as the message that was received and that it has not been tampered with somewhere along the way. A saboteur could wreak havoc on your business

---

2. RFC 2411 'IP Security Document Roadmap', Internet Engineering Task Force, www.ietf.org.
3. RFC 2402 'IP Authentication Header', Internet Engineering Task Force, www.ietf.org.

by simply changing a few part numbers on an order you sent to a supplier. Instead of getting space heaters for your new Alaskan operation, you end up with a load of air conditioners.

● *Replay protection.* In some cases a duplicate message is nothing more than a nuisance, but in the case of electronic commerce, the stakes are much higher. Let's say one of your customers sends an order for 100 hammers. A hacker saves a copy of this message and decides to re-send it to you 100 more times at carefully spaced intervals over the next few days. The folks in Sales might be headed for a celebration until they get the call from an irate customer who has a few choice words for the people who have him up to his eyes in hammers. Replay protection detects, through the use of sequence numbers, that a packet has been seen before and can, therefore, be discarded.

B.7   Just between you and me

In some cases the AH features are sufficient to meet the business requirements, but if privacy is also an issue, then IPSec's **Encapsulating Security Payload**[4] (**ESP**) component should be used. The ESP function (indicated by the presence of an ESP header added to the IP packet) calls for the original message contents to be encrypted before sending them out on the public network. The IPSec specification does not dictate precisely which cryptographic algorithm must be used but, instead, offers a set of choices such as DES, triple DES, etc. that the sender and receiver agree to use during the setup of the tunnel.

B.8   Who has the key?

Cryptography is based upon the assumption that both the sender and receiver know certain predetermined keys that allow them to encrypt and decrypt their communications. But how can both the sender and receiver determine such things as the exact encryption algorithms they will use for privacy and authentication, the encrypt/decrypt keys, the frequency with which these keys will be changed (to keep the hackers off-balance), and other IPSec options? What about the even more challenging problem of how to send these cryptographic details over a non-secured link in order to jump-start the entire process?

Of course you could simply determine all of this manually through 'out of band' communications with the other party. Many of the initial IPSec implementations on the market were based on this arrangement. The advantages with this approach are that it is easier for vendors to build and more likely to interoperate with other VPN solutions owing to this decreased complexity. The disadvantage, however, is that it is more labour intensive for you to set up in the first place.

---

4. RFC 2406 'IP Encapsulating Security Payload (ESP)', Internet Engineering Task Force, www.ietf.org.

This is where the automated key management features of the **Internet Security Association and Key Management Protocol (ISAKMP)** can help. Like its higher-level standard, IPSec, it is essentially a framework of specifications that describe various methods of establishing what are called **Security Associations (SAs)**. According to the spec, ISAKMP 'provides a framework for authentication and key exchange but does not define them'. This allows ISAKMP to be used with a variety of key exchange protocols but, at the time of this writing, the industry has rallied behind only one – Oakley. As a result, you will often see the two names written together as ISAKMP/Oakley or in its newer, shortened form – **Internet Key Exchange**[5] **(IKE)**.

B.9   The envelope, please ...

As discussed earlier from a security standpoint, sending a plain text message over the Internet is like sending a postcard through the mail because its contents can be read by anyone along the delivery path. If a little more security is needed, you could seal the postcard in a special, windowed envelope (the kind that lets you see inside) with your company's logo and return address on the outside. This way the recipient will have a greater degree of certainty that it really came from you (because presumably envelopes with your logo are not readily available to a would-be impostor). Also, the recipient will be able to detect if the envelope has been opened and its contents tampered with.

The cyberspace equivalent (Figure B.2) would be to use IPSec's AH to authenticate the sender and ensure message integrity. The key difference in this analogy is that with the AH function, the window on the envelope exposes not only the address but the message contents as well.

If that's not enough security, you could use a regular, non-windowed envelope to carry your message. This way the receiver could:

● know that the message came from you,

● know whether it had been tampered with, and

● know that no one else had read its contents because this information had been obscured from view during delivery.

FIGURE B.2   IPSec's Authenication Header: a see-through envelope

5. RFC 2409 'The Internet Key Exchange', Internet Engineering Task Force, www.ietf.org.

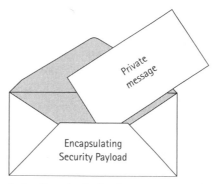

FIGURE B.3   IPSec's Encapsulating Security Payload: an opaque envelope

As illustrated in Figure B.3 IPSec's ESP performs an analogous function by encrypting the message. The ESP could also be used in combination with AH features to provide additional security.

In some cases, though, even that is not enough. Let's say your business partner has a security policy that denies network entry to all unauthenticated traffic. However, you need your message to remain encrypted all the way to the receiver's system in order to ensure end-to-end privacy.

You can satisfy both requirements by **nesting** one IPSec tunnel (or to use the analogy, an envelope) inside another. In other words, perform the AH and ESP processing on the original message to ensure that only the intended receiver can read it and then wrap it in an additional AH envelope designed to be read by your partner's firewall. This would be like putting your postcard in an opaque envelope and then putting it all in an outer, transparent envelope. The mail clerk at the destination site removes the outer envelope and the recipient gets only the inner envelope containing the message. Figure B.4 shows the real-world equivalent of nested IPSec tunnels.

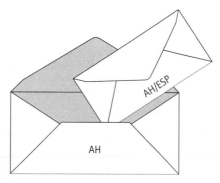

FIGURE B.4   Nested tunnelling: an envelope within an envelope

B.10   And if that weren't enough ...

Let's say that you want to hide not only the contents of your message when it hits the Internet but also your IP address as well as the address of the recipient. You might want to do this in order to hide more information from hackers, thereby making their job tougher. Also, you might need this extra layer of indirection if you've used non-registered IP addresses (e.g. 10.xx.xx.xx) on your internal network, as these can't be routed properly across the Internet. Figure B.5 shows a *tunnel mode* ESP which encrypts not only the message, but also the IP header by **encapsulating** (a term often used synonymously with tunnelling) the entire packet inside the ESP. A new IP header is built which contains different source and destination addresses (e.g. the address of the firewall instead of the client station) which are routable across the Internet and don't reveal internal network details. If you don't need this level of protection, you can use the basic *transport mode*, resulting in lower overhead.

AH also offers transport and tunnel modes, which have a similar effect, as shown in Figure B.6. As with ESP tunnel mode, AH tunnel mode builds a new IP header and the AH authenticates the entire newly built packet. Since AH transport mode relies on the original IP header, it has lower overheads.

Stated simply, transport mode is intended primarily for host-to-host communications, whereas tunnel mode is designed for situations where intermediate gateways (e.g. firewalls) need to be involved in setting up or breaking down the layers of the VPN tunnel.

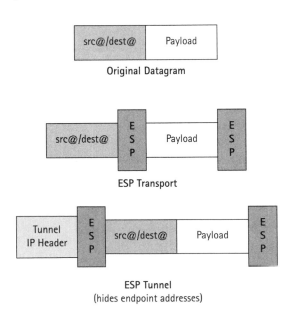

FIGURE B.5   ESP transport and tunnel modes (adapted from 'Please Explain VPNs', Laura Knapp and Tom Hadley, IBM Corp., April 2000.)

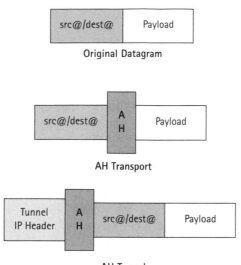

Original Datagram

AH Transport

AH Tunnel
(authentication at an intermediate gateway)

FIGURE B.6   AH transport and tunnel modes (adapted from 'Please Explain VPNs', Laura Knapp and Tom Hadley, IBM Corp., April 2000.)

B.11   The light at the end of the tunnel

If this all sounds rather complicated, then you've obviously been paying attention. Setting up and maintaining VPNs is not a trivial task. However, solutions do exist and there is reason to believe that the situation will get better.

Some of the trickiest details involving VPNs revolve around interoperability issues. Everyone claims to follow the standard but since the standard offers so many options, a multi-vendor turnkey installation is highly unlikely. Interoperability certification and testing from groups such as the International Computer Security Association[6] (ICSA), however, are a step in the right direction. ICSA offers both a general VPN certification and a more specific IPSec certification (which requires automatic key management using IKE, among other things) for products such as firewalls, routers, client systems, and server systems that can serve as VPN endpoints.

The bottom line, though, is that despite its inherent complexities, the potential cost savings (as compared to dedicated lines) and security benefits of VPN solutions are more than enough to justify a long, hard look at this important technology.

6. International Computer Security Association, www.icsa.net.

Glossary

Active content. Programs typically written in Java, JavaScript, or ActiveX, which are often downloaded and executed in a single step by a web browser; differs from *static* content, as typified by web pages built using only HTML tags, which offer a consistent, unchanging document.

ActiveX. A form of active content developed by Microsoft.

Advanced Encryption Standard (AES). The cryptographically stronger successor to the Data Encryption Standard (DES); the selection of the AES algorithm involved submissions from around the world and was overseen by the US government's National Institute of Standards (NIST).

Applet. A program that runs within another program; typically a Java program that is downloaded and executed within a web browser.

Application. A program that utilizes the underlying services provided by the operating system and/or middleware to perform a task for an end user.

Application-level proxy. A firewall technology that involves examining application specific data in order to guard against certain types of improper or threatening behaviours.

Asymmetric cryptography. A form of cryptography involving the use of two different (yet mathematically related) keys so that a message encrypted with one key can only be decrypted with the other key (and vice versa).

Authentication. The process of determining if an entity is who (or what) it claims to be.

Authentication Header (AH). The portion of the IPSec protocol that is intended to determine if the parties involved in the tunnel are who they claim to be.

Bang for the Buck Ratio (BBR). In this book this is a calculation that attempts to determine the cost effectiveness of a given security countermeasure by dividing the cost of compromise or loss (CC) by the cost of protecting (CP) against that loss or compromise; BBR is comparable to a return on investment (ROI) calculation.

Basic Input/Output System (BIOS). The fundamental component of a PC that controls the way data is read from and written to memory, disk storage devices, keyboards, displays, etc.; the BIOS also determines what the system will do when it is first started.

Bulletin Board System (BBS). A computer system typically accessed via dial-in modem(s) that allows for the posting and reading of messages; in some respects, BBSs served as forerunners to certain aspects of the modern Internet.

Certificate Authority (CA). A trusted third party that issues digital certificates.

Checksum. An error detection scheme involving the computation of a fixed-length value based upon the contents of a given message.

Cipher text. The unreadable form of an original *plain text* message after it has been encrypted.

Circuit-level proxy. A firewall technology that involves examining transmitted data for certain types of improper or threatening behaviour without taking into account the specifics of the application involved; SOCKS is a common example of a circuit-level proxy.

Cryptography. A method of 'secret writing' in which a key is used to encode a message, thereby making it difficult for anyone other than the intended receiver to read the message.

Cyberspace. The on-line world of computer networks.

Cyberterrorist. Someone who commits acts of terrorism in cyberspace; for example, a cyberterroist might use the Internet to attack an organization as a means of scaring them into performing (or cease performing) a given action.

Data Encryption Standard (DES). A 56-bit symmetric-key cipher standardized by the US government in the 1970s; for many years DES was considered the 'gold standard' of cryptographic algorithms.

Decryption. The process of converting unreadable *cipher text* back into its original, readable *plain text* form; a form of descrambling.

Defence-in-depth. An approach to security in which multiple layers of countermeasures are created in order to strengthen defences; the idea being that even if an attacker makes it through the first measure of protection, he or she is still faced with yet another hurdle (or hurdles) to overcome.

Denial-of-Service (DoS). A type of attack that results in depriving legitimate users access to resources they are entitled to; the attacker typically gains nothing of value other than the mere satisfaction of disrupting normal operations on the target system.

Digital certificate. An electronic credential consisting of a specially formatted message that can be used to authenticate the identity of a message sender or receiver over a computer network; X.509v3 is a commonly used international standard for digital certificates which provides a means for binding the certificate owner's identity with that owner's public key.

Digital signature. The electronic equivalent to a handwritten signature; typically this takes the form of a hash value calculated for a given message that has been encrypted with the sender's *private key*; the receiver can use this information to determine whether the message has been tampered with, and to verify that it came from the expected sender.

Distributed Denial-of-Service (DDoS). A *denial-of-service* (DoS) attack that emanates from many different locations on a computer network simultaneously; the multiplicative effect of this attack scenario is potentially more devastating than a typical DoS attack.

Domain Name System (DNS). A system of servers in an IP network that can convert alphanumeric domain names (e.g. www.widgets-r-us.com) into their numeric IP address equivalents (e.g. 10.1.2.3).

Dual-homed firewall. A *firewall* that connects to two different networks (e.g. the public Internet and a private intranet) simultaneously; as such it acts as a security gatekeeper that determines which traffic is allowed to pass and which traffic is blocked.

Egress filtering. A security technique in which potentially harmful traffic is blocked from leaving a network.

Elite hacker. One of a reasonably small number of hackers who possess great skill and imagination; elite hackers are able to devise novel attacks which are technically sophisticated and ingenious in their implementation; elite hackers are the true 'geniuses' of the hacking community.

Encapsulation. Embedding one networking protocol inside another; this involves adding information to the beginning (i.e. header) and/or ending (i.e. trailer) of an existing data packet; in the more specific case of virtual private networking, encapsulation is done in order to set up the virtual tunnel.

Encapsulating Security Payload (ESP). The portion of the IPSec virtual private networking protocol which is used predominantly to provide data privacy.

Encryption. The process of converting an original *plain text* message into an unreadable *cipher text* form; a form of scrambling.

Ethernet. A common Local Area Network (LAN) protocol that allows workstations to communicate with other workstations, printers, etc. over a shared physical media.

Ethical hacking. A means for identifying vulnerabilities by having an authorized individual(s) attempt to break into a computer system or network and report their findings to the appropriate personnel.

False negative. When used in the context of biometrics this term refers to the case where an authentication system erroneously *denies* access to an authorized entity.

False positive. When used in the context of biometrics this term refers to the case where an authentication system erroneously *grants* access to an unauthorized entity.

Firewall. A networking component which enforces security policy by selectively permitting or blocking network traffic based upon a predetermined criteria; firewalls are used to provide a degree of isolation (and, therefore, protection) between a trusted network and an untrusted one.

File Transfer Protocol (FTP). A popular protocol used for sending files over an IP network such as the Internet.

Hacktivist. Literally a 'hacker activist'; someone who breaks into computer systems and networks in order to advance a given political or social agenda.

Hashing function. An algorithm that takes as input an original message and produces a fixed-length summary of that message; in order for a hashing function to be effective the result (a.k.a. 'message digest') must be unique to the original message (within an acceptable range of certainty); hashing functions are sometimes thought of as one-way encryption schemes because they cannot be easily reversed (i.e. decrypted).

Hoax virus. A warning for a computer *virus* that does not actually exist; often these appear in the form of email messages which have been forwarded many times and contain dire warnings of impending doom and an urgent plea for the receiver to forward the warning on to others.

Hybrid firewall. A network protection device that includes various firewalling features (e.g. packet filtering, circuit-level proxies, application-level proxies, etc.) in order to guard against multiple forms of attack.

Implantable computer. A computing device that is surgically (or otherwise) implanted into a living being; implantable medical devices for example, heart pacemaker, may contain computing components.

Information Technology (IT). A term referring to the hardware, software, etc. involved in creating, maintaining, and using information; closely related to the term *Information Services* (IS), which is preferred by some organizations.

Intermediate hacker. A hacker who possesses moderate to considerable technical skills; intermediate hackers may devise new exploits but more often rely on the groundwork laid by *elite hackers*.

Internet appliance. A purpose-built device that allows an end user to access Internet resources; unlike a typical general purpose workstation, an Internet appliance may depend entirely upon being connected to the Internet in order for it to function effectively; also, since it may exploit Internet resources to a greater extent, an Internet appliance may lack some of the components and complexity of a full-function PC.

Internet Control Message Protocol (ICMP). A networking protocol that runs over IP and is used to carry error, control, and information messages; the well-known PING command uses ICMP to determine whether another host is reachable via the network.

Internet Key Exchange (IKE). The portion of the IPSec virtual private networking protocol that facilitates cryptographic key exchange and management.

Internet Protocol (IP). The networking protocol that forms the basis of the Internet; other protocols such as TCP and UDP are carried over IP.

Internet Protocol Security (IPSec). A virtual private networking (VPN) protocol standard that can be used to provide data privacy, data integrity, sender/receiver authentication, non-repudiation, and replay protection over a public IP network such as the Internet.

Internet Security Association and Key Management Protocol (ISAKMP). A forerunner to *IKE*.

Java. An object-oriented programming language that is designed to provide computing platform independence; Java programs are compiled into 'bytecodes' which may then be transmitted over a network and executed in a Java Virtual Machine (JVM) designed for that specific platform.

JavaScript. A client-side scripting language loosely based upon Java that is commonly implemented in web browsers in order to provide dynamic content.

KISS principle. Short for 'Keep It Simple Stupid'; in IT security this principle is important because 'complexity is the enemy of security'.[1]

Layer 2 Tunneling Protocol (L2TP). A networking protocol standard that can be used to route non-IP traffic over an IP network and to authenticate senders and receivers; L2TP can be combined with IPSec to provide greater security (e.g. data privacy) if needed.

Macro virus. A computer virus implemented in a scripting language such as Microsoft's Visual Basic Script (VBS) that can be invoked when a user opens an infected document in Excel or Word, for example.

Malware. Malicious software; examples include computer viruses, Trojan horses, worms, etc.

Message digest. The result produced by a *hashing function*.

Message integrity. The notion that a message has not been altered and is, therefore, true to its original intent (a.k.a.'data integrity').

Nesting. Literally putting one thing inside another; with IPSec this refers to creating tunnels within tunnels by wrapping additional headers/trailers around network packets.

Network Address Translation (NAT). A function that can be used to hide the details of an internal network by changing IP addresses as they enter and exit that network; this capability is often included in firewalls and network routers as an additional security mechanism.

Network computer (NC). A type of Internet appliance that relies upon a network connection in order to access key computing resources stored on a server; network computers typically feature a graphical user interface along with a keyboard and mouse but may lack significant local storage (e.g. hard drive) capacity.

Non-repudiation. The legal condition that follows when parties are bound to the terms of an agreement or contract; cryptographic techniques such as *digital signatures* may be used to facilitate non-repudiation, but ultimately the sufficiency of this technology to create a legally binding agreement is a matter of interpretation for the judicial systems having jurisdiction over the exchange.

Novice hacker. A hacker who possesses only minimal technical skills; novices make up the largest group within the hacking community and are often referred to as *script kiddies* since they merely execute the attack programs (i.e. scripts) created by more talented hackers.

Packet filtering. A firewalling technique that selectively allows or denies network traffic to pass from one network to another based upon a pre-determined criteria which can be evaluated using data in the header of the packet (e.g. source address, destination address, port number, protocol, etc.).

Payload. When used in the context of *malware*, the payload is the malicious contents of a computer virus.

Personal Digital Assistant (PDA). Usually a handheld computing device that functions as an electronic calendar, calculator, email client, to-do list organizer, address book, etc.

---

1. Neils Ferguson and Bruce Schneier, 'A cryptographic evaluation of IP5ec.' CRYPTO-GRAM, November 1988, Counterpane Internet Security, Inc., www.counterpane.com.

Pervasive computing. A form of computing that involves ubiquitous access to information through the use of highly portable and/or accessible devices.

Plain text. The original, readable message before *encryption* or after *decryption*.

Point-to-Point Tunneling Protocol (PPTP). A proprietary VPN protocol from Microsoft.

Private key. In asymmetric-key cryptography this is the key that must *not* be divulged to others.

Public key. In asymmetric-key cryptography this is the key that *may be shared* with any entity for whom secure communications are desired.

Relative Value (RV). A value that can be used to compare the relative merits of one security countermeasure versus another; in this book the RV is calculated by dividing the Vulnerability Index (VI) by the Cost of Protection (CP).

Remote Access Trojan (RAT). A *Trojan horse* that accesses other computer systems across a network; malicious software of this type may be used by a hacker to gain a foothold on a compromised system.

RSA. Literally 'Rivest, Shamir, and Adleman', the last names of the men who invented the RSA asymmetric-key encryption algorithm; these initials are also commonly used as a shorthand version of the name of the company (RSA Security, Inc.) which owns the algorithm.

Sandbox. A protected area of a computer system in which programs run with limited privileges; for example Java applets may be confined to a sandbox environment which prevents them from accessing the computer system's permanent storage (e.g. hard disk) or networking services; another example of a sandbox is an isolated network segment used for testing.

Screening router. A device that, in addition to routing network traffic, is configured to reject packets which are not in keeping with the organization's policy; screening routers are often deployed at the outer perimeter of a network and, therefore, serve as the first line of defence against network-oriented attacks; a.k.a. filtering router.

Script kiddies. A derogatory slang term for *novice hackers* who, lacking significant technical skills and imagination, rely entirely on attack tools (i.e. scripts) written by other more skilled hackers.

Secret key. The key used in *symmetric-key cryptography* to encrypt and decrypt a message; it is the 'shared secret' that must be known only to the sender and intended receiver in order for the message to remain private.

Security Administrator Tool for Analyzing Networks (SATAN). A vulnerability scanning tool that can be used to identify network security weaknesses; when SATAN was originally released by Dan Farmer and Wietse Venema in 1995 it launched a heated debate in the IT industry over the ethics of such a tool.

Security Association (SA). A set of security parameters which govern the conduct of end points in an IPSec tunnel; as such SAs represent an agreement between VPN participants as to the cryptographic algorithm, key strength, etc. that will be used for the tunnel.

Server Message Block (SMB). A collection of data that is passed by a client workstation to a Windows NT server during logon.

Shoulder surfing. A 'low-tech' means for discovering passwords and other security information by peering 'over the shoulder' of the intended victim and making note of the keystrokes entered.

Sniffer. With respect to networking this is a tool that listens for and records packets intended for other workstations on a local area network (LAN); sniffers may be used for legitimate reasons by network technicians to diagnose problems, or by hackers to eavesdrop on LAN transmissions in hopes of discovering sensitive information such as passwords.

Sniffing. The act of using a *sniffer* tool to view network traffic not intended for that particular LAN station.

SOCKS. A *circuit-level proxy* used to protect against attacks across a range of application traffic types such as HTTP (web), FTP, telnet, etc.

Spam. junk email; frequently an advertisement for a 'get rich quick' scheme or online pornography

Stateful Packet Inspection (SPI). A firewalling technique that builds upon *packet filtering* technology by taking into account the state (i.e. context) of the session involved in order to decide whether to block or permit a given packet.

Symmetric cryptography. A form of cryptography involving the use of a single 'shared secret' key so that any message encrypted with this key can only be decrypted with that same key; 'symmetry' follows from the fact that the same key is used for both operations,; examples include DES, triple DES and AES.

SYN. A packet sent during the initiation of a TCP session that *syn*chronizes sequence numbers between the two session end points.

SYN/ACK. A packet sent as an *ack*nowledgement to a TCP SYN request.

Thin client. A workstation that lacks the full complement of hardware typically found on a full-function PC but which compensates by relying on resources residing on servers it can connect to.

Token Ring. A Local Area Networking (LAN) protocol.

Transmission Control Protocol (TCP). A connection-oriented protocol that runs over IP; TCP is the most common protocol in use on the Internet.

Triple DES. A cryptographic algorithm involving three separate 56-bit key DES encryptions/decryptions.

Trojan horse. Malicious software whose benign appearance conceals its damaging or thieving intent.

Trusted third party. An entity trusted by both partners in an exchange; a *certificate authority* (CA) can perform this function by issuing digital certificates which are considered trustworthy.

Uniform Resource Locator (URL). The alphanumeric name used on the Internet to uniquely identify a web site; often of the form 'www.companyname.com' where 'companyname' is the name of a given company.

User Datagram Protocol (UDP). A connectionless protocol that runs over IP (contrast with TCP, which is connection-oriented); because of its connectionless nature, UDP is a favourite among hackers as it can be more difficult to trace.

Userid. Literally a 'user identity'; on many computing systems this can consist of eight or more alphanumeric characters that are unique to a given user and are entered by the user during logon.

Virtual Private Network (VPN). A means for communicating securely over a public network; typically the sender (or other VPN endpoint in the sender's network) encrypts the message before sending it over the Internet and the receiver (or other VPN endpoint in the receiver's network) decrypts the message.

Virus. A form of malicious software that copies itself when executed; viruses may also contain a damaging payload which generates an unexpected behaviour such as writing out a message to the computer's display, erasing files, reformatting the hard drive, etc.

Vulnerability Index (VI). In this book, a value that can be used to quantify the magnitude of a given threat; it is calculated by multiplying the cost of compromise or loss (CC) by the probability of compromise (PC).

Vulnerability scanner. A network vulnerability tester which sends data to various IP ports on a host to determine which ones are responsive; vulnerability scanners can be used by hackers to find exploitable vulnerabilities or by security specialists to identify weaknesses needing to be strengthened.

War dialler. Usually a computer program that can be configured to automatically dial a range of telephone numbers and make note of which ones are answered by a computer; the IT security staff can use such a tool to discover previously unknown entry points into their network or hackers can use it to identify attack points.

Wearable computer. A computing device that can be worn by a person as they would an article of clothing or accessory; wearable computers can take the form of a watch, eyeglasses, etc.

Worm. A form of malicious software that replicates itself over and over again and may result in a significant consumption of computing or networking resources; an electronic tape*worm* of sorts.

Bibliography

Anonymous (1997) *Maximum Security, A Hacker's Guide to Protecting Your Internet Site and Network.* Sams.net, Indianapolis. ISBN: 1-57521-268-4.

Associated Press (2000a) Judge critical of army Web site, 5 January.

Associated Press (2000b) Philippines lacks law to fix computer bug, 18 May.

Avolio, F.M. (1997) Firewalls are not enough. Trusted Information Systems, Inc., Networld & Interop Security Symposium, October, Atlanta, GA.

Bellorin, S. (1999) RSA '99 Conference 'Securing the Internet: Is crypto enough?' Panel discussion, 20 January.

Bidzos, J. (1999) RSA '99 Conference Keynote Address. Jim Bidzos, President of RSA Data Security, 18 January.

Blaze, M., Diffie, W., Rivest, R.L., Schneier, B., Shimomura, T., Thompson, E. and Wiener, M. (1996) 'Minimal key lengths for symmetric ciphers to provide adequate commercial security'. January. http://www.bsa.org/policy/encryption/cryptographers_c.html. Business Software Alliance, www.bsa.org.

British Standards Institute (1995) *British Standard 7799, Code of Practice for Information Security Management.* British Standards Institute, London. ISBN: 0-580-26428-9.

Brosnan, J.W. (1998) Hackers testify they can crash Internet service in a half-hour. Scripps Howard News Service, 20 May.

Chen, D.W. (1998) Man charged with sabotage of computers. *The New York Times,* 18 February.

Chess, D. (1997) CAP macro virus widespread. *AntiVirus Online,* IBM Corp., www.av.ibm.com.

Cheswick, W.R. and Bellovin, S.M. (1994) *Firewalls and Internet Security, Repelling the Wily Hacker.* Reading, MA: Addison-Wesley. ISBN: 0-201-63357-4.

CIAC (1997) H-45: Windows NT SAM permission vulnerability. CIAC Information Bulletin, 9 April.

Computer Security Institute (1999) 1999 CSI/FBI Computer Crime and Security Survey. *Computer Security Issues & Trends,* Winter, Vol V, No. 1.

Corby, M.J. (1999) Top-down risk assessment. *Information Security,* ICSA Inc., Vol. 2, No. 1, January.

Cornetto, J. (1998) Bogus e-mail patch reported for Microsoft Outlook. *InfoWorld Electric,* 12 August.

Crouch, C. (2000) Home, Sweet Windows Home. *PC World Online,* 6 January.

Crouch, C. and Mainelli, T. (2000) FBI, industry scramble to stop hack attacks. *PC World Online,* 9 February.

Daily Telegraph (1999), Hackers attack military satellite, 4 March.

Duncan, R. and Ahsan, M. (1999) Information Security Issues: 1998 Survey. Datapro, 15 March.

Felten, E.W., et al. (1997) Web spoofing: An Internet con game. Technical Report 540-96, Department of Computer Science, Princeton University, February.

Fessler, J. (1998) Internet security and the IBM firewall. Networking Systems Technical Conference, Las Vegas NV, September, Jim Fessler, Founder and CEO, Computer ps, Inc.

Franklin, C. (1999) Wearable PCs offer functions, not fashion. *PC World Online,* 23 December.

Garfinkel, S. and Spafford, G. (1997) *Web Security and Commerce.* Cambridge, MA: O'Reilly & Associates.

Giles, L. (trans., ed.) (1994) Sun Tzu on the Art of War. May, Project Gutenberg, http://www.gutenberg.net/history.html.

Grampp, F. and Morris, R. (1984) Unix Operating System Security. *AT&T Bell Labs Technical Journal,* 63(8), October.

Grundschober, S. (1999) Sniffer detector report. Second International Workshop on Recent Advances in Intrusion Detection (RAID '99), West Lafayette, IN, USA, September, www.zurich.ibm.com/Technology/Security/extern/gsal/sniffer_detector.html.

Hamilton, C. (1999) Bang for your buck. *Information Security*, January.

IBM (1997) IBM Firewall V3.1.1 for AIX at a Glance. GC31-8493, IBM Corporation, July.

Infonetics Research (1997) Virtual private networks: A partnership between service providers and network managers. October.

Kaufman, C., Perlman, R. and Speciner, M. (1995) *Network Security, PRIVATE Communication in a PUBLIC World*. Upper Saddle River, NJ: Prentice Hall. ISBN: 0-13-061466-1.

Klein, D.V. (1991) *Foiling the cracker: A Survey of, and Improvement to, Password Security*. Software Engineering Institute, Carnegie Mellon University.

Larsen, A.K. (1999) Study: Security threats from outside on the rise. *InformationWeek Daily*, 5 March.

Loeb, V. (1999) Back channels: The intelligence community. *The Washington Post*, 13 December.

Lusk, H.F. et al. (1982) *Business Law and the Regulatory Environment: Concepts and Cases*. Homewood, IL: Richard D. Irwin, Inc. ISBN 0-256-02603-3.

Masters, B.A. (1999) Teen who hacked into federal sites gets 15 months. *Washington Post*, 20 November.

Merriam-Webster Inc. (1996) *Merriam-Webster's Collegiate Dictionary*.

Microsoft (2000) Microsoft debuts Concept Home. Press Release, Microsoft Corporation, 6 January.

Morrissey, P. (1998) Seven firewalls fit for your enterprise. *Network Computing*, 15 November, www.networkcomputing.com.

MSNBC (1999) Virtual country 'nuked' in cyberwar. MSNBC, 27 January.

Murhammer, M., et al. (1998) *A Comprehensive Guide to Virtual Private Networks, Volume I: IBM Firewall, Server and Client Solutions*, SG24-5201, IBM International Technical Support Organization, Research Triangle Park, NC, USA. www.redbooks.ibm.com. ISBN: 0738400076.

National Institute of Standards and Technology (1995) *An Introduction to Computer Security: The NIST Handbook*. Special Publication 800-12. U.S. Department of Commerce. http://csrc.nist.gov/nistpubs/.

Niccolai, J. (2000) Web attacks losses could pass $1 billion. *PC World Online*, IDG News Service, 10 February.

Poulsen, K. (1999) 'Windfall', *ZDTV Chaos Theory*, www.zdnet.com/zdtv/cybercrime, 12 May.

Reuters (1999a) Clinton backs Milosevic cyber-attack. *TechWeb*, Reuters Ltd, 24 May.

Reuters (1999b) Computer virus costs to business surging – Study. Reuters Ltd, 18 June.

Reuters (2000) Ex-CIA chief's computer scandal. *Wired News*, Reuters Ltd, 3 February.

Rogers, M. (1999) Modern day Robin Hood or Moral Disengagement: Understanding the Justification for Criminal Computer Activity. University of Manitoba, Dept. of Psychology.

Ross, B. (1999) Virtual games. *20/20*, ABC News, 20 December.

Rothke, B. (1999) Firewall fallacies. *Information Security*, ICSA Inc., Vol. 2, No. 1, January.

RSA '99 Conference, 'Securing the Internet: Is Crypto Enough?' panel discussion, Steven Bellovin, AT&T Fellow, 20 January 1999.

Rubin, D. (1999) Most hacks are inside jobs. *PC World News*, Medill News Service, 9 February.

Rushing, R. (1998) How your network can be attacked. Richard Rushing, SecurIT Inc., WebSec'98 – The Conference and Expo on Web Security, August, San Francisco, CA.

Sample, C. (1998) Kicking firewall tires. *Network Magazine*, March, www.networkmagazine.com.

Sanchez-Klein, J. (1998) Cyberfuturist plants chip in arm to test human-computer interaction. CNN.com, 28 August.

Scarponi, D. (2000) Hacker reveals credit card data. The Associated Press, 10 January.

Schneider, F.B. (1999) *Trust in Cyberspace*. National Research Council, National Academy Press, Washington, DC. ISBN: 0-309-06558-5.

Schneier, B. (1996) *Applied Cryptography, Second Edition*. New York: John Wiley & Sons. ISBN: 0-471-11709-9.

Schneier, B. (1998) Cryptography: The importance of not being different. *CRYPTO-GRAM*, 15 April, www.counterpane.com.

Schneier, B. (1999) Why the worst cryptography is in the systems that pass initial analysis. *CRYPTO-GRAM*, 15 March 1999. Bruce Schneier, Counterpane Internet Security, Inc., www.counterpane.com.

Scott, J. (1998) Firewalls: What, why, and how they work. IBM Corporation, November.

Siri, L. (1999) The Internet Auditing Project. August, www.securityfocus.com.

Skoudis, E. (1998) Fire in the hole. *Information Security*, August, www.infosecuritymag.com.

Smith, M. (1998) *Station X, The Codebreakers of Bletchley Park*. London, Channel 4 Books. ISBN: 0-7522-2189-2.

Stephenson, B. (1998) Cryptography: Issues and Terminology for the Layman. IBM Corporation.

Stoll, C. (1987) What do you feed a Trojan horse? Cliff Stoll, Lawrence Berkeley Laboratory, 10th National Computer Security Conference, Baltimore, MD.

Stoll, C. (1990) *The Cuckoo's Egg, Tracking a Spy Through the Maze of Computer Espionage*. New York: Pocket Books. ISBN: 0-671-72688-9.

Swanson, M. and Guttman, B. (1996) *Generally Accepted Principles and Practices for Securing Information Technology Systems*. Special Publication 800-14. National Institute of Standards and Technology, U.S. Department of Commerce. http://csrc.nist.gov/nistpubs/.

Taubes, G. (1996) An immune system for cyberspace. *IBM Research Magazine*, Vol. 34, No. 4.

The SANS Institute (1999) CIO Institute bulletin on computer security, Vol. 2, No. 3, 8 March.

Ungoed-Thomas, J. and Arnaud, S. (2000) Hacker gang blackmails firms with stolen files. *The Sunday Times*, 16 January.

Weil, N. (1999), Pentagon claims hack attack. *PC World Online*, IDG News Service, 5 March.

Winkler, I. (1999) Is your coworker a spy?, *ZDTV Spy Files*, www.zdnet.com/zdtv/cybercrime, 16 February.

Index

Note: Page entries in **bold** show where a term is defined in the book.

H

hackers
  characteristics 23–6, 36–7
  as con men 93–5, 212
  definition of 21
  motivation 21–2, 27–35
  risk analysis 42
  terminology 4, 21
  thinking like 69, 146–50
  Web sites 148–50
hacktivists **31**–3
hardening systems 144
harmful nature of all attacks 70, 208–12
  e-graffiti 208–9
  learning process 212–13
  'unimportant' systems 213–14
hashing function **240**
help desks 118
hoax viruses **177**–82
hybrid firewalls **76**
hypertext, security policies 56, 61

I

IBM
  AntiVirus 181, 182
  Deep Blue 180
  CHRISTMA worm 166–7
  DES 234
  Global Security Analysis Lab 22, 130–1
  Join the Crew hoax 177–8
  Research 11, 22, 130–1
  SmartCard Security Kit 107
ICMP **74**
ICSA 251
identity issues 97–9
  see also authentication schemes; passwords
identity theft 223–4
IDS 213
IETF 131, 245
IKE **248**
implantable computers **228**–9
incident reporting 57, 218
Indonesia 34
industrial espionage 36
information
  as defence 70, 215–19
  firewalls 80
  importance of 17–18, 67
  leaking 100–1
information technology (IT) **2**
  future 221–2
insider hackers 68, 86–7
  characteristics 87–8
  firewalls 88–9

leaking of confidential information 100
  passwords 117
  turnover, staff 89–91
integrated firewalls 84
integrity, message **240**
  VPN 246–7
intermediate hackers **24**, 25
International Computer Security Association (ICSA) 251
Internet, development of 8–9
Internet appliances **230**
Internet Engineering Task Force (IETF) 131, 245
Internet Key Exchange (IKE) **248**
Internet Protocol Security (IPSec) **131**–2, 243, 245–6
  Authentication Header 246–7, 248, 250–1
  Encapsulating Security Payload 247, 249, 250
Internet Security Association and Key Management Protocol (ISAKMP) **248**
intranet
  firewalls 77, 88–9
  SYN flood attacks 159
intrusion detection system (IDS) 213
IPSec *see* Internet Protocol Security
ISAKMP **248**
IT *see* information technology

J

Java 185, **186**, 187
  applets 138, **186**
  applications **186**
  policies, security 59
Java 2 186, 187
JavaScript 185, **186**, 187
  policies, security 59
Java Virtual Machine (JVM) 186, 187
  buffer overflows 138
Jet Propulsion Labs 144
Join the Crew hoax virus 177–8
Jones, Christian 35

K

keyboard-locking screen savers 107
keys, cryptography 195, 233–4
  VPN 247–8
KISS principle **55**
Krawczyk, Hugo 11

L

L0phtCrack 112, 154
  Server Message Block 109, 126–7, 154
L0pht Heavy Industries
  AntiSniff 128–30